One West,
Two Myths II

One West, Two Myths II

Essays on Comparison ━━

Edited by C.L. Higham
and Robert Thacker

UNIVERSITY OF
CALGARY
PRESS

©2006 by C. L. Higham and Robert Thacker
Published by the University of Calgary Press
2500 University Drive NW, Calgary, Alberta, Canada T2N 1N4
www.uofcpress.com

No part of this publication may be reproduced, stored in a retrieval system or transmitted, in any form or by any means, without the prior written consent of the publisher or a licence from The Canadian Copyright Licensing Agency (Access Copyright). For an Access Copyright licence, visit www.accesscopyright.ca or call toll free to 1-800-893-5777.

The University of Calgary Press gratefully acknowledges the Donner Canadian Foundation for its support of this publication. We acknowledge the support of the Canada Council for the Arts and the Alberta Foundation for the Arts for this published work.

 Canada Council for the Arts   Conseil des Arts du Canada

Library and Archives Canada Cataloguing in Publication

One West, two myths II : essays on comparison / edited by C.L. Higham and Robert Thacker.

First published as a special issue of The American review of Canadian studies, based on 3 conferences held 2002-2003.
Includes bibliographical references and index.

ISBN 13: 978-1-55238-204-2
ISBN 10: 1-55238-204-4

1. Canada, Western–History. 2. West (U.S.)–History.
I. Thacker, Robert II. Higham, C. L. (Carol L.) III. Title: American review of Canadian studies.

FC3206.O53 2006   971.2   C2006-905408-8

Cover design by Melina Cusano
Page design and typesetting by Elizabeth Gusnoski

Contents

Acknowledgements   vii

Preface: Sharing the West(s)   ix
C. L. Higham and Robert Thacker

1   Introduction: No Catlin without Kane; or, *Really* Understanding the "American" West   1
    Robert Thacker

2   Turner versus Innis: Two Mythic Wests   15
    R. Douglas Francis

3   One West, One Myth: Transborder Continuity in Western Art   31
    Brian W. Dippie

4   A Northern Vision: Frontiers and the West in the Canadian and American Imagination   63
    William H. Katerberg

5   Transnational Perspectives on the History of Great Plains Women: Gender, Race, Nations, and the Forty-ninth Parallel   85
    Sarah Carter

6   Myths and Realities in American-Canadian Studies: Challenges to Comparing Native Peoples' Experiences   115
    Roger L. Nichols

7   Prairies and Plains: The Levelling of Difference in Stegner's *Wolf Willow*   127
    David L. Williams

8   Whose West Is It Anyway? or, What's Myth Got to Do with It? The Role of "America" in the Creation of the Myth of the West   139
    Lee Clark Mitchell

9   Leading the Parade   153
    Aritha van Herk

Appendices

The Significance of the Frontier in American History   165
Frederick Jackson Turner

Frontierism, Metropolitanism, and Canadian History   193
J. M. S. Careless

Bibliographic Essay   215
C. L. Higham

Index   223

Acknowledgements

Many people helped bring this book to fruition. Dr. Robert Pickering of the Buffalo Bill Historical Center and Dr. Gerry Conaty of the Glenbow-Alberta Institute helped guide the development of the conference that led to both the first and this second volume. Bob, in particular, has provided friendship and support through the technical difficulties of corralling nine authors and their works. The authors themselves have been joys to work with, responding to many e-mails promptly and with patience.

Before appearing as this textbook, Chapters One through Nine originally appeared as a special issue of *The American Review of Canadian Studies* entitled "One Myth, Two Wests." We thank Mark Kasoff, the editor for his permission to reprint these items and Susan Way for her initial editing work on the volume. At the University of Calgary Press, we must thank Walter Hildebrand and John King for their hard work, enthusiasm, and patience.

Patrick Jones at the University of North Carolina-Charlotte created the fine maps found here and we thank him for his patience as we tried to explain theories of Western development to him so he could illustrate them for you. Derek Rodriguez and Frank Mollinek of the Davidson College Library provided technical assistance with scanners and bibliographic searches throughout their production. Craig Ewington gave up several afternoons to help me scan the illustrations.

I must personally thank two people: my co-editor and author, Bob Thacker and my husband, Chris Alexander. Bob signed onto this project sight unseen almost seven years ago and has stuck with it through thick and thin. Chris, who signed on over fifteen years ago, weathered the storms of life and book production with me. And despite being phenomenally busy in his own right he still manages to help me find time and space to work on projects like this. I appreciate his courageousness to load up two kids and a dog and take off for the day while I finish little details.

Preface: Sharing the West(s)

C.L. Higham, Davidson College
Robert Thacker, St. Lawrence University

In perhaps the most quoted passage in his oft-quoted *Wolf Willow* (1962), Wallace Stegner wrote that "The 49th parallel ran directly through my childhood, dividing me in two."[1] As one of us has occasion to say, below, and David Williams asserts here as well, Stegner's book occupies a unique position in understanding the similarities and differences shared by the Canadian and United States western regions as historical and cultural spaces. An unusual book in that it marries history, memoir, and fiction between one set of covers, *Wolf Willow* is all the more unusual in actually straddling the Canada-U.S. border as it runs from the Lake of the Woods to the Rocky Mountains. That is, *Wolf Willow*, like Stegner himself, is divided in two by virtue of its dual appreciation, its parallel understanding, of Western culture as found in Canada along with its appreciation of the Western culture found in the United States – each similar to, yet different from, the other. That border is a fact, certainly, but it is also culturally something of a fiction – drawn in 1818 to divide the Hudson's Bay and Missouri/Mississippi watersheds, the border is both an impediment (witness the ongoing crisis in the cattle industry) and an artificial division between similar Western cultures and landscapes.

This volume, which first appeared as a special issue of *The American Review of Canadian Studies*, was born of much the same impulse as *Wolf Willow*. It avowedly intends to set the histories, myths, and cultures of the two northern North American Wests side by side for purposes of comparison, discernment of differences, and mutual illumination. As is often the case in the academy, this volume derives from a thematically defined conference. But Ours is unusual in that it owes to *three* conferences: the first, entitled "One West, Two Myths," was held at the Buffalo Bill Historical Center in Cody, Wyoming in May 2002; the second, entitled "One West, Two Myths: Comparing Canadian and American Perspectives," was sponsored by the Glenbow Museum and held in Calgary, Alberta in October 2002; the third, entitled "Narrating Frontiers: Transgressions and Exchanges Along North American Borders," was sponsored by the John F. Kennedy Institute for North American Studies, Free University of Berlin, and was held there in July 2003 as a part of the Institute's fortieth anniversary celebrations. As might be imagined, in each case there were both overlapping and new speakers and, given geography – national as well as physiographic – there were different audiences. It is probably fair to say that the farther we were from Wyoming – home, of course, not only to Buffalo Bill but also to that quintessential Western narrative, Owen Wister's *The Virginian* (1902) – the less overwhelming was the popular Myth of the American West.

The idea for these gatherings was Carol Higham's. Attending the 1999 Western History Association meetings in Portland, Oregon, and there participating in several comparative panels, she thought that the time had come for a conference that would focus exclusively on comparing the Canadian and American Wests. During the meetings she buttonholed Lillian Turner of the Buffalo Bill Historical Center, asking whether her museum might be interested in hosting such a conference. A month later, at the Association for Canadian Studies in the United States meetings in Pittsburgh, she asked me, Robert Thacker, as then Editor of *The American Review of Canadian Studies*, if I would be interested in the idea as a special issue. Always on the lookout for such ideas and a Western specialist myself, I enthusiastically endorsed and joined the project.

From there, the idea for the conference and its subsequent volumes spread quickly. I ran into Byron Price, then director of the Buffalo Bill Historical Center, who brought Dr. Robert Pickering, Deputy Director of the Buffalo Bill, into the discussions. Particularly exciting was the way the conferences married the academy with the world of museums – the Buffalo Bill Historical Center and the Glenbow are two of that world's jewels, as conference participants were later able to see. By early 2000, we had a steering committee, speaker lists, and grant ideas. At that point, Gerry Conaty, of the Glenbow Museum, jumped on board – he wondered if we might also hold the conference in Calgary. We were thrilled by this notion and readily agreed because it provided an opportunity to address both Canadian and American audiences about the two Wests. While speakers were approached, Conaty and Pickering wrote grants. Soon we had secured generous funding from the William H. Donner Foundation and the Donner Canadian Foundation. They provided funds not only for the conferences but also for the publication of the special issue of *ARCS* and two other volumes intended for classroom use. We wish to especially thank both Donner Foundations for their *most* tangible support.

May 2002 saw the first conference in Cody at the Buffalo Bill Historical Center. Somewhat open-ended in structure so as to encourage full participation, it quickly turned into a three-day intensive seminar comparing the Canadian and American Wests. Beyond the conference itself, there were late-night discussions at Cody's famous (perhaps infamous) Irma Hotel, a place once owned by Buffalo Bill himself and named after his daughter. Some of that discussion made it to the conference podium the next day. This first conference – which established the form – owed particularly to the Herculean efforts of the staff of the Buffalo Bill who brought considerable conference experience to bear: in particular, Marguerite House, Bob Pickering, and Lillian Turner were the BBHC's core, but Bob Shimp and Jill Osieki were most instrumental, too.

While we were in Cody, two participants who came a very long way added significantly to the discussions: Gerhard Hoffmann (University of Wurzburg) and Heinz Ickstadt (John F. Kennedy Institute for North American Studies, Free University of Berlin). In addition to their participation, they invited us to bring the conference to Berlin. We jumped at that chance too. So, after an equally successful iteration of the conference in October 2002 at the University of Calgary and the Glenbow, where, not surprisingly, the concerns of the audience and points raised for discussion differed considerably from those raised in Cody, many of us were able to reconvene in Berlin in July 2003.

Traveling as it did, the conference sought to maintain as much of the original program as possible. While some speakers were able to attend all three, and several managed two, many were not able to attend more than one. Due to funding and scheduling limitations, a smaller group made the trip to Germany. Thus at each meeting after Cody some new participants were added and, among those who repeated, papers changed as people read each other's work. So the conference continued to evolve and grow over the year and a half of its happening. As this process suggests, too, by speaking to three distinct and interactive audiences – a mainly U.S. one, then mainly Canadian and European ones – perspective on the matter itself, on the relative emphasis of fact, understanding, and meaning, and on ultimate conclusions, changed repeatedly. Each time we spoke, new questions and new ideas emerged from the audience. In Cody – as well it might in a place named after a mythic American Western figure in a museum also named after him – the press of the popular Western was palpably felt, despite numerous instances of demurral from those seeing other Wests. In Calgary the critique of the United States Western Myth was full-blown, with Canada's "other West" – one sharing elements of the mythic American version while leading in other directions and with other emphases – asserted at every turn. And in Germany, finally, far, far away from the geographic North American West but brought up on a culture of the Western stretching well back into the nineteenth century, the North American West became a distant series of Borderlands, reflecting one on the other by way of comparison and contrast, true, but also emblematic of the West as quintessentially North American in the informed European's mind.

What we offer here, finally, is a selection of the papers given at the conferences. In our selection, we have tried to use those which seem to us to be the most comparative and, at the same time, those offering analyses of most interest to the readers new to comparison of the Wests. This volume represents the debates at the three conferences, but the essays have been written for a broader audience, students and non-specialists. It explores issues of exceptionalism, mild versus wild Wests, concepts of myth and frontier with a grounding in the past scholarship, yet focused on ideas and issues warranting more exploration.

This volume demonstrates several important aspects of scholars' understanding of the two Wests. First, almost all of the authors muse about the importance and influence of Frederick Jackson Turner and his frontier thesis. Additionally, many authors compare Turner to the dominant theory in Canada, metropolitanism, but in different contexts. Third, all of the scholars acknowledge the power of the mythic West(s) and its (their) imagery. Some embrace it. Others attack it. And still others acknowledge it but forge onward without it or around it. All the essays, though, demonstrate excitement and curiosity about various forms of studying and comparing the Wests.

To conclude with what this experience has taught us, and speaking here as two scholars who have each written Canada–U.S. comparative studies, we remain convinced that, as in Stegner's phrasing, "The 49th parallel" also runs directly through understandings of Canada's West and the United States West, "dividing" scholars into (at least) two groups. Illustrating this bifurcation, one of the readers of this manuscript objected to any designation of Canadians as "Americans" – Robert Thacker does this in his introductory essay as a way, ultimately, of privileging the Canadian point of view. Yet the Press's reader – likely a Canadian, given this objection – did not seem to countenance this: any application of the term "American" to Canadian North Americans is objectionable, apparently. Such assertions, minor and even silly, demonstrate the need for such work as is offered here, work we very much hope to continue. The three conferences from which these papers were drawn began a discussion, one that had happened before but needs to happen again, and more frequently. So this volume is an addition to the literature of Canada-U.S. Western comparisons, as the other two which have already appeared have been. We very much hope that others will use, and respond to, the comparative work we offer here.

Note

1   Wallace Stegner, *Wolf Willow: A History, a Story, and a Memory of the Last Plains Frontier* (1962; New York: Penguin, 1990), p. 80.

chapter one

Introduction: No Catlin without Kane; or, *Really* Understanding the "American" West

Robert Thacker, St. Lawrence University

Let me begin by invoking three moments from the history of the North American West. The first occurred in late 1801; the second, in 1842 or early 1843; the third took place in 1881. Together, these three moments set the stage for this volume of essays, an attempt to probe the commingling of Canada's West with that of the U.S. West in history, image, and myth, to adapt the phrasing of Henry Nash Smith's subtitle in *Virgin Land* (1950). Any story, any history, is a combination of verifiable fact, descriptive image, and believed (or disbelieved) mythology, and nowhere has this been more evident that in the North American West as it was explored, settled, and understood from the sixteenth century to the present.

Three moments. John L. Allen, author of the excellent *Passage Through the Garden: Lewis and Clark and the Image of the American Northwest* (1975), has also written of Thomas Jefferson's reaction to the publication, in London, of Alexander Mackenzie's *Voyages from Montreal, on the River St. Lawrence, through the Continent of North America to the Frozen and Pacific Oceans in the Years 1789 and 1793* (1801). He says that late in 1801 the President "was worried" because the publication of Mackenzie's book "had stirred the imagination of the Western world and jolted Jefferson's thinking on the geography of the western interior of North America." As a consequence, Jefferson ordered his own copy of the book from Philadelphia, he began "poring over" his

I

collection of "books and maps on western North America," and he told his personal secretary, Meriwether Lewis, "to begin making preparations for an American exploration to the Pacific." More than this, Jefferson also informed the Spanish, British, and French ministers to the United States of his intentions to send Lewis west, "as he put it," to "'unite the discoveries' of the explorers of Rupert's Land with those of an American party farther south."[1] That is just what Lewis and Clark eventually did – unite the versions of the geographical reality of the North American West then understood in Europe, in British North America, and in the United States. This is a first moment.

The second occurred sometime over the winter of 1842–43 in London, where Paul Kane, who was there after studying art in Italy, met George Catlin and saw Catlin's art on display in Egyptian Hall, Piccadilly. The American was then basking in the fame that was his for a short time, a notoriety fuelled by his best-selling book, *Letters and Notes on the Manners, Customs, and Conditions of the North American Indians*, which had been published in 1841. Kane, inspired by this meeting and by Catlin's images, decided to embark on a similar project in Canada. He returned there and made an initial summer sketching trip to the northern Great Lakes country in 1845 before securing the support of the Hudson's Bay Company for his transcontinental trip, 1846–48. As J. Russell Harper explains, Sir George Simpson – Inland Governor of the Company – "wrote a circular letter to all Hudson's Bay Company officers in 'Ruperts Land and Elswhere,' directing that the artist be given free transportation of company boats and 'hospitalities' at all posts. Kane, a guest of the Hudson's Bay Company, could go without cost anywhere in the vast territories it controlled."[2] It was a wonderful deal. Kane, in fact, arrived on the Pacific coast in the same HBC brigade that brought the official news of the Oregon Treaty (1846). That is, he was there *just* as vast changes were afoot.

The third moment is a brief one, barely mentioned in the biographical accounts of North America's most-famous Western painter, Frederic Remington. In 1881, Remington made his first trip west to Montana, the trip from which he sent back – drawn on a piece of wrapping paper – his first illustration to appear in *Harper's Weekly* (in February 1882). During that trip he crossed the Canada-U.S. border on horseback and there, according to one commentator, "saw his first Mounted Police – bringing in a Blackfoot suspected of murder. He transferred the scene to paper at the next stop – the Indian's expression of resignation as he walked ahead with a rope around his neck, the officers in their frogged British coats and Scotch caps, the troopers in small forage caps."[3]

One can't make too much of this last moment biographically. At the time, Remington was nineteen and seemed to take in very little of what he saw – his biographers Peggy and Harold Samuels wonder how he could not have remarked on the great Buffalo slaughter then going on in east-central Montana; and according to Ben Merchant Vorpahl, "the trip marked" Remington "as improvident, puerile, cranky."[4] His immediate family wondered about him and worried over him – and with good reason, for nothing Remington had done by 1881 or would do over the next few years suggested success, or even much promise. He squandered his sizable inheritance, first on a sheep farm and then on a Kansas City bar. Yet Remington had seen the West and, once his inheritance was nearly gone, he went back there in order to set about making something of the West as his subject during the late 1880s. Even so, as the Samuels write, "Remington was actually the last of the great Western artists to go West.[5]"

Alexander Mackenzie and Thomas Jefferson, George Catlin and Paul Kane, Frederic Remington and the North West Mounted Police: the U.S. West intertwined with the Canadian West – there are thousands of other such moments, innumerable cruxes, and myriad border-crossings. The problem, ever and always, is in how we "Americans" understand these things. (Canadians, of course, are also "Americans" in the sense of being of this continent.) Each of us, Canadians and United States people, living within a national myth born of exceptionalism, seek to assert our country's historical narrative – especially the narrative of West: expansion – "Westward the Course of Empire Takes Its Way" – or, in Canada, the Laurentian thesis propounded with respect to the Canadian Pacific Railway (completed in 1885): Pierre Berton's "The National Dream" (or Gordon Lightfoot's "Canadian Railroad Trilogy").[6] Yet these parallel narratives, historically intertwined as they were, and are, have too infrequently crossed, too infrequently been probed and understood as the interconnected fact-based stories they are.

The significance of Jefferson's response to his worried moment over Mackenzie's transcontinental success is clear: the massed bulk of the University of Nebraska Press's *The Journals of the Lewis and Clark Expedition* (1983–99, 13 volumes) looms, the narrative versions of Lewis and Clark have piled up (though they were slow to start – the first, by Biddle, did not appear until

1814), James Fenimore Cooper's Leatherstocking series stands mythologizing them yet, especially in its third volume, *The Prairie* (1827). And two words – *Undaunted Courage* – have recently again broadcast Lewis and Clark throughout the United States through Stephen Ambrose's popular retelling of the story of their voyage of discovery.[7]

Yet early in Wallace Stegner's *Wolf Willow* (1962) – arguably *the* paradigm border-crossing Western text, a paradigm as autobiography, as history, as art – there is an invocation of the Lewis and Clark expedition on the upper Missouri in May 1805: "They came watchfully," Stegner writes, "for they were the first. They came stiffened with resolution and alert with wonder.... Every river and creek that came in from south or west brought word of the Stony Mountains and the passes that might lead to the Great South Sea; every stream from north or northwest was a possible trail to the Saskatchewan in Prince Rupert's Land. More and more, as they moved westward, the country that lay between them and these desired goals was not merely unknown, it was unrumored." Stegner's invocation of Lewis and Clark here – one that is both precise and careful – serves him an important narrative purpose: he places them on the Milk River bluffs (so called because Lewis and Clark renamed them for Euro-Americans), staring northward toward the Cypress Hills, the mythic place of his boyhood in Saskatchewan to which he returns through *Wolf Willow*. Standing at the apex of the continent, Lewis and Clark, Stegner writes, "would have been looking down the imperceptible hill that led to Hudson Bay."[8]

Such a careful placement of these paradigmatic explorers in a paradigmatic text by a writer who was a literal border-crosser, and so also something of a paradigm himself, is indicative. Stegner was born in the United States, he self-identified as American but, having spent his "litmus years" (*pace* W.O. Mitchell) in Saskatchewan, he offers a bifurcated sensibility, an ambivalent nationalism. *Wolf Willow*, ironically, is a book more valued in Canada than in the United States. Beyond this, Stegner was also a disciplinary border crosser – arguably, much of *Wolf Willow* and of his other publications is history, despite his status as an important novelist.[9] The history Stegner is telling in *Wolf Willow* – and narrative history takes fully a third of the text – is a recovery project: when he was growing up near Eastend, Saskatchewan, he says, history was always somewhere else, and his education tried to make him a European (24–25).

Coming back an established writer and academic on a Guggenheim toward the end of the 1950s, Stegner writes the history he never knew when he was a boy living on what he calls in his subtitle "the last plains frontier." Native peoples, Lewis and Clark's nearby passage, the Hudson's Bay Company, the Métis, whisky traders, the North West Mounted Police, settlers and ranchers – each passes by as Stegner mounts his transborder recovery project. All of this is his, and it is encapsulated by the odour of the weed Wolf Willow, he says, an "odor that I have not smelled since I was eleven, but have never forgotten – have *dreamed*, more than once." "If I am native to anything," Stegner concludes his first chapter, "I am native to this" (18, 20).

Stegner literally returned to Eastend, Saskatchewan for purposes of *Wolf Willow* and, re-seen, that place was the locus of his imaginative "last plains frontier," a place he calls Whitemud in the book. I want to broaden this ubiquitous notion of "frontier" before I return to Catlin, Kane, and Remington. Writing about Cormac McCarthy's *Blood Meridian*, Jonathan Pitts invokes Frederick Jackson Turner and asserts that:

> The frontier has been displaced and reconstituted so convincingly in our likeness that we cannot help but read it as our history, as a reflection of our presence. It is literally impossible to see our absence, for where we are not we will inevitably be, and where we once were we can never leave. To open the American eye is to see that which is inevitably and originally American. With the closing of the American frontier comes the opening, as in a God's-eye view, of the American landscape, of the American eye. In this optical democracy, in this intellectual and spiritual equilibrium, everything is necessarily luminous.[10]

Pitts's articulation here of Emersonian ideas refracted through the Turnerian prism and focused upon the American West as place – what he calls "optical democracy" – is also indicative. The parade of artists who visited the West to paint it and its peoples – Catlin, Kane, and Remington only the most prominent among them – made physical the imaginative processes involved – "necessarily luminous." William H. Goetzmann offered this as an apt phrasing: "The West as Romantic Horizon" and, more famously, F. Scott Fitzgerald invoked the "capacity for wonder" of the first European sailors to see Long Island – North America, "a fresh, green breast of the new world"[11]

Fitzgerald, and Pitts too with his references to "that which is inevitably and originally American," each strive for meaning in the U.S. West and, doing so, find the "necessarily luminous" there. Put another way, they engage the Myth of the American West and, concurrently, the myth of United States exceptionalism. Just as Stegner strives to connect his physical boyhood place near the Cypress Hills in southwest Saskatchewan with the West's pervasive myths, renderings he only later came to know, so others have wrested mythic meaning from the West of their imaginations. This West is a place within those North American imaginations that has ever been, and is still "necessarily luminous" indeed. And in some very significant ways, all of this mythologizing began with George Catlin, Paul Kane, and the other Western artists – most pervasively Remington and Russell, a fact well known among scholars and enthusiasts alike. But any such imaginative luminosity – in the North American West or any place else – is a construction, and things are constructed for purposes: to persuade, to control, to sell, or to otherwise take some advantage.

As he describes Thomas Jefferson's reactions to the news of Mackenzie's book in 1801, Allen makes it clear that while the President sought greater knowledge of the geographical realities of the North American West, Jefferson did so ever with his eye on matters of territorial control and trade. Equally, and as Brian W. Dippie has masterfully detailed in his *Catlin and His Contemporaries: The Politics of Patronage* (1990), George Catlin's romantic quest was fuelled by the artist's felt need to support himself and his art through the financial backing of government patronage. The complex web of ambitions, jealousies, and stymied plans Dippie offers in that fine book is as daunting as it is characteristic of human overreaching. For his part, Kane serves as contrast to Catlin in the story Dippie tells – the Canadian, he writes, "secured" "public and private commissions of the sort Catlin only dreamed of" – beyond the free support of Sir George Simpson and the Hudson's Bay Company, Kane had paintings commissioned by the Canadian colonial government. When a book, putatively his, entitled *Wanderings of an Artist Among the Indians of North America* (1859) appeared, its existence owed itself in some measure to the politics surrounding the question of a parliamentary renewal of the Hudson's Bay Company charter. That did not happen, for Rupert's Land went to the new Dominion of Canada. The rest, as is said, is history. Complementing Dippie's scholarship on Catlin, I.S. MacLaren has been writing since the late 1980s on Kane to elaborate the verifiable facts of that artist. The assessment that emerges from his work is caught by Dippie's comment that "One of Kane's patrons thought his personality a sufficient guarantor of the accuracy of his Indian scenes: he was too unimaginative to invent what he painted"[12]

Frederic Remington, the last of the painters to see the West, and in some ways the most luminous of the lot, sought none of the patronage Catlin failed to secure and Kane received. Instead, his interests, focus, and timing were impeccable – the West he found and offered through his illustrations in *Harper's Weekly*, *Century*, and other publications was just what the public wanted and needed: a Mythic West which, if it still existed at all, was receding into the distant past yet, ironically, remaining to ennoble and mythologize the U.S. West's history.

Seeing his first Mounted Policemen in 1881, just as he was inchoately groping for the purposeful career that was to become his, Remington caught a glimpse of a myth already alive and growing – that of the North West Mounted Police. Though he didn't know it at the time, Frederic Remington was home – in the Mounted Police he found a subject he was to use regularly in the following years – there were to be over three hundred Remington "Mounties." Stegner, recovering this history in *Wolf Willow*, writes in a chapter called "Law in a Red Coat" that "Never was the dignity of the uniform more carefully cultivated, and rarely has the ceremonial quality of impartial law and order been more dramatically exploited." (101).[13] When Remington saw Mounted Policemen arresting an alleged Blackfoot murderer in 1881, he saw them before they had collided with another mythic force in 1885 during the North West Rebellion: the messianic Métis leader, Louis Riel. In 1881, Riel was in exile in Montana – where he became an American citizen. When he returned to Canada and led the North West Rebellion, Riel severely tested the myth of the Mounted Police. (They had already been tested by the Sioux under Sitting Bull, who had fled to Canada in 1877 after the Greasy Grass/Little Big Horn battle of June 1876, which saw the destruction of Custer and his troops – indeed, the presence of these people in Canada became one of the first international disputes between the two countries.) And not surprisingly, that rebellion drew Remington back to the North West to illustrate its aftermath for *Harper's*. In one montage published in *Harper's Weekly*, for instance, he portrays "Louis Riel's Captor."[14]

Again: Alexander Mackenzie and Thomas Jefferson, George Catlin and Paul Kane, Frederic Remington, and the North West Mounted Police: the U.S. West intertwined with the Canadian West. The problem, ever and always, is in how we "Americans" understand these things. By pursuing separate visions and versions of West, by embracing our separate myths, by asserting our separate exceptionalities, we have largely sidestepped the more complex – and border disregarding – story. Owing to its connection to the Mounted Police, Sitting Bull's "flight to Canada" is reified in Canada but largely ignored in the United States; conversely, despite being "the individual in Canadian history about whom the most has been written," Riel's American years were first explored systematically only in 1999.[15] So such disregard goes both ways.

A recent illustration that embraces the complexity I am speaking of, and will serve as central text here, is Guy Vanderhaeghe's *The Englishman's Boy* (1996). It won Canada's Governor General's Award for Fiction and, as criticism has since shown, has found a quick currency.[16] Vanderhaeghe, a Saskatchewan writer who had previously established himself as the author of stories about sensitive, perplexed men, headed off in a new direction with *The Englishman's Boy*, a direction he has continued to pursue with *The Last Crossing* (2002). *The Englishman's Boy* is historical fiction that combines a narrative of the 1873 Cypress Hills massacre of a group of Assiniboine by revenge-seeking American wolfers with a fictional narrative of Hollywood's 1920s rendering of this event into a film entitled *Besieged* – moving into analysis of the ultimate myth machine: Hollywood. Alternating one with the other as they do, Vanderhaeghe's two narratives mediate and meditate on the relations between a historical happening and any telling of it, imaginative or otherwise.

The Cypress Hills Assiniboine Massacre was the precipitating event for the creation of the North West Mounted Police in 1873. Following Stegner, Vanderhaeghe's narrator calls the creation of the Mounted Police "A mythic act of possession."[17] That's what it was. As Stegner goes on to say after the passage on the creation of the Mounted Police, "One of the most visible aspects of the international boundary was that it was a color line: blue below, red above, blue for treachery and unkept promises, red for protection and the straight tongue" (101). And Vanderhaeghe was – no doubt consciously – focusing on the Cypress Hills incident as perhaps something of a homage, even, to Stegner's *Wolf Willow*, doubtless the best-known book to come out of the Cypress Hills. By evocatively recreating the Cypress Hills massacre, Vanderhaeghe returned to the "last plains frontier" of Stegner's subtitle: in his book, the historical act, the historical fact, is rendered now, rendered complex, rendered human. With the Englishman's boy, we are there; Vanderhaeghe begins:

> Even from such a distance Fine Man could smell their camp, the fried-pig stink of white men. He took up a pinch of dirt, placed it under his tongue, and made a prayer. Keep me close, Mother Earth, hide me, Mother Earth. It was light as day, the moon's bright face a trader's steel mirror, the grey leaves of the sage and wolf willow shining silver, as if coated with hoarfrost. Under a full moon, it was dangerous to steal horses – even from foolish white men. (1)

This is the precipitating moment of the Cypress Hills massacre – though we don't know that yet – the point of departure that begins the crossing of the frontier – first by Fine Man and the other Natives with their stolen horses and then by the wronged wolfers, seeking those horses and their revenge through Native deaths. Chapter by chapter, the wolfers are textualized – described but not explained – detailed in their act of riding north. They are reminiscent of Larry McMurtry's riders in *Lonesome Dove*, but there the riders head north to Montana as if that is as far as they can go. These riders ride north consciously toward a frontier that, in 1873 circumstances, is never really seen to have been crossed. It is what the Native people called "The Medicine Line," demarcated (at least on the plains) between the U.S. and British "possessions" in 1818, surveyed just the year before this action, in 1872. An intersection of the Missouri and Hudson's Bay watersheds, the forty-ninth parallel ran through Stegner's childhood, he writes in *Wolf Willow*, dividing him in two (81).

Like Stegner in *Wolf Willow*, Harry Vincent, Vanderhaeghe's first-person narrator of the novel's other narrative, recalls his younger self when he was working as a title-writer in 1923 in Hollywood at Best Chance Pictures. Looking back from 1953 Saskatoon, Vincent sees "the South Saskatchewan River, the frozen jigsaw pieces bumping sluggishly downstream, the cold, black water streaming between them" (5). In 1923, plucked from the obscurity of title-writing, Vincent is taken up by the studio's owner, Damon Ira Chance, and set to pursue the firsthand account of one Shorty McAdoo, a person who was among those 1873 riders, and who ultimately participated in the massacre. Chance, a racist xenophobe out to out-D.W. Griffith D.W. Griffith, wants

Harry to discover the facts of the massacre and write a screenplay. Setting Vincent to the task, he says, "'You mark my words, Harry, there'll come a day when the public won't swallow any of our stories unless they believe them to be real. Everybody wants the real thing, or thinks they do. Truth is stranger than fiction, someone said. It may not be, but it's more satisfying. Facts are the bread America wants to eat. The poetry of facts is the poetry of the American soul'" (19). Vincent does what he was asked but, not surprisingly, Chance proves to be megalomaniacal, wrong in his assertion here, and dead.

At the heart of *The Englishman's Boy* lies an irony that Vanderhaeghe exploits very effectively. It is the same division that animates Stegner in *Wolf Willow*: a bifurcated perspective. Chance is seeking to write cinematic "American" poetry through Canadian facts, gotten by a Canadian from an Englishman, written by a Canadian screenwriter. Vanderhaeghe crosses a frontier, privileging the Canadian point of view of the American western mythos so as to offer a view, as it were, from above. This is the same crossing, the same privileging, I would argue, that has made much of Margaret Atwood's fiction so effective – she is *in* America but not *of* it. A (North) American who is not *American*. This is part of what makes *Wolf Willow* such a haunting book: the bifurcated sensibility, the conflicting cultural claims, the separate versions of history.

Looking down once more at the South Saskatchewan River as the novel closes, Vincent remembers that "Chance believed character didn't count for much in history. But looking at the river, I remind myself the map of the river is not the river itself. That hidden in it are deep, mysterious, submerged, and unpredictable currents. The characters of all those wolfers, Canadian and American, cast longer shadows than I had any inkling of that endless night in which McAdoo made his confession, crouched on a cot in a desolate bunkhouse, an old man reliving his pain and guilt thousands of miles from an obscure dot on the Saskatchewan prairie" (326).

Students of western landscape are drawn to moments like this, to moments in texts of epiphany when, as Pitts says, "everything is necessarily luminous." that is, when the texts we read manage words so aligned that themselves, commingle character, landscape, circumstance, and moment within a configuration that glows. There is that moment in *Wolf Willow* when Stegner rediscovers "all around" "that odor that," and he continues in his own voice, "I have not smelled since I was eleven, but have never forgotten – have *dreamed*, more than once. Then I pull myself up the bank by a gray-leafed bush, and I have it. The tantalizing and ambiguous and wholly native smell is no more than the shrub we called wolf willow, now blooming with small yellow flowers" (18). (Not for nothing is this selfsame shrub evident in Vanderhaeghe's opening paragraph: "Homage, Wallace Stegner.") This wolf willow "brings" Stegner "home": "If I am native to anything," he asserts, "I am native to this" (19, 20).

I would take this point a step further, to conclude: this sensibility is "Canadian," I would hold, by virtue of its contingent duality: to speak, as Emerson, as Turner, and as many others have of "the American landscape" and "the American eye," and "the American frontier" is to imagine a homogeneity that no Canadian could countenance – recent criticism on all these matters has only confirmed as much. Such a frontier-crossing sensibility is part of what animates Vanderhaeghe's *The Englishman's Boy* and it is the very purpose of Stegner's *Wolf Willow*. To have a Canadian point of view, especially an English-Canadian point of view, is to be "on the frontier," to be above *America* but part of America, to have to cross frontiers.

So once again: Alexander Mackenzie and Thomas Jefferson, George Catlin and Paul Kane, Frederic Remington and the North West Mounted Police. These are the moments I have chosen to discuss here, and in my choice there is randomness, certainly. Yet as the essays which follow here show, the very idea that the "Canadian West" can be understood without reference to the "American West," that the North American Western mythology owes only to United States history, is impossible. The stories, the histories, and the myths are utterly interconnected, interdependent. And owing to the felt pull of the nation-state and its concomitant demand for national history, thoroughgoing scholarly comparative analysis of the Canadian West seen in relation to the American West is a nascent thing despite the massed bulk of Western histories from each side of the border. Bringing together several scholars who have already made this attempt and are continuing that work now, this volume seeks to both broadcast this comparative work and encourage even more.

Questions to Ponder

1. What is the difference between the physical Wests and the imagined Wests of authors and artists?
2. What is the "Mythic West"?
3. How did an artists' funding influence his or her view of the West?
4. What images do the United States' and Canadian Wests have in common?
5. What images are unique to each West?

Notes

1. John L. Allen, "To Unite the Discoveries: The American Response to the Early Exploration of Rupert's Land," in *Rupert's Land: A Cultural Tapestry*, ed. Richard C. Davis (Waterloo: Wilfrid Laurier University Press, 1988), pp. 79, 80.
2. Quoted in I.S. MacLaren, "'I Came to Rite Thare Portraits': Paul Kane's Journal of His Western Travels, 1846–1848." *American Art Journal* 21 (1989): 11. See also Brian W. Dippie, Terrese Thau Heyman, Christopher Mulvey, and Joan Carpenter Troccoli, [title of article?] *George Catlin and His Indian Gallery*, ed. George Gurney and Therese Thau Heyman (Washington: Smithsonian American Art Museum, 2002).
3. Robin McKown, *Painter of the Wild West: Frederic Remington* (New York: Julian Messner, 1959), pp. 43–44.
4. Peggy and Harold Samuels, *Frederic Remington: A Biography* (New York: Doubleday, 1982), pp. 34, 94; Ben Merchant Vorpahl, *Frederic Remington and the West*. Austin: University of Texas Press, 1978), pp. 34, 30.
5. Samuels, *Frederic Remington*, 94.
6. See Frances W. Kaye, "An Innis, Not a Turner." *American Review of Canadian Studies* 31 (2001): 597–610.
7. Stephen Ambrose, *Undaunted Courage: Meriwether Lewis, Thomas Jefferson, and the Opening of the American West* (New York: Simon & Shuster, 1996).
8. Wallace Stegner, *Wolf Willow: A History, a Memory, and a Story of the Last Plains Frontier* (1962. New York: Penguin, 1990), p. 42. Subsequent page numbers in parenthesis are from this edition.
9. See Robert Thacker, "Erasing the Forty-Ninth Parallel: Nationalism, Prairie Criticism, and the Case of Wallace Stegner," *Essays on Canadian Writing* 61 (1997): 179–202.
10. Pitts, Jonathan, "Writing On: *Blood Meridian* as Devisionary Western," *Western American Literature* 33 (1999): 18.
11. F. Scott Fitzgerald, *The Great Gatsby*, ed. Matthew J. Bruccoli (1925. Cambridge: Cambridge University Press, 1991), p. 140. See also William H. and William N. Goetzmann, *The West of the Imagination* (New York: W.W. Norton, 1986); and William H. Goetzmann and Joseph C. Porter, *The West as Romantic Horizon* (Omaha: Center for Western Studies, Joslyn Art Museum, 1981).

12 Brian W. Dippie, *Catlin and His Contemporaries: The Politics of Patronage* (Lincoln: University of Nebraska Press, 1990), p. 275.
13 See Robert Thacker, "Canada's Mounted: The Evolution of a Legend," *Journal of Popular Culture* 14 (1980): 298–312; and "The Mystery of Francis Jeffrey Dickens, N.W.M.P., and Eric Nicol's *Dickens of the Mounted*," *Great Plains Quarterly* 12 (1992): 19–30.
14 Frederic Remington, "Sketches of the Canadian Mounted Police, 1887–1888," *Harper's Weekly* (13 October 1888): 780.
15 See Thacker, "Erasing," pp. 193–97; and J. M. Bumsted, "Louis Riel and the United States." *The American Review of Canadian Studies* 29 (1999): 17–41.
16 See Alison Calder, "Unsettling the West: Nation and Genre in Guy Vanderhaeghe's *The Englishman's Boy*." *Studies in Canadian Literature* 25 (2001): 96–107; and David Williams, "Film-nations vs. Print-nations: The Politics of Metonymy in *The Englishman's Boy*," in *Imagined Nations: Reflections on Media in Canadian Fiction* (Montreal and Kingston: McGill-Queen's University Press, 2003), pp. 183–201.
17 Guy Vanderhaeghe, *The Englishman's Boy* (Toronto: McClelland & Stewart, 1996), p. 326. Subsequent page numbers in parenthesis are from this edition.

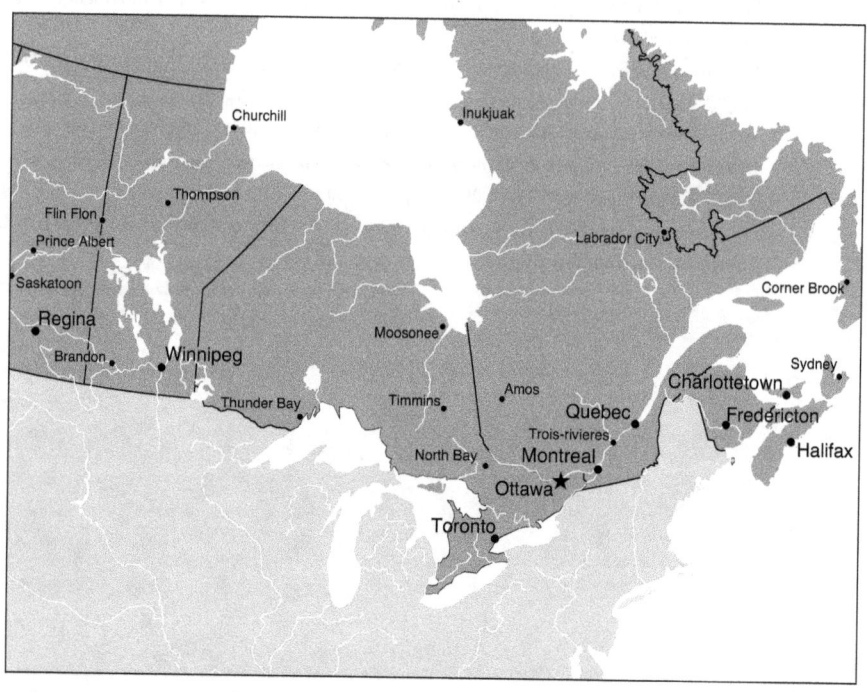

Provinces of Central Canada

chapter two

Turner versus Innis: Two Mythic Wests

R. Douglas Francis, University of Calgary

One of the challenges to comparative Canadian/American studies of the West is to understand the differences. Although the word "compare" means recognizing both similarities and differences, the tendency often is to see the similarities only: to reduce things down to their common denominator. In keeping with the conference theme of "One West, Two Myths," the challenge is to focus not on the "one West" but rather on the "two myths."

My point of departure is to understand the two myths by sketching out some essential differences between them and noting the implication of those differences for understanding the history of the Canadian and the American Wests. Then I go on to explore ways of getting beyond the current Canadian myth by suggesting a new myth for the Canadian West.

The historiographies of the Canadian and American Wests have evolved over time, but in that evolutionary process, one historian in the United States and one in Canada stand out as *the* historians who have been most influential in shaping the historical interpretations, and hence the mythologies, of their respective West. In the United States, that individual is, of course, Frederick Jackson Turner; in Canada, it is Harold Adams Innis. Although the interpretations of both historians have been challenged of late, the difficulty of getting beyond and supplanting their interpretations is indicative of the stronghold that both views hold in the respective history of the two Wests.

The two interpretations are distinguished by a couple of significant ideas. The Turner frontier thesis is noted for its emphasis on the progressive development and advancement of the American West as representative of the progressive development of American society and civilization as a whole. In the oft-quoted words of Turner: "The existence of an area of free land, its continuous recession, and the advance of American settlement westward, explain American development."[1] Although Turner's focus was on the West – the area west of the Mississippi River, his assumption is that developments here are characteristic of developments in other regions of the country. Indeed, his argument is that the frontier began on the Atlantic coast and then systematically moved westward along with westward settlement, "civilization" meeting "the wilderness" in each successive wave of westward migration. Each time that civilization met the wilderness – that point where the frontier was reborn – America came of age. To quote Turner:

> American development has exhibited not merely advance along a single line, but a return to primitive conditions on a continually advancing frontier line, and a new development for that area. American social development has been continually beginning over again on the frontier. This perennial rebirth, this fluidity of American life, this expansion westward with its new opportunities, its continuous touch with the simplicity of primitive society, furnish the forces dominating American character. The true point of view in the history of this nation is not the Atlantic coast, it is the Great West.... In this advance, the frontier is the outer edge of the wave – the meeting point between savagery and civilization.[2]

Turner goes on to emphasize the "purity" of America as the frontier advances:

> The fact is, that here is a new product that is American. At first, the frontier was the Atlantic coast. It was the frontier of Europe in a very real sense. Moving westward, the frontier became more and more American.... The result is that to the frontier the American intellect owes its striking characteristics. That coarseness and strength combined with acuteness and inquisitiveness; that practical, inventive turn of mind, quick to find expedients; that masterful grasp of material things, lacking in the artistic but powerful to effect great ends; that restless, nervous energy; that dominant individualism, working for good and for evil, and withal that buoyancy and exuberance which comes with

freedom – these are traits of the frontier, or traits called out elsewhere because of the existence of the frontier.[3]

Two points worth emphasizing, and which are commonplaces of Turner's frontier thesis: first, that the "true America" and "pure American" is in "the Great West," as Turner notes. Secondly, that the "Great West" and the characteristics Turner identified within it have defined the qualities and values of America as a whole – "the American character." Out of the West, according to Turner, had come American independence, individualism, democracy, egalitarianism, inventiveness, coarseness, idealism, and progress. The Great West thus became for Turner and his followers that "mythical region" that was more "real" than the "real West," the physical area west of the Mississippi Valley, because it had become "a region of the mind" and part of a national mythology. The mythical West became by transformation the defining region of America, so much so, and so readily identifiable, that the creation of an "imagined West" became a national preoccupation and obsession in the twentieth century. As Richard White, a member of the New Western American historians, notes: "The creation of an imagined West by those who lived in a place and sought to bond themselves to it seems readily understandable, but the creation of an imagined West by those who lived outside the West and have few or no ties to the place itself is more mysterious. Yet it is the critical issue, for the nationally imagined West has been far more powerful than the locally imagined West."[4] In American mythology, the West looms very large as *the* dominant region that has shaped America. The United States becomes the West writ large.

A different and less well-known perspective of the West has emerged north of the forty-ninth parallel. Initiated by the economic historian Harold Innis, and given popular form by Donald Creighton, it has been called the "Laurentian thesis,"[5] and has evolved, through the works of J.M.S. Careless in particular, into the metropolitan-hinterland school of thought, metropolitanism being a nice counter-perspective and contrasting term to frontierism. Careless explains metropolitanism as follows: "Briefly this implies the emergence of a city of outstanding size to dominate not only its surrounding countryside but other cities and their countrysides, the whole area being organized by the metropolis, through control of communications, trade, and finance, into one economic and social unit that is focussed on the metropolitan 'center of dominance' and through it trades with the world. Political activity, too, may often become centred on the metropolis."[6] This interpretation of history argues that the most creative and major developments in the history of Canada occurred *not* on the frontier nor in the West, but in the metropolitan centres of central Canada, most notably Montreal and Toronto in the Laurentian lowlands.

Innis first enunciated this perspective of Canadian history in his "Conclusion" to *The Fur Trade in Canada*, published in 1930. He began his "Conclusion" with the bold assertion:

> Fundamentally the civilization of North America is the civilization of Europe and the interest of this volume is primarily in the effects of a vast new land area on European civilization. The opening of a new continent distant from Europe has been responsible for the stress placed by modern students on the dissimilar features of what has been regarded as two separate civilizations. On the other hand communication and transportation facilities have always persisted between the two continents since the settlement of North America by Europeans, and have been subject to constant improvement.[7]

Note that for Innis, North American civilization is an extension of European civilization, through communication and transportation facilities, with the focus being on Europe as opposed to North America. Nowhere was this linkage truer than in Canada, which continued its historic ties to Britain well into the twentieth century. The linkage resulted in dependency of North America on metropolitan centres in Europe. As Innis noted: "The importance of metropolitan centers in which luxury goods were in most demand was crucial to the development of colonial North America."[8] This dependency remained throughout Canadian history, Innis argued, through a series of "staple trades" from fish, furs, timber, and wheat to minerals, and fossil fuels. It resulted in centralized control, which in the case of Western Canada meant control from the centre: the dominant metropolitan centres of Montreal and Toronto economically and Ottawa politically. Innis noted the resulting differences in terms of the pattern of development in Canada and the United States by comparing the Canadian pattern, implicitly more than explicitly, with that of the Turnerian frontier thesis in the United States:

Canada came under the sweep of the Industrial Revolution at one stroke whereas the westward movement of the United States was a gradual development. There are no transcontinental railroads controlled by one organization in the United States. In Canada transcontinental roads are distinct entities controlled in eastern Canada. Similarly in financial institutions the branch bank system with headquarters in the east has been typical of Canada but not of the United States. No such tendency toward unity of structure in institutions and toward centralized control as found in Canada can be observed in the United States. The Canadian government has a closer relation to economic activities than most governments.[9]

In his "Conclusion" to his *History of the Canadian Pacific Railway*, published in 1923, Innis noted the negative impact of this centralized transportation system on the Canadian West:

> [T]he tax which has been paid by western Canada as a result of the particular attitude of eastern Canada has provoked a movement [the Progressive Movement] the strength of which is difficult to estimate.... On the whole, important as the movement in western Canada must become for the future development of the country, the dominance of eastern Canada over western Canada seems likely to persist. Western Canada has paid for the development of Canadian nationality, and it would appear that it must continue to pay. The acquisitiveness of eastern Canada shows little sign of abatement.[10]

In a review article on Canadian historiography, J.M.S. Careless noted the shift in perspective of the West that occurs when one turns from the frontier to the Laurentian perspective: "Indeed, it [the Laurentian School] primarily studied the effects of the East on the West, and largely regarded business men and conservative urban political elements as agents of national expansion who might well be more far-sighted in their outlook than were their agrarian opponents."[11]

In this interpretation, the importance of cities, or metropolitan centres, evolves outwards like concentric circles. From the perspective of the Canadian West, that means that each metropolitan centre in the West – Calgary, Edmonton, Saskatoon, etc. – dominates the area around it – its hinterland –

Calgary for southern Alberta; Edmonton for northern Alberta; Saskatoon for south-central Saskatchewan, etc. Winnipeg, as the largest and most influential city in the early development of the West and historically the "gateway to the West," becomes the dominant metropolitan centre of the entire Canadian West, making the region and its smaller urban centres its "hinterland." But the entire Western region, including Winnipeg, becomes a hinterland for metropolitan centres outside its borders: Paris during the French regime; London during early British rule; Montreal and Toronto after Canadian acquisition of the West in 1869/70; and New York and Chicago more recently.

The underlying assumption of the metropolitan-hinterland paradigm is that there are essentially two types of regions: heartlands (regions of dominance) and hinterlands (regions of subservience). Prairie analysts within this perspective have consistently seen the Prairie West as a hinterland to metropolitan centres outside its borders; to my knowledge, no western historian has attempted to argue that the West was a heartland within the context of metropolitanism, a region of dominance to other regions outside its borders. According to the metropolitan school of thought, creativity, power, and dominance lie elsewhere other than in the West, and consistently within the Canadian context, in the metropolitan centres of central Canada. The Canadian West is subservient, an extension of creative forces elsewhere. Thus, unlike the frontier thesis, where the creative centre of the American nation lay in the Great West, the metropolitan thesis sees the creative centre of Canada in central Canada, and sees the West as a subordinate region in terms of shaping a national identity.

To be sure, there are positive aspects to Innis's theory vis-à-vis Turner's, some of which have been noted by Frances Kaye in her insightful article "An Innis, Not a Turner."[12] For one thing, the Canadian West does not become a monolithic region in the metropolitan-hinterland perspective that the American West becomes in the frontier thesis. While the Canadian West is seen as a hinterland region as a whole, the metropolitan-hinterland perspective allows for sub-regional differences within the West as each metropolitan centre develops its own unique relationship with its surrounding hinterland area. Turner assumes that each new "frontier wave" recreates a civilization that is similar to the previous wave, only more "purely American" in orientation. Innis also, unlike Turner, acknowledged the existence of a Native or First Nations civilization in Canada in general and the Canadian West in particular, that European migrants interacted with, and initially borrowed from, in order to survive in the harsh climate and unfamiliar terrain of North America. He does go on to note (and lament) the disappearance of this "North American civilization" as a result of the onslaught of European civilization with its superior technology. But, unlike Turner, Innis at least acknowledges the existence of a Native civilization prior to the coming of the Europeans that contributed to the European civilization that ultimately dominated in North America:

> The history of the fur trade is the history of contact between two civilizations, the European and the North American, with especial reference to the northern portion of the continent. The limited cultural background of the North American hunting peoples provided an insatiable demand for the products of the more elaborate cultural development of Europeans. The supply of European goods, the product of a more advanced and specialized technology, enabled the Indians to gain a livelihood more easily – to obtain their supply of food, as in the case of moose, more quickly, and to hunt the beaver more effectively.
>
> Unfortunately the rapid destruction of the food supply and the revolution in the methods of living accompanied by the increasing attention to the fur trade by which these products were secured, disturbed the balance which had grown up previous to the coming of the European. The new technology with its radical innovations brought about such a rapid shift in the prevailing Indian culture as to lead to wholesale destruction of the peoples concerned by warfare and disease.[13]

Turner's frontier thesis reflected the attitude of the American frontiersman and settlers/homesteaders whose history he attempted to understand and explain. As they pushed westward, they pushed aside anything and anyone who got in the way of the advancing American frontier and the "civilization" that it brought with it. The wilderness, and its Native inhabitants, succumbed or were conquered. As has often been noted, to American settlers, the only good Indian was a dead Indian. Innis's Laurentian thesis reflected a different attitude among Canadian fur traders, who depended on the Native population for survival and for the success of the fur trade. Innis at least acknowledged as early as 1930 the importance of the First Nations people with their own "North American civilization" in shaping and defining the nature of a "Canadian civilization," a term Innis used to distinguish Canada from the United States.

Still, the overall image of the Canadian West in the metropolitan-hinterland paradigm is a negative one. The Canadian West as a hinterland, a region subservient to regions of dominance outside its borders, contrasts unfavourably with the much more positive perspective of the American West in the Turnerian schemata as a creative region that defined the finest attributes of the nation. In the Turnerian myth, the West is an Edenic garden where all within are virtuous, contented, and fulfilled individuals. The ideal inhabitant in the garden of the West – the "Adam" – and it is "Adam" not "Eve" who is the truly "godly" inhabitant of the American Edenic West – is the yeoman farmer. The myth is a story of success, of triumph, what Northrop Frye, the Canadian literary theorist of mythology, would classify as the "myth of freedom."[14] In the Innisian mythology, the Canadian West is the wilderness, the area to which Adam and Eve were banished when they were expelled from the "Garden." Or using another biblical reference, Canada in general became identified with what Jacques Cartier called "the land that God gave Cain" – the barren land that contrasted unfavourably with the lush, fertile land that Cain's brother, Abel, received. It was a region that had few redeeming qualities, a region of "staples" or "natural resources" that could be exploited for the benefit of profiteers elsewhere. The Canadian West became, to paraphrase a description of Canada given by Goldwin Smith, a late-nineteenth-century Canadian critic, "the hewers of wheat and the drawers of oil" for eastern Canadians, Europeans, or Americans, a development that western Canadian historians remind us has stunted the growth of the region ever since, resulting in perpetual western Canadian protest, the most recent being the Canadian Alliance Party.

One has to remember that just as the Turner frontier thesis presented a perspective that gave meaning to all of American history, so too the Innisian Laurentian thesis presented a perspective on Canadian history as a whole. That perspective on Canada was as negative as it was on the region of the West within Canadian development. Canada was seen as a vast hinterland for metropolitan centres outside its borders to exploit and dominate, whether Paris, London, New York, or Chicago, or any other major American city that has close links with Canada. The powerlessness that the Canadian West has felt throughout its history as a hinterland to central Canada is true of Canada as a whole in its history, feeling resentful of first British, and then American, dominance, causing Innis to note sardonically that the history of Canada has been one of "colony to nation to colony" – from a colony of Britain prior to

World War I to a brief moment of independence and nationhood in the interwar years to a colony of the United States in the post-World War II era. The irony is that Innis formulated his Laurentian thesis in the interwar years, at the very moment when Canada was supposedly "celebrating" its independence. Yet it was his theory – and the mythology that it created – that perpetuated the image of Canada as a hinterland, an area of subservience and dependency on "foreign" countries. To this day, Innis's interpretation of Canadian history holds sway as the most convincing explanation of Canada's past. Canadian historians chip away at it, but the Laurentian thesis seems as strong and enduring as the granite rock of the Laurentian Shield from which the theory derives its name. It has been as difficult to challenge and supplant Innis's theory as the New Western American historians have found the Turner thesis to be.

But if both the Turner and the Innis perspectives are *only myths*, then like all myths, they are only one way of constructing reality and making sense of the world, or in this case that part of the world, the North American West, that interests us; they are not absolute truths (with a capital "T"). Such myths need to be challenged and supplanted.

Of the two myths under consideration, the metropolitan-hinterland one has been least questioned. Indeed, it is worth taking a leaf from the work of the New Western American historians who have succeeded in undermining one aspect of the frontier thesis: its monolithic view of the American West. These historians continually remind Americans that there were many different groups who inhabited the American West, groups who do not fit into the Turnerian perspective of white Anglo-Saxon Protestant (WASP) male homesteaders, such groups as women, blacks, Hispanics, and Native Americans.[15] As Richard White reminds us: "[Western] myths are constantly in competition just as various groups within the West were always in competition."[16]

Now it would be unfair to suggest that Western Canadian historians have not done the same for minority groups within the Canadian West. First Nations, ethnic, and women historians, to name but a few, have been presenting the history of their respective interest groups, telling the story, giving a voice to these minority groups, noting their contribution to the history of the Canadian West. Yet, the story is still most often told within the familiar Innisian paradigm, i.e., these groups as subservient minorities dominated by the majority group within the region, or by dominant groups in metropolitan centres outside the region, against which the minority group has had to struggle.

A recent book that has stirred considerable interest among Western American historians (and some Western Canadian historians too) might serve as a fine example of what I have in mind. The book is Jon Gjerde's *Minds of the West: Ethnocultural Evolution in the Rural Middle West, 1870-1917* (1997).[17] Note that Gjerde talks about the "minds of the West" in the plural, emphasizing that the American West was not of one mind nor did it have a common perspective or uniform population. In this way alone, Gjerde challenges Turner's view of the American West as a monolithic region. Gjerde compares the ideas, beliefs, and values of the "foreign mind," that of the Catholic and Lutheran newcomers from continental Europe in the mid-nineteenth century, to the traditional "Puritan mind," the *mentalité* of the native-born Protestant Americans of British stock, in the Upper Middle West – the states of Illinois, Wisconsin, Iowa, Nebraska, and North and South Dakota. He does not assume, however, that these "mind sets" were fixed from the point of transition of immigrants from Europe to the American West, but notes that values and beliefs became transformed "on the frontier." At the same time, however, these immigrants did not completely abandon their values and beliefs from the Old World and adopt wholeheartedly the beliefs and values of the host society, a wholly American perspective as Turner believed; these European immigrants contributed to a new "Western American mind set," but one that was a fusion of Old World and New World values.

If one compares Gjerde's *Minds of the West* with an earlier American study of the Western American mindset, Henry Nash Smith's *Virgin Land: The American West as Symbol and Myth* (1950), the contrast and current trends in American historiography are evident. Smith assumes that the American West is of one mind, a mindset that was epitomized in Turner's frontier thesis. As Smith notes:

> The present study traces the impact of the West, the vacant continent beyond the frontier, on the consciousness of Americans and follows the principal consequences of this impact in literature and social thought down to Turner's formulation of it. Whatever the merits of the Turner thesis, the doctrine that the United States is a continental nation rather than a member with Europe of an Atlantic community has had a formative influence on the American mind and deserves historical treatment in its own right.[18]

Smith sketches out this "American mind" in broad strokes. To be sure, he notes the nuances, the altering perspective, of that American mindset in different periods. But a unity and commonality of thought prevails in the end. And it is appropriate that Smith ends his study with a chapter on "The Myth of the Garden and Turner's Frontier Hypothesis," because Turner's frontier hypothesis is very much the backdrop to Smith's study, representative of the thinking of the region as a whole, he argues. This is not to denigrate Smith's study; it is a classic in American history and deserves to be considered as such. However, it examines only one version of the American West, one Western American myth. Gjerde's study looks at at least two different mindsets, two Western American myths, and a study similar to his is needed for the Canadian West. Better yet would be a comparative study of similar groups in the American and Canadian Wests to see to what extent the differing environment on both sides of the forty-ninth parallel and the differing intellectual and cultural milieux across the border have affected the outlook of immigrant groups who settled in the two Wests. As well, such a study could explain in what way these immigrant groups shaped the *mentalité* or psyche of the two western regions, thus contributing to the unique and different perspectives of the Canadian and American Wests. Here is a challenge to comparative Canadian/American studies.

These reflections need to be drawn to a close. Maybe one way to do so is to return to the myth of the Canadian West, and to suggest a possible new Western Canadian myth. In his little collection of essays entitled *The Educated Imagination*, Northrop Frye suggests that an appropriate myth for the modern age might be the biblical Tower of Babel. To quote Frye's reflections on this myth:

> The particular myth that's been organizing this talk and in a way the whole series, is the story of the Tower of Babel in the Bible. The civilization we live in at present is a gigantic technological structure, a skyscraper almost high enough to reach the moon. It looks like a single world-wide effort, but it's really a deadlock of rivalries; it looks very impressive, except that it has no genuine human dignity. For all its wonderful machinery, we know it's really a crazy ramshackle building, and at any time may crash around our ears. What the myth tells us is that the Tower of Babel is a work of human imagination, that its main elements are words, and that what will make it collapse is a confusion of tongues. All had

originally one language, the myth says. The language is not English or Russian or Chinese or any common ancestor, if there was one. It is the language of human nature that makes both Shakespeare and Pushkin authentic poets, that gives a social vision to both Lincoln and Gandhi. It never speaks unless we take the time to listen in leisure, and it speaks only in a voice too quiet for panic to hear. And then all it has to tell us, when we look over the edge of our leaning tower, is that we are not getting any nearer heaven, and that it is time to return to the earth.[19]

In another essay, Frye notes that the myth of the Tower of Babel became "related to Mesopotamian ziggurat, the temple in the midst of the city that provided the means of ascent to the gods, a kind of artificial mountain transplanted to a flat country."[20]

In the period of settlement at the turn of the twentieth century, the image of the Canadian West as a "Tower of Babel" was evoked by opponents of multicultural and multilingual immigration into the Canadian West as an indication of all that was wrong with the settlement of the West with groups that spoke different languages and adhered to strange customs. They took the biblical myth literally, believing that what would cause the Tower of Babel – and by analogy the Canadian West – to collapse was a "confusion of tongues," and thus advocated instead the imposition of one language – English – and one culture – British-Canadian – on the West.

Yet, the myth of the Tower of Babel with its many voices, its sense of creation from human imagination and ingenuity, its "main elements of words," and its "stairway to heaven" in a "flat country" seems an appropriate one for the Canadian West. It situates the creative imagination in the West itself, and acknowledges a multiplicity of voices, and the importance of words – myths – in creating the region's identity. Could not such a myth as the Tower of Babel offer an alternative to the Innisian mythology? If adopted, we might come to realize that the Canadian West was a much richer, deeper, more complex, and more exciting region in the past than we have come to believe. We might also discover that there was not just "one West," and only "two myths," but many Wests and a multiplicity of myths. Discovering and chronicling these many Wests and multiplicity of myths might well be the greatest challenge of comparative Canadian/American studies of the West.

Questions to Ponder

1. How does Turner define the West? Is this accurate about today's West or the historical West?
2. What happens when you apply Turner's thesis to Canada?
3. What is the metropolitan theory?
4. What happens when you apply the metropolitan theory to the United States West?
5. How does the West affect the East and vice versa in the United States and Canada?

Must Reads

Frye, Northrop. *The Educated Imagination*. Massey Lectures. Toronto: Canadian Broadcasting Corporation, 1963.

Gjerde, Jon. *The Minds of the West: Ethnocultural Evolution in the Rural Middle West, 1830–1917*. Chapel Hill: University of North Carolina Press, 1997.

Innis, Harold. *The Fur Trade in Canada: An Introduction to Canadian Economic History* [1930] rev. ed. Toronto: University of Toronto Press, 1965.

Limerick, Patricia Nelson et al., eds. *Trails: Toward a New Western History*. Lawrence: University Press of Kansas, 1991.

White, Richard, *"It's Your Misfortune and None of My Own": A History of the American West*. Norman: University of Oklahoma Press, 1991.

Notes

1 Frederick Jackson Turner, "The Significance of the Frontier in American History," in *The Frontier Thesis and the Canadas: The Debate on the Impact of the Canadian Environment*, ed. Michael S. Cross (Toronto: Copp Clark, 1970), p. 12.
2 Ibid., pp. 12–13.
3 Ibid., pp. 13, 22.
4 Richard White, "The Imagined West," in *It's Your Misfortune and None of My Own: A History of the American West* (Norman: University of Oklahoma Press, 1991), p. 619.
5 Harold Innis formulated the Laurentian thesis in *The Fur Trade in Canada: An Introduction to Canadian Economic History* [1930], rev. ed. (Toronto: University of Toronto Press, 1956); and the implications for the West in *A History of the Canadian Pacific Railway* [1923], rev. ed. (Toronto: University of Toronto Press, 1971). Donald Creighton developed the thesis in *The Commercial Empire of the St. Lawrence, 1760–1850* [1937], rev. ed. (Toronto: University of Toronto Press, 1956).

6   J.M.S. Careless, "Frontierism, Metropolitanism, and Canadian History," in *Approaches to Canadian History*, ed. Ramsay Cook, Craig Brown, and Carl Berger (Toronto: University of Toronto Press, 1967), p. 79.
7   Innis, *The Fur Trade in Canada*, p. 383.
8   Ibid., p. 384.
9   Ibid., p. 401.
10 Innis, *History of the Canadian Pacific Railway*, p. 294.
11 Careless, "Frontierism, Metropolitanism, and Canadian History," p. 78.
12 Frances W. Kaye, "An Innis, Not a Turner," *American Review of Canadian Studies* 31, no. 4 (Winter 2001): 597–610.
13 Innis, *The Fur Trade in Canada*, p. 388.
14 For a discussion of this myth, see Northrop Frye, *The Critical Path: An Essay on the Social Context of Literary Criticism* (Bloomington: Indiana University Press, 1971).
15 For a good sample of the writings and ideas of the New Western Historians, see the essays in Patricia Nelson Limerick, Clyde A. Milner II, and Charles E. Rankin, eds., *Trails: Toward A New Western History* (Lawrence: University Press of Kansas, 1991).
16 White, "The Imagined West," p. 617.
17 Jon Gjerde, *The Minds of the West: Ethnocultural Evolution in the Rural Middle West, 1830–1917* (Chapel Hill: University of North Carolina Press, 1997).
18 Henry Nash Smith, *Virgin Land: The American West as Symbol and Myth* [1950], rev. ed. (New York: Random House), p. 4.
19 Northrop Frye, *The Educated Imagination*. Massey Lectures (Toronto: Canadian Broadcasting Corporation, 1963), pp. 67–68.
20 Northrop Frye, "The Koine of Myth: Myth as a Universally Intelligible Language," in *Northrop Frye: Myth and Metaphor, Selected Essays, 1974–1988*, ed. Robert D. Denham (Charlottesville: University Press of Virginia, 1990), p. 11.

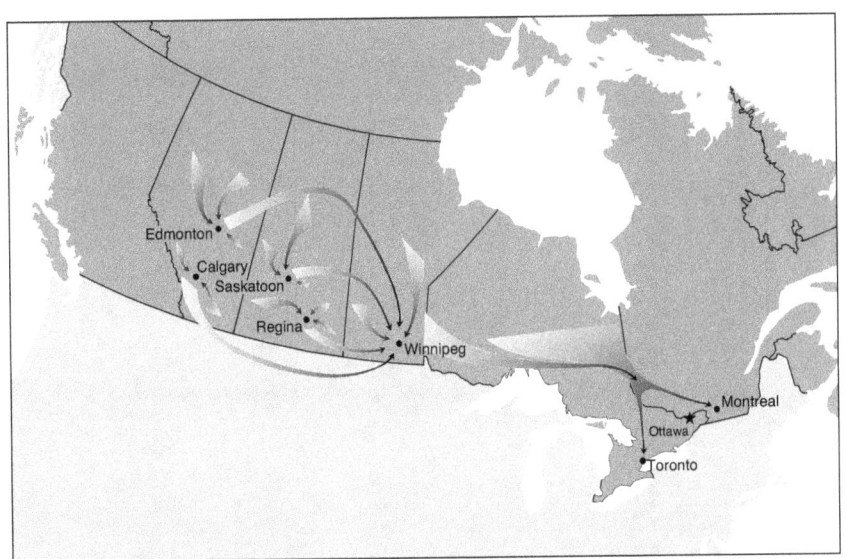

A Visual Representation of the Theory of Metropolitanism

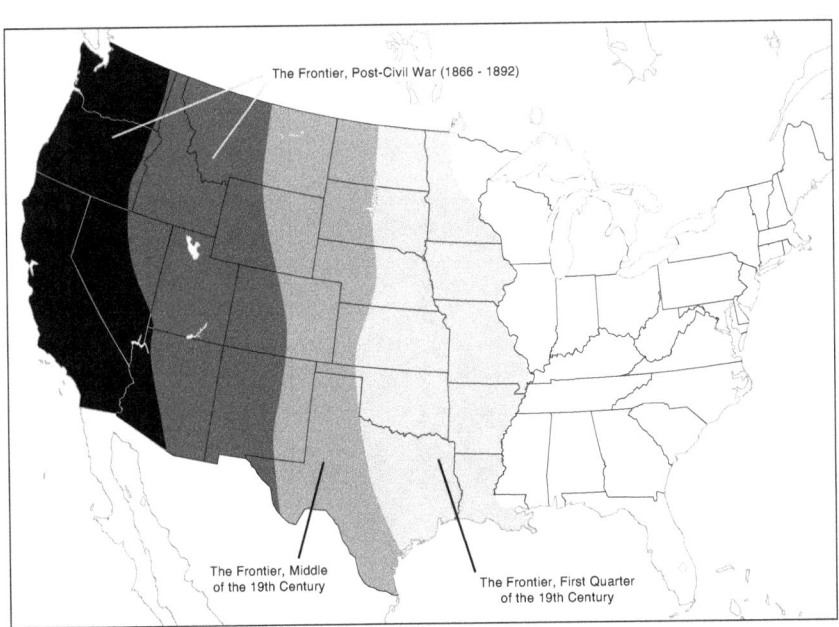

A Visual Representation of Turner's Frontier Thesis

chapter three

One West, One Myth: Transborder Continuity in Western Art

Brian W. Dippie, University of Victoria

In American and Canadian literature, the notion of One West, Two Myths seems plausible. The large "W" Western – formula fiction in which violence resolves a conflict between good and evil – expresses distinctly American cultural values, the argument goes, constituting a Puritan morality play. And it is also possible to argue for subtle differences in the presentation of the American and Canadian Wests even in a grimly realistic, transnational literature like the prairie or farming novel in which the heavy hand of environmental determinism would seem to impose sameness.[1] The theme of the Melting Pot, for example, appears more pronounced in such American novels as Willa Cather's *O Pioneers!* (1913) and *My Ántonia* (1918) and O.E. Rolvaag's *Peder Victorious* (1929) than in comparable Canadian prairie novels also concerned with the immigrant experience such as Martha Ostenso's *Wild Geese* (1925) and Frederick Philip Grove's *Our Daily Bread* (1928).

Does the same hold true of imagery? Is there, in Canadian representations of the West, more emphasis on farming and family, on an Arcadian idyll rather than on the whoop-and-holler action, violent conflict, and rugged individualism so prominent in American Western art? Of course, the promotional literature and the accompanying illustrations issued by railways and governmental agencies on both sides of the border emphasized the fecundity of the land and abundant cereal crops or fruit trees or whatever was particular to the area being promoted. And there is a whole prairie school of art showing wheat fields and grain elevators silhouetted against towering skies. Notably, in his useful anthology *Images of the West: Changing Perceptions of the Prairies, 1690–1960*, Douglas Francis devotes attention to the idea of the Canadian West as the promised land, the garden of the world; cowboys and cattle are conspicuous by their absence.[2] Indeed, the coats of arms of two of the three Prairie Provinces – Alberta and Saskatchewan – feature grain. Only Manitoba's displays a ruminant, a majestic buffalo, leaving cattle shut out entirely.[3] But if Alberta's coat of arms is content to honour its farming potential at the expense of its grazing industry, it does include the snow-capped Rockies. Tourist imagery, naturally, emphasizes nature at its grandest, with soaring mountain peaks and all the possibilities for alpine recreation – from trail hikes and rides, skiing and climbing, to simple contemplation of the scenery from the veranda of a hotel set on the shore of a glimmerglass lake.[4] Hunting and fishing in the West produced its own body of literature and illustration squarely within the venerable tradition devoted to outdoors adventure.[5] But heritage was also always part of the tourist sales pitch: an Old West, gone with the wind and magic in memory. Nostalgia doted on the picturesque. In the imagery popularized by Western art, cowboys and Indians ruled on both sides of the border.

It has become something of a truism in the historiography of the Canadian West to insist that its ranching frontier was distinctive from that of the American West. A strong British tradition, enforced by the arrival of the North-West Mounted Police in 1874, outweighed American elements, the reasoning goes, producing a respect for law and order that virtually eliminated the "wild and woolly" antics so prevalent to the south.[6] What might be referred to – politely – as the Lewis G. Thomas school of ranching history, followed his pathbreaking 1935 Master's thesis on "The Ranching Period in Southern Alberta." As a member of a southern Alberta ranch family himself, educated in Okotoks and Calgary and then at the University of Alberta and Harvard, and an unabashed anglophile, Thomas was convinced that the refined culture of the ranch community in southern Alberta was quite distinct from the rougher, cruder American culture below the border.[7] He and his followers acknowledged strong American influences in the earliest history of the Canadian range and in practical matters of cattle management, but otherwise discounted them.[8] In effect, the Americans exported the cowboy, but the ranchman was a distinctively Canadian fusion of respectable Central Canadians and the British gentry. This led to the entrenchment of a contrasting mythology: the Mild West north of the border, and the Wild West south of it.[9]

Recently, Warren Elofson has challenged the basis of these competing national mythologies by arguing that neither West lived up to its mythic billing. That is, Canada's "mild" West was wilder than the myth allows, while the American West was never as wild as its myth would have it.[10] Indeed, a substantial literature has long existed poking gaping holes in – and fun at – the idea of the American Wild West. John Barrows, who cowboyed awhile in Montana's Judith Basin in the same years as Charles M. Russell, was at pains to point out that the local roundup was "a tame affair ... dominated by eastern cattlemen,"[11] while Walt Coburn, the son of a Montana rancher, wrote "blood and thunder" Westerns but always acknowledged how much tamer the reality was.[12] Even Russell himself, Montana's celebrated "Cowboy Artist," had fun with the idea of a shoot-'em-up West. Writing from Hollywood in 1926 he observed: "thair are more two gun men here now than the history of the west from north to south ever knew ... if the old west had of been as tough as the mooves make it thaeyd be run[n]ing buffalo yet on the Great Falls flat."[13] American historians like Lewis Atherton and Gene Gressley in the 1960s tried to redirect attention from the cowboy, a picturesque but relatively inconsequential hired hand, to "cattle kings" and the more substantial investor/managerial elite – "bankers and cattlemen," as Gressley put it – in the spirit of rescuing American Western history from Wild West moonshine. "Glamor, romance, and legend tend to obscure business aspects of the ranching industry," Atherton stated. In addressing the heavy British investment in the American cattle industry ("At least thirty-three limited companies registered in Great Britain between 1879 and 1888 with the primary intention of investing in American ranching."), he provided another parallel to the Canadian cattle industry.[14]

Arguing for the distinctiveness of southern Alberta ranch culture, Sheilagh Jameson observed that hunting coyotes with hounds was a popular Foothills sport, affirming the "predominantly British middle class background" of Alberta ranchers.[15] But the Portland, Oregon-based magazine *West Shore*, on its cover for October 5, 1889, featured a well-dressed Montana rancher riding after a pack of hounds which are nipping at the heels of their quarry. Titled "Coursing Cayotes in Montana," the illustration not only undercuts the assumption of Alberta distinctiveness, but also challenges the American myth of the Wild West. Today, the milder elements of the American West serve to

"*Coursing Cayotes in Montana,*" *West Shore no. 174 (5 October 1889), cover. Author's Collection.*

establish the social history objectives of the New Western History, in which ordinary folk and families were the norm, not free-riding cowboys on a drunken spree with pistols a-blazing.[16]

But Western art resists revision. It works the wild side of the ledger, isolating the romantic and stirring at the expense of the mundane and monotonous. In 1890 Charlie Russell, still night wrangling for a living, painted his version of the *West Shore* cover, *Cowboy Sport – Roping a Wolf*. By shifting from a genteel ranchman with his pack of hounds to a couple of rough-hewn cowboys giving chase at full gallop, lassos twirling, a hat flying off, he transformed the entire feel of the subject.[17] It is this image, the Russell image, that has stuck in the popular imagination. When an Alberta rancher like George Lane wanted a painting of his own encounter with wolves, he naturally turned to Russell. The resulting watercolour, with Lane blasting away with his pistol at the attacking animals, is pure Wild West melodrama – a lupine Custer's Last Stand.

Charles M. Russell, Cowboy Sport – Roping a Wolf (1890, oil on canvas). Courtesy The Sid Richardson Collection, Fort Worth, Texas.

As one of the "Big Four" – the Alberta cattlemen responsible for underwriting the first Calgary Stampede – Lane serves as a proper segue into the subject of Western imagery on both sides of the border. Before 1912, Calgary's Dominion Exhibition had been a reasonably sedate agricultural fair with limited cowboy elements. Its poster for 1908 showed progress as an obstacle: a barbed wire fence and a sheaf of grain blocking the path of a cowboy who reins in his horse, apparently ready to accept the inevitable. "Another Trail Cut Off," the poster read: "Visit Alberta before the golden opportunities, picturesque riders and Indians are gone."[18] The same theme was revisited in a poster for the 1912 Calgary Industrial Exhibition. "Keeping His Hand In," it said, and this time the cowboy was galloping along the wire fence, having lassoed a sheaf of grain on the other side.[19] That September, the Calgary Stampede debuted.

Influences on the 1912 Stampede were strongly American. Guy Weadick, born in Rochester, New York in 1885, was the Stampede's founder and energetic manager in its early years. He staged a second Stampede in Winnipeg in 1913 and, after a hiatus caused by the Great War, brought it back to Calgary in 1919 where, beginning in 1923, it became an annual event. Guy Weadick, the advertising read in 1919: "The Guy That Put the Punch In Cowpuncher."[20]

With roots in American vaudeville (a "rope act" with his wife Florence LaDue) and broad experience as an entertainer, Weadick had a showman's instinct for what the public wanted even before the public realized it. The Stampede was a case in point. As Weadick recalled, he "brought the idea of 'The Stampede' to Calgary as an attraction for this part of the continent, and induced the 'Big Four' to financially sponsor it after various Calgarians had predicted that such an attraction would never be a success in Calgary."[21] And he made sure that the 1912 Stampede – "A Peerless Presentation of the Pioneer Past" – was a borderless affair, with American contestants and bucking horses known by reputation, contract performers, including the Pendleton, Oregon Mounted Cowboy Band, a contingent of vaqueros brought all expenses paid from Mexico, and such acknowledgments of Alberta's history as: an encampment of two thousand costumed Indians from the Blackfoot, Blood, Stoney and Sarcee reserves, a reunion of veterans of the 1874 Mounted Police attired in period uniform, and a replica of Fort Whoop-up, the notorious American whisky post at the confluence of the Old Man and St. Mary's Rivers that led to the Mounties coming west in the first place. The wild old days were key to the Stampede's appeal, and the Stampede's West, like Charlie Russell's cowboy, "ranged from the timber rims in the East to the shores of the Pacific from Mexico north to snow bound land."[22]

Weadick made a number of good decisions in publicizing the first Calgary Stampede. He used the drawings of Edward Borein, a California cowboy artist, to illustrate Stampede advertising, establishing a partnership that in 1919 created the most recognizable image associated with the Calgary Stampede, Borein's etching of a towering horse and rider bucking straight at the viewer, "I-See-U."[23] And he invited Borein's friend, Montana's Charlie Russell, to hold an exhibition of his original art at the Stampede. It was a beneficial partnership that made Russell an integral part of successive Stampedes – his work illustrated posters in both 1912 and 1919 – and his artistic vision of the Old West a Canadian vision, too.[24]

Charles M. Russell was born in St. Louis in 1864. The year he turned sixteen, his family allowed him to spend the summer on a sheep ranch in the Judith Basin. "Kid Russell" fell in love with the land and, by 1882, the cowboy way of life. As a night wrangler on the spring and fall roundups he sketched what he saw, and by 1887 had established a local reputation as the "cowboy artist." He quit the range in 1893 to take up his art full time, and three years later married Nancy Cooper. In 1897 they settled in Great Falls. It was still their home when Russell died in 1926.²⁵

Long before then, Nancy's business sense and drive had made her husband famous. His original paintings commanded thousands of dollars, and the public knew his work through countless calendar, postcard, and colour print reproductions. Thus when Guy Weadick invited Russell to Calgary in 1912, he was inviting a bona fide attraction. The publicity was clear. "Without any question the magnificent exhibition of Charles Russell's pictures in the art exhibition, depicting scenes of early cowboy life call forth paens of praise.... Whether his efforts be in either water colors or oils, the amount of light and shade, coupled with fine technique, that he puts into his work are worthy of the efforts of an R.A."²⁶

Russell was already familiar with Alberta. In 1888 he had spent a summer on High River with a friend. "I have reached my stop[p]ing place," he wrote in a letter that June: "I am s[t]aying at a cattle ranch on high rive[r] I am not doing aney thing now as I got here to late for the roundup I like the county pritty well so far there is lots of Indians here they visit us nearly every day."²⁷ The experience in Alberta changed Russell. Eventually the Cowboy Artist would be equally famous as a painter of the old-time Plains Indian. He had renewed his acquaintance with Alberta in 1903 when, having succumbed to the "lure of the North," he took the train up to "Fort Edmonton," as he styled it, in hopes of finding a fur post with trappers and Indians and dog teams – the frontier reborn, in short. In the period 1906–10 Russell often crossed into Alberta since he co-owned a ranch in the Sweet Grass Hills five miles below the border. The Montana-Alberta border opened both ways and people moved across it freely, received ideas in tow. Russell's West was the Northern Plains. His Indians were Plains Indians and, after his experiences in Alberta, frequently Blackfeet. Their reservation straddled the border. His cowboys were the Montana cowboys of his day who roamed the northern range. In attending the 1912 Calgary Stampede, then, Russell was on familiar ground.²⁸

Among the paintings Russell exhibited in Calgary were several showing cowboys at work and just as strenuously at play, old-time Indians moving magisterially across a land they still owned, man-animal confrontations, and action galore. They proved irresistible. Thirteen of the twenty paintings listed in Russell's "Special Exhibition" catalogue were sold. The buyers, by definition, were wealthy – "gentlemen" of a ranching persuasion, or Central Canadians and Englishmen lured by the romance of the West epitomized by William F. "Buffalo Bill" Cody's entertainment sensation the Wild West, and by the stories and pictures that appeared in English boys' annuals well into the twentieth century of a still exciting frontier "out there" where Red Indians and white settlers often came to mortal blows.[29] Even Lewis G. Thomas had reference to Russell's work: "None of the innumerable water-colours, oils and sketches, which the women of the [Alberta] ranches, like their English sisters, delighted in making ever equalled the works in which C.W. [sic] Russell depicted so vitally the life of the American range."[30] In fact, Canadian ranchers turned to Russell, through reproductions and a sprinkling of originals, to provide images of life on their range as well.

George Lane was one of the Stampede's "Big Four" – the men who provided the financial backing that made it all possible. Born in the Midwest in 1856, Lane, like Russell, migrated to Montana when he was just sixteen. There he rode for some of the large cattle outfits before moving north to Canada in 1884 to manage the Bar U Ranch – and eventually, to own it. Lane clearly relished the American cowboy mythos with its rugged individualism, though unlike Russell he was a progressive when it came to western settlement and boasted as much about Alberta's farm potential as he did about its ranching heritage.[31] Still, Lane identified with the camaraderie and fun of the good old days on the range. A rider being bucked into a roundup camp's morning fire to the dismay of the cook was a Russell staple by 1912, best known through his 1908 watercolour *Bronc to Breakfast*. Lane "wouldent have aney thing elce," Russell noted, "so I painted him one."[32] Lane ordered *Camp Cook's Troubles* right after the Stampede, and tradition has it that his only criticism was that an axe in the foreground did not have its handle mended – a fact of life in every cow camp he remembered. Russell was happy to make the correction.

Seeing the two paintings side by side demonstrates that Russell's cowboy imagery knew no boundaries. For him, cowboys on either side of the Forty-ninth Parallel, like the Indians and wildlife, were interchangeable. Indeed, he made only one direct concession to the Canadian market after his success at the first Calgary Stampede. That fall, and once each year for the next three years, he painted a major oil painting featuring the Mounted Police. In them, Russell sometimes reworked his typical subject matter. On exhibition at the Calgary Stampede in 1912 was an oil titled *The Call of the Law* (1911), showing a sheriff arresting two horse thieves. Russell subsequently gave it a

Canadian twist in *When Law Dulls the Edge of Chance* (1915), replacing the sheriff with Mounted Policemen. At first glance, it is a specifically Canadian painting. In fact, it shows Russell adapting a Montana theme to a Canadian setting. Russell's West readily folded Canadian and American content into a single construct.[33]

Russell returned to Calgary in 1919 to exhibit at the Victory Stampede, as it was called, marking the end of the Great War. Patrick Burns, a self-made man with a packing house and ranching empire, was one of the "Big Four" who again bankrolled the Stampede.[34] He bought another Mounted Police painting with a genuinely Canadian theme, *Whiskey Smugglers Caught with the Goods* (1913). George Lane, in turn, bought *The Queen's War Hounds* (1914), and arranged for the purchase of *When Law Dulls the Edge of Chance* for presentation to the Prince of Wales, who was touring Canada at the time and had decided to purchase the ranch next to Lane's Bar U. In appreciation, Lane persuaded the citizens of High River to present the Prince with a Russell painting to adorn his new Alberta ranch house. In fact, the painting ended up in England, at the Imperial Institute, where it was destined to join other Canadian works. "The picture has been on view here for two months and has attracted considerable attention," an official wrote Russell in 1920. "Our Canadian Section is now under reorganization, but the picture will afterwards be shown, together with the other presents which his Royal Highness the Prince of Wales has contributed to our Galleries."[35] That "our Canadian Section" says it all. To the extent that Russell's work shaped the content of the Western myth, it was a borderless myth.

Russell was one of the two most influential artists to depict the American West at the end of the nineteenth century. Frederic Remington was the other. Both, in their very different ways, were master myth-makers. Remington, who was born in 1860 in Canton, New York, just across the St. Lawrence River from Canada, grew up loving outdoor activities and daft about horses and soldiers; his father was a cavalry officer in the Civil War. The West became his substitute battlefield. He first visited in 1880 and, as an artist-correspondent, frequently thereafter. But apart from a brief residence in Kansas and Kansas City, New York City remained his home base until his death in 1909. More than any other artist he defined the Old West for his generation. His work appeared in all the leading American periodicals, and as early as 1892 a journalist could observe: "It is a fact that admits of no question that Eastern people have formed their conceptions of what the Far-Western life is like, more from what they have seen in Mr. Remington's pictures than from any other source."³⁶

Remington played a seminal role in shaping the image of two key actors in the Western drama: the Indian-fighting soldier and the cowboy. His cowboy sketches and paintings illustrated an influential series of essays by Theodore Roosevelt, an aspiring politician with a ranch in Dakota, published in *Century Magazine* in 1888. Roosevelt described cowboys; Remington gave them visual form. "They are smaller and less muscular than the wielders of ax and pick," Roosevelt wrote,

> but they are as hardy and self-reliant as any men who ever breathed – with bronzed, set faces, and keen eyes that look all the world straight in the face without flinching as they flash out from under the broad-brimmed hats … their appearance is striking … and picturesque too, with their jingling spurs, the big revolvers stuck in their belts, and bright silk handkerchiefs knotted loosely round their necks over the open collars of the flannel shirts. When drunk on the villainous whisky of the frontier towns, they cut mad antics, riding their horses into the saloons, firing their pistols right and left, … and indulging too often in deadly shooting affrays….³⁷

Just so did Remington show them. Drawing on the photographs of L.A. Huffman of Miles City, Montana, he covered the range of cowboy subjects: cow camp and roundup routine, including, roping, branding, night herding and horse breaking; hazing a tenderfoot; a stampede; Indian encounters; and saloon brawls and shoot-outs.

Like every other artist who "did" the West, Russell was influenced by Remington. But because their Western myths were different, he reworked Remington themes and poses to his own ends. Remington celebrated the taming of a savage land, the "winning of the West"; Russell lamented what was lost in the process.³⁸ Thus his initial foray into painting the North-West Mounted Police in 1888 conveyed a downbeat understanding of defeat and dispossession. Two Mounted Policemen escort three Blood Indians to Fort Macleod, a scene approximating one Russell had actually witnessed. While the police are jaunty enough, their prisoners appear glum.³⁹ *Canadian Mounted Police bringing in Red Indian Prisoners* is steeped in pathos. Russell returned to the subject in 1912 in *Single Handed*, showing the arrest in an Indian camp of a warrior by a lone constable. Of course the tone was different by then. Reality had been swallowed up in golden romance; policing the Indians, in retrospect, had become a testament to white valour and native admiration for such valour. No guns blazing and swords slashing madly; no cavalry charge scattering a war party. Just Indians watching silently, studying the policeman for a flinch that will dispel the aura created by his daring. Indeed, Russell – who almost never painted soldiers – loved painting the North-West Mounted Police. He respected their even-handed enforcement of the law, and showed them going about their business, armed and purposeful, but never actually firing their weapons.

In contrast, Remington's treatment of a similar subject, published in 1888, *Arrest of a Blackfeet Murderer*, was action-packed. Galloping horses and riders charge at the viewer. It appears as though a whole troop of Mounted Policemen are apprehending a single culprit – reversing the point of Russell's *Single Handed*, and linking Remington's depiction directly to his cavalry action scenes. Remington had visited Western Canada in 1887 and added Blackfeet and the Mounted Police to his stock of picturesque Western types. His Mounted Policemen and soldiers were interchangeable; both could be plugged into his mythic Wild West. How generic, and adaptable, was Remington's West? His illustrations for Roosevelt's 1888 cowboy essays included *A Bucking Bronco*. Here was a subject that captured the cowboy ideal – a national ideal, in the view of both men – in compressed, exciting form. "A true 'cow town' is worth seeing," Roosevelt wrote, because "It would be impossible to imagine a more typically American assemblage...."[40] Wallace Coburn, Montana's "Cowboy Poet" whose 1899 book of verse *Rhymes from a Round-Up Camp* was illustrated by "my old friend and fellow range rider" Charles M. Russell, echoed Roosevelt's tribute in "The Cow-Boy":

> No other land can claim his like,
> He's a native American, born and bred,
> A product of God's noblest land,
> The land for which his fathers bled.[41]

Fittingly, given the cowboy's Americanness, Remington's *A Bucking Bronco* was directly cribbed in an early poster advertising Buffalo Bill's Wild West,

"America's National Entertainment."[42] "Cowboy Evangelist" Buckskin Brady, in a book published in Toronto in 1905, also used the same image to illustrate this sentiment:

> The first few days of the spring round-up, when all the horses are aching to take the tickle out of the cowboys' spurs, it is great sport to see the boys starting for circle in the morning. Talk about Buffalo Bill's outlaw horses! but here's where you have to come to see the real Wild West, because the country is rough and a bronc never picks out a nice piece of ground on which to have his fun.[43]

Since Brady, like Roosevelt, was born in New York and cowboyed in the Dakotas, using a Remington illustration to represent his experiences made sense. But in the same period Remington's picture also illustrated a postcard published in Canada captioned "Ranching in the Canadian West. Broncho Breaking."

Why use an American image to illustrate a Canadian subject? Perhaps a cowboy is just a cowboy, and one size fits all. But the cowboy extolled by Roosevelt and depicted by Remington – and by Russell, for that matter – was ideologically charged. He was not a neutral figure; he was an expression of core American values. There is another answer. By 1910 the cowboy was a mythic figure on both sides of the border. Owen Wister's wildly popular novel *The Virginian* (1902) had much to do with it. For Wister, the cowboy represented a racial rather than a national principle. In 1895, in an essay illustrated by Remington that appeared in *Harper's Monthly*, "The Evolution of the Cowpuncher," Wister had asserted what required no proof: the cowboy was the embodiment of the Anglo-Saxon masculine ideal. "To survive in the clean cattle country," he wrote, "requires spirit of adventure, courage, and self-sufficiency; you will not find many Poles or Huns or Russian Jews in that district; it stands as yet untainted...."[44]

Remington echoed this judgment. Cowboy culture drew a line between East and West. "Every one knows that...[the western bronc] 'bucks,'" he wrote in 1889,

> and familiarity with that characteristic never breeds contempt. Only those who have ridden a bronco the first time it was saddled, or have lived through a railroad accident, can form any conception of the solemnity of such experiences. Few Eastern people appreciate the sky-rocket bounds, and grunts, and stiff-legged striking....[45]

*"Ranching in the Canadian West. Bronco Breaking."
Undated "Private Postcard," no publisher, ca.
1910, Author's Collection.*

Appropriately, for his very first work in bronze, Remington sculpted *The Broncho Buster* (1895). "I wish that the manhood of the cow-boy might come more into fashion further East," he subsequently observed.[46] Roosevelt, in turn, left no doubt about where the cowboy stood in the hierarchy of America's working class. "Except while on ... sprees," cowboys "are much better fellows and pleasanter companions than small farmers or agricultural laborers; nor are the mechanics and workmen of a great city to be mentioned in the same breath."[47]

When it came to Western myth, the distinction to be drawn was not between life north and south of the Forty-ninth Parallel, but between East and West. Wister might be a Philadelphian educated at Harvard, Remington a New Yorker who attended Yale, and Roosevelt a New Yorker and a Harvard man. However, their collective creation – "cowboy land," America's mythic heartland – could

A Rainy Morning in Cow Camp (1904). Postcard, W. T. Ridgley Calendar Co., Great Falls, ca. 1904; reproduced in Rhoda Sivell, Voices From the Range (1911) as Range Call. Author's Collection.

not exist in the "polluted" East.[48] But it could exist in Canada. Rhoda Sivell was a Medicine Hat, Alberta poet whose 1911 collection of Western verse, *Voices from the Range*, was published in Toronto and Winnipeg by The T. Eaton Company. Its credentials, in short, were solidly Canadian. But the only artists to illustrate the first edition were American – Remington and Russell. Remington's *A Running Bucker* served as the book's frontispiece illustrating Sivell's poem about a "Broncho Buster" who, when he "was in the saddle – /With the horse a-rearing so," displayed his mastery, riding

> … him to a finish,
> Though he'd buck, and twist, and squeal,
> And plunge around in circles,
> Just enough to make you reel.

In turn, Russell's evocative watercolour *Rainy Morning in the Cow Camp*, a 1904 painting that was exhibited at the 1912 Calgary Stampede, illustrated "The Range Call":

If ever you hear the range call,
The voice that speaks soft and sweet;
That wins you back to the prairie,
Away from the gas-lit street;
If once you hear her calling,
You sure then have got to go,
For the old range is waiting for you,
And you've got to love her so.[49]

Sivell might not be much of a poet, but her choice of imagery was astute. Visually, when it came to cowboys, the American and Canadian versions transcended national distinctions. They were touchstones to a common myth.

Indians, too, served as touchstones to that myth. Where there were cowboys, there were Indians, whose participation in entertainments like the 1912 Calgary Stampede aroused the usual opposition. Some Indian agents on both sides of the border, committed to governmental policies of assimilation, opposed exhibitions that encouraged Indians to dress in traditional costume and play at old times. They thundered dire warnings about the regressive effects of Stampedes, Wild West shows and costumed parades, though the very grounds on which the advocates of assimilation opposed them made them all the more appealing to Indian participants. Just as the cowboy had been displaced by the farmer as the harbinger of pioneer progress and relegated to the realm of myth – that "isle of ghosts and of strange dead memories," as Theodore Roosevelt put it – the Indian, too, represented the past.[50] He was a ghost whose lingering presence affirmed the bustling, progressive civilization that had displaced him. He could join it by abandoning such vestiges of his old way of life as tipis, feathers and the other picturesque reminders of yesterday like the buffalo skulls that dotted the land where plows now turned over the soil and farmers planted their crops. Or he could stand aside and observe, with resignation, the new forces that had doomed his way of life.[51] In this guise, as the representative of a "vanishing race" – more precisely, a vanishing culture – the Indian, decked out in traditional finery, filled an obvious allegorical role for artists interested in sounding a nostalgic note as they celebrated, regretfully or otherwise, civilization's triumphant advance.[52]

George Catlin had set the tone for a kind of artistic salvage operation back in the 1830s when he created an Indian Gallery consisting of some six

S. Hunter, "What It Must Come To," *Toronto News, 20 June 1885*, reproduced in Bob Beal and Rod Macleod, *Prairie Fire: The 1895 North-West Rebellion* (1984). Author's Collection.

hundred paintings, mostly portraits but also landscapes and many scenes showing manners, customs, and costumes of the western tribes. Subjects like the buffalo hunt lured American and Canadian artists alike, and Paul Kane, painting in the 1840s, is often considered the Canadian Catlin. The Indian as artistic subject has been heavily investigated in terms of the Euro-American construction of the "Indian." But most revealing are allegorical representations of the "vanishing race," since they express ideology overtly.[53]

Few sculptures are more familiar than James Earle Fraser's allegorical masterpiece *The End of the Trail*, originally modelled in 1894 and refined for exhibition at the Panama-Pacific International Exposition in San Francisco in 1915. Fraser wanted his two-and-a-half times life size equestrian statue – Indian and pony, heads drooping, facing oblivion – to stand above the Pacific's booming surf, where nature would complete the symbolism of a dying way of life. Working in the fertile years for artists that came with the closing of the frontier, Fraser was still squarely within a much older allegorical tradition, literary and visual. It was

Frederick Opper, *"Move On, Maroon Brother, Move On!"* Bill Nye's History of the United States *(London: Chatto and Windus, 1894). Author's Collection.*

given poignant form in William Cullen Bryant's 1824 poem "An Indian at the Burying-place of His Fathers":

> They waste us – aye – like April snow
> In the warm noon, we shrink away;
> And fast they follow, as we go
> Towards the setting day, –
> Till they shall fill the land, and we
> Are driven into the western sea.[54]

Artists like Tompkins Matteson in *The Last of the Race* (1847) and John Mix Stanley in *The Last of Their Race* (1857) had shown Indians huddled on the shores of the Pacific with a setting sun to underscore the symbolism.[55] This was such a familiar "high art" motif that nineteenth-century cartoonists on both sides of the border readily adopted it. An editorial cartoon in the *Toronto News*

Charles M. Russell, *The Last of His Race (1899)*, Pen Sketches (Great Falls: W. T. Ridgley Publishing, 1899). Author's Collection.

for June 20, 1885, the year of the second Riel Rebellion, bore the caption "What It Must Come To." Prime Minister John A. Macdonald is shown as a policeman using his billy club to nudge a group of Indians to the edge of a cliff. Pressing behind them are the advancing multitudes representing "civilization," spelled out in the smoke of a train engine; before them looms the Pacific Ocean. The setting sun bears a message, "Westward Ho." "Here, you copper colored gentlemen," the Officer says, "no loafing allowed, you must either work or jump."[56] An American variation on the same theme, a drawing by Frederick Opper published in 1894, showed civilization in the form of a policeman using his club to prod a ragged Indian in a U.S. government issue blanket, rye bottle in hand, toes curling over the cliff's edge, the waves below awaiting him as the setting sun sheds crocodile tears. Its title: "Move On, Maroon Brother, Move On!"[57]

Artists doted on the theme. Indians were forever bowing their heads in sorrowful recognition of their redundancy. The hunting way of life, like the once great herds of buffalo, had vanished, and the old-time Indian was doomed to disappear. Buffalo skull allegories abounded. Montana's Russell offered his version in a pen and ink drawing, *The Last of His Race* (1899), and Western

John Innes, Reverie [Memories] (1922). Calendar reproduction. Author's Collection.

Canada's John Innes in a painting, *Reverie [Memories]* (1922). In both, an old Indian man brooding on a buffalo skull recalls past glories. A spectral buffalo hunt completes the symbolism. The cost of progress, sentimentally calculated, was a theme that expressed a common set of assumptions on both sides of the border.[58]

Reaching back to another rich allegorical tradition, Russell in 1898 painted a matched set of watercolours, *1858 – Blackfoot Brave* and *1898 – Blackfoot Brave*, contrasting a proud pre-reservation buffalo hunter and his conquered counterpart reduced to peddling buffalo horns to feed his family. They echo Catlin's famous before-and-after painting *Wi-jun-jon, Pigeon's Egg Head, The Light, Going to and Returning from Washington* (ca. 1838). By representing civilization's corrosive effects on the uncorrupted noble savage, such allegories affirmed the notion of a Vanishing Race. Loss measured gain, with moral judgment implied, but also with a sense of inevitability. Other artists celebrated the passing of the old order. Charles Fripp, for example, published a very different set of images in the *London Daily Graphic* in 1889, "The Dying North-West," showing a traditional Indian and "The New North-West," featuring a sturdy pioneer. Here transformation is depicted in a positive light. Indeed, allegorical

"Jasper National Park and the Triangle Tour"
({Montreal}): Canadian National Railways,
[ca. 1924]), cover. Author's Collection.

art usually shed a tear for the olden days, then embraced a clear-eyed vision of progress.

Artists on both sides of the border portrayed progress's triumphant march as a procession in which a column of representative figures move by, the Indian always in the lead. In the nineteenth century, American artists tended to show the representatives of civilization literally scattering wildlife and Indians before them. Civilization in this guise is unambiguously aggressive. In the twentieth century, the same theme assumed a more benign aspect: the old order yields place to the new in an orderly, measured fashion. The cover of a Canadian National Railways promotional booklet from the 1920s showed two Indians followed by an explorer, a trapper, a farmer, a Mounted Policeman, and a cowboy. Behind, a settler drives a covered wagon. It was unnecessary to elaborate the obvious: in the wake of the prairie schooner would come the railroad, as passengers leafing through the booklet and about to experience "The Romance of the Rockies" from a comfortable observation car well knew.[59] By depicting historical development as a literal progression, artists were in line with pageants and parades. The 1912 Calgary Stampede parade, for example, began with Indians "in full regalia" followed by Hudson's Bay factors and Red River carts, missionaries, whisky traders, the North-West Mounted Police, cattlemen, cowboys and chuckwagons, and then floats honouring labour, business, and schoolchildren. Moving from the past to the future, the parade traced the progress that Calgary had made "in a few short years…. It was genuine; it carried sentiment; it was historical; it was educational and above all it was Western."[60] Not Canadian, not American: Western.

Can the elements that make for a good Stampede be extrapolated to represent the West? Leroy V. Kelly, at the end of his raucous pioneering history of "the Ranchers and Indians of Alberta," answered in the affirmative. He concluded with the 1912 Calgary Stampede and praised its "great picture of Western days" for presenting "to the later-comers to the Province a vivid and never-to-be-forgotten illustration of Western life, of the work and the play of the cowboys and ranchmen when the ranges were open and the cattle were wild."[61] Ermeline Ference, writing in the shadow of Lewis G. Thomas, answered in the negative in an essay on "Alberta Ranching in Literature." The Calgary Stampede was no more a truthful "picture of Western days" than Zane Grey's novels were history. But she made an interesting concession: "Although most of the literature on ranching in southern Alberta refutes the conception that the American myth applies to the Canadian West as well, the myth has become naturalized into the Canadian environment insofar as the modern rodeos, and particularly the Calgary Stampede, have capitalized on the picturesque events of the life and spirit of the ranchers and cowboys of past decades." But stampedes, she concludes, "are exaggerations of reality."[62] Exactly – just like the mythic West that, drawing on the imagery of artists on both sides of the border, has entrenched itself in the popular consciousness. When it comes to the visual imagery of the American and Canadian Wests, it can be said, emphatically: One West, One Myth.

Questions to Ponder

1. What are the elements of Russell's West?
2. Did Russell paint a Canadian West, an American West or simply a mythic West?
3. How does Remington's physical distance from the West define it?
4. How are Russell's and Remington's Wests different?
5. How do the artists use Indians as subject?

Must Reads

Dippie, Brian W., and Peter H. Hassrick. "Capturing Western Legends: Russell and Remington and the Canadian Frontier," *Alberta History* 52 (Spring 2004).

Elofson, Warren M. *Frontier Cattle Ranching in the Land and Times of Charlie Russell*. Montreal and Kingston: McGill-Queen's University Press/University of Washington Press, Seattle, 2004.

Evans, Simon, Sarah Carter, and Bill Yeo, eds. *Cowboys, Ranchers and the Cattle Business: Cross-Border Perspectives on Ranching History*. Calgary: University of Calgary Press, 2000.

Livingstone, Donna. *The Cowboy Spirit: Guy Weadick and the Calgary Stampede*. Vancouver: Greystone Books, 1996.

Thomas, Lewis G., ed. by Patrick A. Dunae. *Ranchers' Legacy: Alberta Essays*. Edmonton: University of Alberta Press, 1986.

Notes

1 See Walter Prescott Webb, *The Great Plains* (Boston: Ginn and Company, 1931), pp. 470–73, for the linkage between environmental determinism and the farm novel.

2 Douglas Francis, ed., *Images of the West: Changing Perceptions of the Prairies, 1690–1960* (Saskatoon: Western Producer Prairie Books, 1989); and see Jason Patrick Bennett, "Apple of the Empire: Landscape and Imperial Identity in Turn-of-the-Century British Columbia," *Journal of the CHA 1998 Revue de la S.H.C. NS* 9 (2000): 63–92, for the promotional literature of fruit ranching, and Ronald Rees, *New and Naked Land: Making the Prairies Home* (Saskatoon: Western Producer Prairie Books, 1998), which devotes a chapter to "Ranchers and the Prairie Landscape" that acknowledges the cowboy's romantic appeal as a nomadic type, and the ranchers as constituting a culturally homogeneous community who accommodated themselves to the land, in contrast to the farmers, who in the Canadian West represented ethnic diversity and, as genuine settlers, moulded the land to their purposes.

3   The absence of the grazing industry on the Prairie Province crests is pointedly evident when, marking their Golden Jubilees, those of Alberta and Saskatchewan were featured on the cover of *Canadian Cattlemen* 18 (July 1955). As for Manitoba, it is worth noting that after Charles M. Russell exhibited at the Winnipeg Stampede in 1913 the idea was floated by some local businessmen "in a vague way that it might be possible that the Provincial Government of Winnipeg would want a big picture, either mural decoration or painting of buffalo, their coat of arms for their new State House in Winnipeg." Nancy C. Russell to A.E. Cross, 23 August 1913, Calgary Brewing and Malting Company Papers, Glenbow ArchivesMuseum, Calgary.
4   E.J. Hart, The Selling of Canada: The CPR and the Beginnings of Canadian Tourism (Banff, AB: Altitude Publishing, 1983).
5   Karen Wonders, "A Sportsman's Eden," *The Beaver* 79 (October–November 1999): 26–32; *The Beaver* 79 (December 1999/January 2000): 30–35, 37.
6   See John Jennings, "Policemen and Poachers: Indian Relations on the Ranching Frontier," in *Frontier Calgary: Town, City, and Region 1875–1914*, ed. Anthony W. Rasporich and Henry C. Klassen (Calgary: University of Calgary Press, 1975), pp. 87–99. Jennings admits that the newspaper rhetoric in southern Alberta regarding Indian "rascals" and "pests" was similar to that in the Western papers south of the border, but argues that the Mounted Police provided a stability that "almost completely insulated" Alberta ranchers "from negative contact with the Indians," and headed off the kind of reprisals that led to Indian wars in the American West. A rejoinder to Jennings is provided by another essay in the same collection, T. Thorner, "The Not-So-Peaceable Kingdom: Crime and Criminal Justice in Frontier Calgary," ibid., pp. 100–113. "There were numerous complaints regarding the efficiency of the Mounted Police," Thorner notes, adding that "Many of the original ranchers in the area returned to Montana because of the lack of protection," p. 106. The Indians also lost their high regard for the Mounties over time, while the white population was never as law-abiding as tradition holds when it came to the prohibition on liquor in the North-West. A middle of the road position is advanced in R.C. Macleod, *The North-West Mounted Police and Law Enforcement, 1873–1905* (Toronto: University of Toronto Press, 1976), pp. 144–48, which contends that while the police sometimes catered to local prejudices against Indians and shared a few themselves, they administered justice in an even-handed manner in order to demonstrate that police actions "were based on a rational system of laws which operated to the benefit of all." For a direct comparison between the American and Canadian relations with Western Indians, arguing that the use of the police instead of the army meant an "emphasis on preventive rather than punitive law" in Canada, see John Jennings, "The Plains Indians and the Law," in *Men in Scarlet*, ed. Hugh A. Dempsey (Calgary: Historical Society of Alberta, [1976]), p. 54. Canadian Indian horse-stealing remained a problem, however, and created tensions south of the border until the Mounted Police began cracking down in the early 1880s. See Brian Hubner, "Horse Stealing and the Borderline: The NWMP and the Control of Indian Movement, 1874–1900" (1995), reprinted in *The Mounted Police and Prairie Society, 1873–1919*, ed. William M. Baker (Regina: Canadian Plains Research Center, University of Regina, 1998), pp. 53–70; and Michel Hogue, "Disputing the Medicine Line: The Plains Crees and the Canadian-American Border, 1878–1885," *Montana: The Magazine of Western History* 52 (Winter 2002): 2–17.

7   See Lewis H. Thomas, "Lewis Gwynne Thomas," in *Essays on Western History: In Honour of Lewis Gwynne Thomas*, ed. Lewis H. Thomas (Edmonton: University of Alberta Press, 1976), pp. 1–12, and Patrick A. Dunae, Introduction to Lewis G. Thomas, *Ranchers' Legacy: Alberta Essays*, ed. Patrick A. Dunae (Edmonton: University of Alberta Press, 1986), pp. xi–xxv, which notes, interestingly, that Thomas's "first paid academic job" was a contract in the summer of 1934 "to interview people in the Okotoks area on their attitudes towards Americans. The results ... reinforced Lewis's growing awareness that southern Alberta was not simply a northern extension of the American frontier."

8   This position has been subjected to increasing revisionist scrutiny: see Simon Evans, "Tenderfoot to Rider: Learning 'Cowboying' on the Canadian Ranching Frontier during the 1880s," in *Cowboys, Ranchers and the Cattle Business: Cross-Border Perspectives on Ranching History*, ed. Simon Evans, Sarah Carter, and Bill Yeo (Calgary: University of Calgary Press, 2000), pp. 61–80, which cites some of his earlier pertinent essays; Joy Oetelaar, "George Lane: From Cowboy to Cattle King," in ibid., pp. 43–59; and Kristi Benson, "Cowboys and Cattle Barons: Status and Hierarchy on Alberta's Early Corporate Ranches," *Alberta History* 48 (Autumn 2000): 2–9, which argues for "a social syncretism" combining "American and eastern/British styles of living and working." For southwestern Saskatchewan's ranching history, with its undeniable American influences, see Barry Potyondi, *In Palliser's Triangle: Living in the Grasslands, 1850–1930* (Saskatoon: Purich Publishing, 1995), ch. 3, and for a balanced overview, Hugh A. Dempsey, *The Golden Age of the Canadian Cowboy: An Illustrated History* (Saskatoon: Fifth House, 1995).

9   See Thomas, *Ranchers' Legacy*, ed. Dunae, especially pp. 6, 42–43, 96–97, 171–83; Patrick A. Dunae, *Gentlemen Emigrants: From the British Public Schools to the Canadian Frontier* (Vancouver: Douglas & McIntyre, 1981), especially ch. 5; David H. Breen, *The Canadian Prairie West and the Ranching Frontier, 1874–1924* (Toronto: University of Toronto Press, 1983), pp. 12–14, 30, 68–69; James H. Gray, *A Brand of Its Own: The 100 Year History of the Calgary Exhibition and Stampede* (Saskatoon: Western Producer Prairie Books, 1985), ch. 1; Rees, *New and Naked Land*, pp. 138–42. Breen addresses the American comparison directly in "The Turner Thesis and the Canadian West: A Closer Look at the Ranching Frontier," in *Essays on Western History*, ed. Thomas, pp. 147–56, finding little in common between the two cattle frontiers. "Though some of the first ranchers in the Canadian southwest were American, they were always a small minority and as a body they carried practically no social or political weight," he writes: "The Canadian range was never in the hands of 'wild and wooly' Westerners, either American or Canadian" (p. 152). His conclusion: "Ironically, the old Canadian cattle kingdom, usually considered to have been simply an economic and social adjunct of the American west, was in fact one of the main bulwarks of 'British' tradition in the southwestern prairie region" (p. 156). Sheilagh S. Jameson, "The Social Elite of the Ranch Community and Calgary," in *Frontier Calgary*, ed. Rasporich and Klassen, pp. 57–70, drums home the notion of a "unique" Alberta community not to be confused with the American version. Its "tone," she argues, "developed from an attitude of respect for law and an interest in things cultural; it was far removed from that which is generally associated with settlement of an agricultural frontier and it bore little resemblance to the popular picture of the Wild West. This society, the ranch elite, influential and pervasive in nature, had a significant effect on the emergent settlement of Calgary." A passage in the *Calgary Herald* for 12

November 1884 said it all: "Calgary is a western town, but not ... in the ancient sense of the word. It is peopled by native Canadians and Englishmen ... who own religion and respect law. The rough and festive cowboy of Texas and Oregon has no counterpart here. [There are] two or three beardless lads who wear jingling spurs and walk with a slouch.... The genuine Alberta cowboy is a gentleman." This oft-quoted observation sets the tone for the Lewis G. Thomas school's perspective. It was a reaction to L.V. Kelly's breezy, anecdotal history *The Range Men: The Story of the Ranchers and Indians of Alberta* (Toronto: William Briggs, 1913), pp. 241, 245, which lovingly recited "wild West" incidents and, in dismissing the English in Alberta as remittance men, heaped "solid contempt" upon them: "The British training of feeling sure that all things learned in England were certainly better than any other teaching, the slow-moving brains of some, the lack of initiative, of originality, marked the general run of them as hopeless for Western life, where necessity is ever forcing and developing the inventive genius, the adaptability, and the power to make one thing do work for a dozen other articles." There was a minor literature devoted to the English in the West. See, for example, C.L. Johnstone, *The Young Emigrants: A Story for Boys* (London: Thomas Nelson and Sons, 1898), set principally in Saskatchewan, and W.H.P. Jarvis, *The Letters of a Remittance Man to His Mother* (Toronto: Musson Book Co., 1909), set in Manitoba. The latter urged English readers to abandon their airs and adjust to conditions in the Canadian West if they wanted to make a success. Both books featured cover illustrations of an inexperienced rider on a bucking bronco – an initiation rite that, properly handled, could serve as a passport to local acceptance.

10   Warren M. Elofson, *Cowboys, Gentlemen & Cattle Thieves: Ranching on the Western Frontier* (Montreal and Kingston: McGill-Queen's University Press, 2000); and "Law and Disorder on the Ranching Frontiers of Montana and Alberta/Assiniboia, 1870–1914," *Journal of the West* 42 (Winter 2003): 40–51; and *Frontier Cattle Ranching in the Land and Times of Charlie Russell* (Montreal and Kingston: McGill-Queen's University Press, and University of Washington Press, Seattle, 2004). Interestingly, American writers beginning in the 1880s chose to differentiate the northern range and its respectable cowboys from their wild Texan precursors: Rufus Fairchild Zogbaum, "A Day's Drive with Montana Cow-boys," *Harper's Monthly* 71 (July 1885): 188–93, which portrays the cowboys as honest workmen; Joseph Nimmo, Jr., "The American Cow-boy," *Harper's Monthly* 73 (November 1886): 880–84, whose description of the "gentler brethren of the northern ranges" anticipates the "Mild West"; and Arthur Chapman, "The Cowboy of Today," *World's Work* (8 September 1904): 5278: "In the main, the cowboy of today is much better behaved than the puncher of the days of the old cattle-trail.... There is less drinking of bad whisky and less attention to the fascinations of the gaming-table.... As a result of all these things, the cowboy is clean, honest, and self-reliant." This is in accordance with the idea advanced by Terry G. Jordan, *North American Cattle-Ranching Frontiers: Origins, Diffusion, and Differentiation* (Albuquerque: University of New Mexico Press, 1993), summarized in "Does the Border Matter?: Cattle Ranching and the 49th Parallel," in *Cowboys, Ranchers and the Cattle Business*, ed. Evans, Carter, and Yeo, pp. 1–10, which contends that the northern cattle range on both sides of the border was essentially an adaptation of Midwestern cattle culture. For a classic meditation on transboundary issues that gets at the rancher, the homesteader, and competing and complementary nationalities, see Wallace Stegner, *Wolf Willow: A History, a Story and a*

Memory of the Last Plains Frontier (New York: Viking Press, 1972 [1955]); and for a recent, nuanced history, drawing on both Stegner and Charles M. Russell, whose lawn Stegner cut on a brief stay in Great Falls during his peripatetic childhood, see Beth LaDow, *The Medicine Line: Life and Death on a North American Borderland* (New York: Routledge, 2001).

11 John R. Barrows to James B. Rankin, 3 April, 21 March 1938, James B. Rankin Papers, Montana Historical Society, Helena. Barrows continued: "the roundup as a whole was characterized as a bunch of 'pumpkin rollers,' or 'corn huskers,' or 'straight legs,' and the use of cots and mattresses by some of the elders, caused the roundup to be called a 'feather bed roundup.' They had no trouble either with Indians or outlaws." As for Russell, Barrows characterized him as drawn to the picturesque side of cowboy life: "Generally speaking, the cowboys were affectedly genteel. Ninety percent of them tried to maintain the illusion that they were wild members of an aristocratic family, while ten percent claimed that they were, 'born on a desert island and suckled by a cow whale.'... As a cowboy, Charley specialized in night herding horses.... He had no special skill as a rider or roper. We were all armed, of course, but I never heard of him being mixed up in any rough stuff." Barrows's *Ubet* (Caldwell, Idaho: Caxton Printers, 1934) is a readable and revealing memoir of ordinary life in 1880s Montana.

12 Walt Coburn to Frank Linderman, 18 December 1923, Frank B. Linderman Collection, University of Montana, Missoula. Speaking of the Eastern publishers of Western stories, Coburn continued: "they want lots of riding, shooting, gore-wading yarns and in order to keep the pr[o]verbial wolf from the proverbial door, I give it to 'em – with trimmings. In self defense, wish to say that I've put in enough range atmosphere to let the reader know that I'm not a pilgrim.... I'm biding my time until the day comes when I can do something that will be really decent. I believe that I can do it but at present I'm not situated financially so that I can devote the time to it. If the public was composed of Montana folks (not the dry-land variety, but the real folks) I could cut loose and write what I like, but when the editor and readers at the editorial office are people who still maintain that the man west of North Dakota packs a notched gun and talks like a kid in the third grade, we have to play up to the idea. It's not pleasant to be classed with these damned short-horn writers that don't know a running iron from a fountain pen, but I need the money. When that dreamed of Some Day appears on the horizon I'll write a story that you won't be ashamed to read. Until then – well, I'll do my darndest to not be a disgrace to the old state whose settlers were the best of the best. And that, as some guy has said, is that!" Coburn got his opportunity in two books that are long on realism: *Pioneer Cattleman in Montana: The Story of the Circle C Ranch* (Norman: University of Oklahoma Press, 1968) and *Western Word Wrangler: An Autobiography* (Flagstaff, AZ: Northland Press, 1973). On this issue, see Wallace Stegner, "Coming of Age: The End of the Beginning" (1990), reprinted in *When the Bluebird Sings to the Lemonade Springs: Living and Writing in the West* (New York: Random House), 1992, pp. 135–42. Stegner warred with the fictive cowboy's dominance in Western literature; he understood Coburn's dilemma but rejected his solution.

13 C.M. Russell to Frank Brown, 4 April 1926, *Charles M. Russell, Word Painter: Letters, 1887–1926*, ed. Brian W. Dippie (Fort Worth: Amon Carter Museum in association with Harry N. Abrams, New York, 1993), p. 388. But Russell did keep tally on the violence that claimed some of his rowdier rangeland acquaintances, documenting six shooting deaths in sketches he sent to Harry T. Duckett in July 1901, ibid., p. 44. Russell explained this fascination

when he wrote to Berners B. Kelly, 22 February 1920, ibid., p. 289, about his first extended trip to Los Angeles, noting that along a country road "a band of riders" might suddenly burst "from a grove of live oaks ... for looks thair shure scary all heeled to the teeth and spuring dow[n] the slope with guns smoking thair is flashes of silver where the sun dances on the horse jewelery of this bunch...the leader of this band is Bill Hart Tom Mix ore som other moovie gun man to fancyfull to be real but to an old romance loving boy like me its the best thing Iv seen in Calif."

14 Lewis Atherton, *The Cattle Kings* (Bloomington: Indiana University Press, 1961), pp. 151, 190; Gene M. Gressley, *Bankers and Cattlemen* (New York: Alfred A. Knopf, 1966); and see the influential essay by Earl Pomeroy, "Toward a Reorientation of Western History: Continuity and Environment," *Mississippi Valley Historical Review* 41 (March 1955): 579600. Gressley, in profiling Eastern American investors and their Western managers, notes: "the intense activity from 1882 to 1885 was the high point of investment in the range cattle industry; the nadir came in 1886–8, with a short period of recovery in 1888–9 and a much stronger resurgence in 1898–1901. After 1900 the cattle industry on the plains underwent a radical metamorphosis. Ranching increasingly became a locally contained business, with its financing centered in the community or the regional banking institutions" (p. 111). Gressley follows Earl Pomeroy's "reorientation" in asserting the impact of Eastern culture in the West, arguing that this was one of the substantial legacies of the investor speculation in Western cattle: "the Eastern investor left behind the memories of a way of life that Western society would attempt to emulate from then on" p. 295. In the same period, Robert Dykstra, *The Cattle Towns* (New York: Alfred A. Knopf, 1968), ch. 3, provided a corrective to the tradition of Kansas cattle town violence – a topic convincingly revisited in his "Overdosing on Dodge City," *Western Historical Quarterly* 27 (Winter 1996): 505–14.

15 Jameson, "The Social Elite of the Ranch Community and Calgary," p. 65; and see A. Herbert Eckford, "Wolf Hunting in the Days of the 'Open Range' in Alberta," *Canadian Cattlemen* 9 (June 1946): 48, which almost claps its hands and shouts, "What jolly sport!"

16 See Patricia Nelson Limerick, Clyde A. Milner II, and Charles E. Rankin, eds., *Trails: Toward a New Western History* (Lawrence: University Press of Kansas, 1991), in particular the essays by Peggy Pascoe and Elliott West.

17 Russell offered another version of this subject, *Cowboy Sport – Roping a Wolf* in the very first book of cowboy art, *Studies of Western Life* (New York: The Albertype Co., 1890). Montana cattleman Granville Stuart later provided accompanying text: "This is a frequent occurrence during the semi-annual roundups. A wolf is started from some ravine, and instantly with a yell every cowboy near by spurs his horse and dashes after it at headlong speed, utterly regardless of the broken dangerous ground, loosing their lariate from their saddles as they run, the deadly noose is soon swinging swiftly around their heads as they close in on the frightened animal, who strains every nerve to escape. Often several misthrows are made, till some lucky fling catches it around the neck or body and it is dragged some distance.... Its career is then ended by a pistol shot and the march is resumed with the horses as much on the 'qui vivre' for another wolf as the cowboys themselves." Cowboys roping a wolf became a favourite Russell theme; he painted a version as late as 1925. The one drawing he did with hounds and a wolf, *The Wolf Hunt*, in Wallace D. Coburn, *Rhymes from a Round-Up Camp* (Great Falls, MT: W.T. Ridgley Press, 1899), p. 64, is a study in the ferocity of the

pack mentality that captures the frenzy of the kill – far removed from the sedate tradition of English fox-hunting art, or Coburn's closing lines:

> Well done, brave hounds! Thy savage prey
> Was shrewdly caught and killed today. (p. 68)

18   Gray, *A Brand of Its Own*, p. 25.
19   Max Foran, with Edward Cavell, *Calgary: An Illustrated History* (Toronto: James Lorimer & Company, and National Museum of Man, 1978), p. 69.
20   Advertisement, Calgary *Daily Herald*, 2 August 1919.
21   "Guy Weadick Comments on Clem Gardner's Impressions as Contestant at 1912 Stampede," *Canadian Cattlemen* 8 (September 1945): 60; and see Donna Livingstone, *The Cowboy Spirit: Guy Weadick and the Calgary Stampede* (Vancouver: Greystone Books, 1996). Weadick never forgot that in 1912 he was rebuffed by the manager of the Calgary Exhibition, who told him that the exhibition grounds would be unavailable and "stated that the public was not interested in cowboy activities, claimed that people had seen too much of it and furthermore that the public was interested in the development of Calgary into a modern city and they were not interested in the things of the past." Other "leading citizens" echoed this judgement, but Weadick, irrepressible at twenty-seven and convinced he had a good idea, found an ally in George Lane, who liked the concept and at once involved two other cattlemen, A.E. Cross and Pat Burns, in a discussion that also brought in A.J. McLean and a firm commitment to back the venture up to $100,000. [Kenneth Coppock], "Guy Weadick: Dean of Rodeo Producers," *Canadian Cattlemen* 9 (September 1946): 113. Subsequently, Weadick and the Exhibition manager, E.L. Richardson, enjoyed a good working relationship until Weadick's bitter parting after the 1932 Stampede.
22   "Guy Weadick Comments on Clem Gardner's Impressions as Contestant at 1912 Stampede," p. 105; C. M. Russell to Walt Coburn, 27 January 1915 in *Charles M. Russell, Word Painter*, ed. Dippie, p. 214. Coburn's cowboy poetry was well-represented in the official program, "The Stampede at Calgary, Alberta, 1912, September 2, 3, 4 & 5"; in inviting Coburn to participate, Weadick wrote: "We want riders and ropers from every cattle state in the union, Old Mexico and the Dominion of Canada to attend this meet." *Great Falls Daily Tribune*, 18 August 1912.
23   See Calgary *Daily Herald*, 3 September 1912; and Harold G. Davidson, *Edward Borein, Cowboy Artist: The Life and Works of John Edward Borein, 1872–1945* (Garden City, NY: Doubleday, 1974), pp. 74–98. Borein's work was especially prominent in the 1919 Stampede advertising: *Calgary Daily Herald*, 2, 9, 16, and 20 August, "Victory Stampede Edition" supplement which offered an appraisal of the artist and his art, "Cowboy Artist Has Had a Most Varied Career."
24   See Hugh A. Dempsey, "Charlie Russell and Guy Weadick," *Russell's West* 5, no. 1 (1997): 14–19; and *Charles M. Russell, Word Painter*, ed. Dippie, for the commentaries accompanying Russell's letters to Weadick.
25   *Fort Benton River Press*, 6 April, 3 August, 6 September 1887; *Weekly Herald Helena*, 26 May 1887; *Daily Independent Helena*, 10 June, 1 July 1887; and see John Taliaferro, *Charles M. Russell: The Life and Legend of America's Cowboy Artist* (Boston: Little, Brown, 1996).

26 *Calgary Daily Herald*, 4 September 1912; and see *Calgary Morning Albertan*, 2, 7 September 1912.
27 C.M. Russell to Ben R. Roberts, [June 1888], *Charles M. Russell, Word Painter*, ed. Dippie, p. 14.
28 See Hugh A. Dempsey, "Tracking C.M. Russell in Canada, 1888–1889" (1989), reprinted in *Charlie Russell Roundup: Essays on America's Favorite Cowboy Artist*, ed. Brian W. Dippie (Helena: Montana Historical Society Press, 1999), pp. 221–38; ibid., pp. 8–10, 1314; *Charles M. Russell, Word Painter*, ed. Dippie, pp. 126–27, 139; and Dippie, "Charles M. Russell, Cowboy Culture, and the Canadian Connection," in *Cowboys, Ranchers and the Cattle Business*, ed. Evans, Carter and Yeo, pp. 11–27.
29 See Joseph G. Rosa and Robin May, *Buffalo Bill and His Wild West: A Pictorial Biography* (Lawrence: University Press of Kansas, 1989); Paul Reddin, *Wild West Shows* (Urbana: University of Illinois Press, 1999), chs. 3–5; Lorain Lounsberry, "Wild West Shows and the Canadian West," in *Cowboys, Ranchers and the Cattle Business*, ed. Evans, Carter and Yeo, pp. 139–52; and, for a typical example of the English annuals, *The Boy's Own Annual* (London): "Boy's Own Paper" Office, [1910], made interesting by its cover illustration of a rancher fending off attacking wolves with his six-gun, its scowling, war-bonneted, war-painted Indian with rifle and tomahawk on its spine, and a four-panel story on the end-papers of an Indian attack on a settler's cabin that is avenged in the final panel when the cowboys, alerted by a brave son, capture two of the culprits.
30 Lewis G. Thomas, "The Ranching Tradition and the Life of the Ranchers"(1935), in *Ranchers' Legacy*, ed. Dunae, p. 37.
31 Great Falls *Daily Tribune*, 13 December 1918; and see Oetelaar, "George Lane: From Cowboy to Cattle King." Russell never reconciled himself to the farmer. His New York illustrator friend Philip Goodwin, who specialized in outdoor subjects, gave support to the notion of a "Mild West" when he wrote from Twin Buttes, Alberta, in 1909, "Even out here the ranchmen are farmers." Philip R. Goodwin to his mother, 9 August 1909, Philip Goodwin Collection, Harold McCracken Research Library, Buffalo Bill Historical Center, Cody, Wyoming. In Russell's lexicon, this was the acme of insult.
32 C.M. Russell, undated note ca. 1916 to Joe De Yong, Joe De Yong Papers, C.M. Russell Museum, Great Falls.
33 For Russell's treatment of the Mounted Police, see Dippie, "Charles M. Russell, Cowboy Culture, and the Canadian Connection," pp. 23–25; and for another parallel between a Mounted Police painting and in this instance a Russell Indian subject, *The Queen's War Hounds* and *The Lost Trail*, see Brian W. Dippie, "'… I Feel That I Am Improving Right Along': Continuity and Change in Charles M. Russell's Art," *Montana: The Magazine of Western History* 38 (Summer 1988): 43, 48, 51.
34 See Paul Voisey, "In Search of Wealth and Status: An Economic and Social Study of Entrepreneurs in Early Calgary," in *Frontier Calgary*, ed. Rasporich and Klassen, pp. 222–41, for Burns and another of the Big Four, A.E. Cross.
35 Wyndham R. Dunstan to C.M. Russell, 31 May 1920, Helen E. and Homer E. Britzman Collection, Taylor Museum for Southwestern Studies of the Colorado Springs Fine Arts Center.

36 William A. Coffin, "American Illustration of To-day," *Scribner's Magazine* 11 (March 1892): 348; and for a brief treatment of Remington's career and influence, see Brian W. Dippie, *The Frederic Remington Art Museum Collection* (Ogdensburg, NY: Frederic Remington Art Museum, and Harry N. Abrams, New York, 2001), pp. 13–30, the basis for the discussion that follows.

37 Theodore Roosevelt, "Ranch Life in the Far West," *Century Magazine* 35 (February 1888): 502.

38 See Brian W. Dippie, "'Cowboys Are Gems to Me': Remington, Russell, and the Cowboy in Art," *South Dakota History* 32 (Fall 2002): 217–42, for a recent treatment of this topic.

39 Phil Weinard, who rode to Alberta with Russell in 1888, recalled that "From Stand Off to Ft. McLeod the C.M.P. were taking a Blood Indian as prisoner, we rode alongside of them for some time and Charlie got his first impression of a C.M.P. with an Indian handcuffed and under arrest." Phil Weinard to James B. Rankin, 4 January 1938, Rankin Papers; and see Phil Weinard to Homer E. Britzman, 14 February [1939], Britzman Collection, which specifies that there were two Mounted Policemen accompanying the prisoner.

40 Roosevelt, "Ranch Life in the Far West," p. 500.

41 Coburn, Rhymes from a Round-up Camp, pp. 2, 9.

42 Jack Rennert, *100 Posters of Buffalo Bill's Wild West* (New York: Darien House, 1976), p. 20.

43 Buckskin Brady, *Stories and Sermons* (Toronto: William Briggs, 1905), pp. 108–9.

44 Owen Wister, "The Evolution of the Cow-puncher," *Harper's Monthly* 91 (September 1895): 604. Wister's Anglo-Saxonism was so pronounced that he made the Englishman at home not only in genteel Alberta but in the Wild West as well: "Directly the English nobleman smelt Texas, the slumbering untamed Saxon awoke in him, and mindful of the tournament, mindful of the hunting-field, galloped howling after wild cattle, a born horseman, a perfect athlete, and spite of the peerage and gules and argent, fundamentally kin with the drifting vagabonds who swore and galloped by his side."

45 Frederic Remington, "Horses of the Plains," *Century Magazine* 37 (January 1889): 342.

46 Frederic Remington, "Life in the Cattle Country," *Collier's Weekly* (26 August 1899), in *The Collected Writings of Frederic Remington*, ed. Peggy and Harold Samuels (Garden City, NY: Doubleday, 1979), p. 388.

47 Roosevelt, "Ranch Life in the Far West," p. 502.

48 Theodore Roosevelt, *An Autobiography* (New York: Macmillan, 1913), ch. 4, "In Cowboy Land," which says of Dakota Territory in 1883, when Roosevelt became a rancher: "It was still the Wild West in those days, the Far West, the West of Owen Wister's stories and Frederic Remington's drawings, the West of the Indian and the buffalo-hunter, the soldier and the cow-puncher."

49 Rhoda Sivell, *Voices from the Range* (Toronto: William Briggs, 1912), pp. 33, 51. A third illustration in some printings, *The Cow-Girl*, was the work of John Innes, thereby adding a Canadian artist to the mix. A native of Ontario, Innes (1864–1941) worked as a cowboy in Alberta at the Bar U Ranch, but spent most of his career in Vancouver. See John Bruce Cowan, *John Innes: Painter of the Canadian West* (Vancouver: Rose, Cowan & Latta, 1945).

50 Roosevelt, *An Autobiography*, p. 94.

51 See Edward Roper, *By Track and Trail: A Journey through Canada* (London: W. H. Allen & Co., 1891), facing p. 378: "Wild and Tame Indians – A Contrast." Interestingly, Roper sympathized with the traditional Indians, not the progressives.

52 Shelley Hulan, "Amelia Paget's *The People of the Plains*: Imperialist and Ethnocritical Nostalgia," *Journal of Canadian Studies / Revue d'études canadiennes* 37 (Summer 2002): 47–67, is of interest, but it creates a false dichotomy. The two nostalgias cannot be so readily separated. Both informed the Calgary Stampede's presentation of Indians, a point arrived at by a different route in Robert M. Seiler and Tamara P. Seiler, "The Social Construction of the Canadian Cowboy: Calgary Exhibition and Stampede Posters, 1952–1972," *Journal of Canadian Studies / Revue d'études canadiennes* 33 (Fall 1998): 76: "The sets of oppositions inscribed in the posters we studied do not come across as irreconcilable, as one might think." For the use of Indians in Alberta tourist promotions, see Jon Whyte, *Indians in the Rockies* (Banff, AB: Altitude Publishing, 1985); Patricia Parker, *The Feather and the Drum: The History of Banff Indian Days, 1889–1978* (Calgary: Consolidated Communications, 1989); and Keith Regular, "On Public Display," *Alberta History* 34 (Winter 1986): 1–10. The Rev. John McDougall was effective in rebutting those who opposed Indian participation, writing in 1910 that the Indian Commissioner and the Inspector of Indian Agencies for Alberta "view the Indian not as a fellow man, a being just as capable as themselves in distinguishing between right and wrong, but as an inferior to be treated as a child." (Regular, pp. 6–7, quoting McDougall in the *Calgary Albertan*, 28 October 1910). This perspective – once out of favour in the academic literature, which routinely condemned Indian involvement in stampedes, festivals, touring shows and the like – has gained new respect. As Regular observes, "All indications suggest that the Indians did not feel particularly exploited by their association with the exhibitions…. The problem was … the product of the rigid rules of a clumsy and inflexible bureaucracy and the insensitive minds of bureaucrats and religious zealots, who perceived their way as best for all" (p. 9). Also see Daniel Francis, *The Imaginary Indian: The Image of the Indian in Canadian Culture* (Vancouver: Arsenal Pulp Press, 1992), ch. 5; L.G. Moses, *Wild West Shows and the Images of American Indians, 1883–1933* (Albuquerque: University of New Mexico Press, 1996); and, for an example of the older critique, Peter Geller, "'Hudson's Bay Company Indians': Images of Native People and the Red River Pageant, 1920," in *Dressing in Feathers: The Construction of the Indian in American Popular Culture*, ed. S. Elizabeth Bird (New York: Westview Press, 1996), pp. 65–77.

53 See Brian W. Dippie, Therese Thau Heyman, Christopher Mulvey, and Joan Carpenter Troccoli, *George Catlin and His Indian Gallery*, ed. George Gurney and Therese Thau Heyman (Washington: Smithsonian American Art Museum, and New York: W. W. Norton, 2002); Brian W. Dippie, "'Flying Buffaloes': Artists and the Buffalo Hunt," *Montana: The Magazine of Western History* 51 (Summer 2001): 2–17; and Brian W. Dippie, "The Moving Finger Writes: Western Art and the Dynamics of Change," in Jules David Prown et al., *Discovered Lands, Invented Pasts: Transforming Visions of the American West* (New Haven, CT: Yale University Press, 1992), pp. 89–115.

54 Quoted in Brian W. Dippie, *The Vanishing American: White Attitudes and U.S. Indian Policy* (Middletown, CT: Wesleyan University Press, 1982), p. 13; and see pp. 218–20 for "The End of the Trail."

55 See Dippie, "The Moving Finger Writes," pp. 89–115; and Julie Schimmel, "Inventing 'the Indian,'" in *The West as America: Reinterpreting Images of the Frontier*, ed. William H. Truettner (Washington, DC: Smithsonian Institution Press, for the National Museum of American Art, 1991), pp. 168–74.

56 Cartoon by S. Hunter reproduced in Bob Beal and Rod Macleod, *Prairie Fire: The 1885 North-West Rebellion* (Edmonton: Hurtig, 1984), p. 69.

57 *Bill Nye's History of the United States* (London: Chatto and Windus, 1894), p. 317.

58 See Dippie, *The Vanishing American*, passim; and Francis, *The Imaginary Indian*, chs. 2–3.

59 "Jasper National Park and the Triangle Tour " (Montreal: Canadian National Railways, [ca. 1924]). The title page reproduces a drawing of an Indian in feather bonnet stoically watching a wagon train passing below, an allegorical motif so heavily worked by then that it required no elaboration. For an American example of the first motif see Ila Turner McAfee's 1930s mural "The Scene Changes" in Marlene Park and Gerald E. Markowitz, *Democratic Vistas: Post Offices and Public Art in the New Deal* (Philadelphia: Temple University Press, 1984), p. 39; and for the second, the program cover of "An Historical Pageant of Illinois" (Evanston, 1909), in David Glassberg, *American Historical Pageantry: The Uses of Tradition in the Early Twentieth Century*. (Chapel Hill: University of North Carolina Press, 1990), p. 141.

60 [Kenneth Coppock], "Guy Weadick: Dean of Rodeo Producers," *Canadian Cattlemen* 9 (December 1946): 149; and see Lounsberry, "Wild West Shows and the Canadian West," pp. 151–52. By the third successive Stampede the format was set; see "Souvenir Programme: Calgary Exhibition, Jubilee and Stampede," 6–11 July 1925, Calgary, pp. 53–91, for "Calgary's Historical Pageant" in twenty-seven "episodes."

61 Kelly, *The Ranch Men*, p. 439.

62 Ermeline Ference, "Alberta Ranching in Literature," in *Frontier Calgary*, ed. Rasporich and Klassen, p. 85. In following Thomas's lead, Ference bogs down in self-contradiction. Having asserted that Alberta's ranch literature refuted "the idea that the American myth also pertains to the Canadian West," she offers evidence, derived from poetry and fiction, establishing the emergence of a cowboy hero in Canada, too. She explains this away in the novels of John Mackie by noting that his "concentration on the thrilling and breath-taking was probably the result of Mackie's awareness of what the reading public desired in a novel." This was the very point Walt Coburn made about his American Westerns.

chapter four

A Northern Vision: Frontiers and the West in the Canadian and American Imagination

William H. Katerberg, Calvin College

An Englishman-become-Canadian named Robert Service was the favourite poet of Ronald Reagan, notes Daniel Francis in his book on myth, memory, and Canadian history.[1] Service, who was a ranch hand and later a bank teller, moved to the Yukon in 1904, soon after the Gold Rush ended, and reinvented that recent history in poetry. His first poem was "The Shooting of Dan McGrew," a frontier tale of the sort that inspired Reagan, the cowboy actor and president.

In the poem, Service set up a classic Western barroom scene, with music and booze, two gun-slinging frontiersmen, and the none-too-respectable woman caught between them.[2] It starts:

> A bunch of the boys were whooping it up in the Malamute saloon;
> The kid that handles the music-box was hitting a jag-time tune;
> Back of the bar, in a solo game, sat Dangerous Dan McGrew,
> And watching his luck was his light-o'-love, the lady that's known as Lou.

> When out of the night, which was fifty below, and into the din and the glare,
> There stumbled a miner fresh from the creeks, dog-dirty, and loaded for bear.

> He looked like a man with a foot in the grave and scarcely the strength of a louse,
> Yet he tilted a poke of dust on the bar, and he called for drinks for the house.

> There was none could place the stranger's face, though we searched ourselves for a clue;
> But we drank his health, and the last to drink was Dangerous Dan McGrew.
>
> There's men that somehow just grip your eyes, and hold them hard like a spell;
> And such was he, and he looked to me like a man who had lived in hell;
> With a face most hair, and the dreary stare of a dog whose day is done,
> As he watered the green stuff in his glass, and the drops fell one by one.
> Then I got to figgering who he was, and wondering what he'd do,
> And I turned my head – and there watching him was the lady that's known as Lou.

As the poem goes on, the strange miner from the wilds of the Yukon takes over the piano and plays a savage Northern tune. The poem's narrator says:

> Were you ever out in the Great Alone, when the moon was awful clear,
> And the icy mountains hemmed you in with a silence you most could hear;
> With only the howl of a timber wolf, and you camped there in the cold,
> A half-dead thing in a stark, dead world, clean mad for the muck called gold;
> While high overhead, green, yellow and red, the North Lights swept in bars?
> Then you've a hunch what the music meant … hunger and night and the stars.

The stranger's music ends with tones of revenge and a lust to kill. At the end of the poem, in good Western fashion, gunplay erupts, and the reader is left with the body count.

> And the stranger turned, and his eyes they burned in a most peculiar way;
> In a buckskin shirt that was glazed with dirt he sat, and I saw him sway;
> Then his lips went in in a kind of grin, and he spoke, and his voice was calm,
> And "Boys," says he, "you don't know me, and none of you care a damn;
> But I want to state, and my words are straight, and I'll bet my poke they're true
> That one of you is a hound of hell … and that one is Dan McGrew."
>
> Then I ducked my head and the lights went out, and two guns blazed in the dark,
> And a woman screamed, and the lights went up, and two men lay stiff and stark.
> Pitched on his head, and pumped full of lead, was Dangerous Dan McGrew,
> While the man from the creeks lay clutched to the breast of the lady that's known as Lou.

> These are the simple facts of the case, and I guess I ought to know.
> They say that the stranger was crazed with "hooch," and I'm not denying it's so.
> I'm not so wise as the lawyer guys, but strictly between us two –
> The woman that kissed him and – pinched his poke – was the lady that's known as Lou.

"The Shooting of Dan McGrew," and Ronald Reagan's love of Service's poetry, clearly illustrate how easily Western myths and frontiers cross borders.[3] A classic "American" story, the poem describes Canada's Northern frontier, a place where, thanks to the Mounties and a ban on pistols, such shootouts did not occur. On the one hand, then, the poem suggests the influence of American myth on how Canadians imagine their own frontiers. On the other hand, it points to the participation of Canadian writers in "American" culture, even when writing about what is ostensibly a "Canadian" subject. Finally, it illustrates the overlap of "Western" and "Northern" mythology in the Canadian imagination.

In the spirit of crossing borders my paper explores several themes. First, it compares and contrasts specific features of Western mythology in Canada and the U.S. But the position of the West in the larger Canadian imagination is significantly different than in the U.S. Thus, second, I argue that the frontier West in American culture typically is a land all its own, with its own logic and dynamic, where people go to escape the burdens of the civilized world. But in the Canadian imagination, frontiers usually are tied to the larger world, as peripheries shaped and controlled by distant cities and capitals. Third, if the West symbolizes something fundamental about the entire American nation, in Canada the imagined West must be understood in relation to the mythic power of the North. Finally, the paper concludes by comparing the fields against which Western myths are set in Canada and the U.S. If the foil for the Canadian West in the nineteenth century and the first half of the twentieth was the American "Wild West," in recent decades that foil has become the metropolitan core of central Canada.

"Mild West" vs. "Wild West"

A simple way to distinguish the two myths of the West is to use Daniel Francis's phrase, "Mild West."[4] Unlike the "Wild West" of American myth, with its Indian wars, rustlers, outlaws, and vigilante hangings, the "Mild

West" of Canadian myth was for the most part peaceful. With the regrettable "exception" of brief rebellions by the Métis and a few reluctant Indian allies, the new Canadian government dealt peacefully and honestly with the region's aboriginal inhabitants, normally signing treaties before the arrival of a significant number of settlers, entrepreneurs, and labourers. Canadian law and order – defined in the British North America Act by the motto, "peace, order, and good government" – effectively forestalled the culture of gunplay and violence typical of the American West and its ideal, "life, liberty, and the pursuit of happiness." The North West Mounted Police symbolize this difference like nothing else.[5] John A. Macdonald's Conservative government created the force in 1873 to assert Canadian sovereignty in the region and to clear out American whisky traders causing trouble among the Indians. Their deployment was spurred by the Cypress Hills Massacre of twenty or more Assiniboine by wolf hunters from the U.S. who had been chasing horses, purportedly stolen by local Indians.[6] So trusted were the Mounties that when Sitting Bull and the Sioux fled after the battle at the Little Big Horn, they migrated north to Canada, where they agreed to keep the "Queen's peace." The NWMP even lectured a delegation of U.S. cavalry officers, insisting that Sitting Bull had caused no trouble in Canada. The Mounties also barred guns and kept gamblers and other American ne'er-do-wells in check during the gold rush era in the Yukon. Episodes like these have been captured in the *Heritage Minutes* series that has played widely on Canadian television.[7] No other country in the world, perhaps, has placed a police force quite so centrally placed among its national symbols.

Needless to say, history and the myths themselves are more complicated than these two categories – Mild West and Wild West – allow. The American West was not as "exceptionally" violent as pop culture has it, and the Canadian West not so peaceful.[8] Vigilante justice took place in Canada, on occasion even led by NWMP officers.[9] The Métis uprisings and the execution of their leader, Louis Riel, were not marginal exceptions that proved the rule, but central events in the region's development. Deeper in the past, Hudson's Bay Company policy was to respond to Indian violence blood for blood, several times over, and if necessary against the nearest Indians at hand, their guilt aside.[10] In the end, the development of the West amounted to much the same for aboriginal peoples on both sides of the border.[11] And, in both countries, governments and corporations used police, soldiers, and even private detective agencies to combat labour unions and other workers' movements. More could be said here about the comparative myth-history of the West – in terms of the role of the state, Canadian borrowing from American homesteading policies, conceptions of ethnic diversity, or themes of conquest and survival.[12] But in the realms of myth and history, differences between the West in Canada and the U.S. are easily overplayed.

The common imaginative, mythic ground shared by Canadians and Americans regarding the West is especially apparent in its most basic forms – in notions of development, new world adaptation, and imperialist destiny. In the early nineteenth century, Americans and Canadians often viewed the Prairie West as a wasteland unsuited for settlement. In the second half of the century, both re-envisioned the region as marvellously endowed by the Creator, or Nature, for economic development and settlement, and thus enacted policies to foster individual investment and Nation Building. Alike, they assumed that the region was there to be taken, from Aboriginal peoples who had wasted its resources by leaving it a wilderness and failing to develop true civilization. And, both viewed raw nature as incomplete, even sinful, without the hand of civilized humanity to "redeem" it.[13] The seemingly boundless resources and opportunities available in the frontier West inspired in Canadians and Americans a common belief in the unique vitality of the New World, even if, as we shall see, Americans more strongly emphasized their distance from the Old World, and Anglo-Canadians remained concerned to keep faith with their British cultural inheritance. Finally, in common, both justified the process of conquest with imperialist, racialist, and often religious visions of national destiny – in ideals of creating democratic, Anglo-Saxon, Christian societies that represented the leading edge of Progress and the Kingdom of God.[14]

To be sure, Anglo-Canadian dreams of the Dominion as an equal partner with Britain differed from American notions of manifest destiny, but they did so in the details more than in scope. Some Canadian imperialists believed that the moral and the spiritual vitality of the British Empire depended on its New World frontiers. This "Turnerian" environmentalism, of sorts, was distinctively Canadian in its notion that the Dominion would help to fulfill a destiny that God had first given to Britain. Especially hopeful Canadian imperialists might even have fancied that the centre of the Empire would move West to Canada. Such visions emphasized both the promise of material progress in the Canadian West and the conviction that Canada had treated its Indians with more Christian justice and British fair play than had the U.S. In the imperialist imagination, then, the Canadian myths of the West had the same basic function as those associated with the American West, even as they carefully distinguished the Canadian project from that of the U.S.[15]

The Canadian "Frontier Thesis"

The "small differences" between Western "imperialism" in the U.S. and Canada stemmed from the latter's self-conscious fidelity to its British cultural heritage, but also reflected broader differences in the Canadian experience and the imaginative reconstruction of the frontier, in the West and elsewhere in the Dominion.[16] One way to think about these differences is to compare the prevailing versions of the American and Canadian "frontier thesis." To be sure, academic histories are not the same thing as popular or political culture; but they too can play a "myth-historical" role.[17]

The "frontier thesis" proper is rightfully identified with the turn-of-the-century American historian, Frederick Jackson Turner. In his famous essay of 1893, he argued that "an area of free land, its continuous recession," and the advance of settlement westward explain American life. The U.S. had evolved in a unique fashion because its institutions had adapted to changes required "in crossing a continent, in winning a wilderness, and in developing at each area of this progress out of the primitive economic and political conditions of the frontier into the complexity of city life." This struggle between wilderness and civilization had repeated itself again and again in the West, forcing pioneers to cast off European ways, thus making immigrants into a new people.[18] Turner described the "striking" features of the American character vividly: "That coarseness and strength combined with acuteness and inquisitiveness; that practical, inventive turn of mind; that dominant individualism, working for good and for evil, and withal that buoyancy and exuberance which comes with freedom."[19] This American myth-history thus separated the frontier from the Old World and emphasized adaptation rather than cultural inheritance. To be sure, some American historians and culture producers did emphasize the influence of the larger world and the past on American life, but Turner's kind of story prevailed in the American imagination. The frontier had made America "exceptional," giving it a history and course of development all its own.[20]

Canadian historians also espoused New World themes, such as the significance of frontier environments, the transformation of Old World traditions, the frontier's impact on social conflicts, and its contribution to democratic ideals. If they always insisted that Canadian frontiers remained different (e.g., because of British traditions of order, as represented by the ubiquitous Mountie) or agreed that Turner's thesis did not apply to Canada in its entirety, they also adapted his frontier thesis to Canadian life and emphasized common North American experiences. In this vein, in his widely read book, *Colony to Nation*, A.R.M. Lower said that "North American democracy was forest-born."[21] Nonetheless, the prevailing Canadian frontier thesis explained Canada's Old World inheritance. Together, the "staples thesis" of Harold A. Innis and the "metropolitan-hinterland" paradigm of J.M.S. Careless provide the basis for a Canadian frontier thesis.[22] In contrast to the independent dynamics of American frontier evolution, both Canadians pointed to the interaction between "new world" frontier hinterlands, or peripheries, and "old world" metropolitan centres.

The basics of Innis's "staples thesis" can be found in his book, *The Fur Trade in Canada*. "Fundamentally the civilization of North America is the civilization of Europe," Innis contended, "and the interest of this volume is primarily in the effects of a vast new land area on European civilization."[23] Like Turner, Innis noted the need for early settlers to borrow from the "cultural traits" of the Indians. However, sudden change is always difficult and the "depreciation of social heritage is serious." The weight of his story thus was on the "primary importance" of migrants to frontiers maintaining the "cultural traits to which they [had] grown accustomed."[24]

The staples thesis explains the economics of this cultural maintenance. Colonists on the frontier depended on the homeland to hold up their way of life. They needed readily available natural products to sell "in the home market in order to purchase other goods essential to the maintenance and improvement of the current standard of living." Manufactured goods "supplied by the home country enabled" migrants to keep up their standard of living and adjust "to the new environment without serious loss."[25] The economics of adaptation and maintenance thus fostered a dependent relationship that served both the colonial hinterland and the metropolitan centre. Colonial goods were luxuries (furs and gold) or bulk products (fish and lumber) not available in adequate quantities in the Old World. Subsequent staple industries built on the original ones. In nineteenth-century colonial Canada, pulp and paper, wheat, and non-precious metals thus built on the fish and fur trades. The exploitation of these staple products required the development of appropriate means of transport, such as the canoe and later the railroad. All of this required capital investment and institutions of trade and commerce – resources and services largely controlled by metropolitan centres.[26]

"The economic history of Canada" thus "has been dominated by the discrepancy between the centre and the margin of western civilization," Innis observed. Consequently, "Agriculture, industry, transportation, trade, finance, and government activities tend to become subordinate to the production of the staple for a more highly specialized manufacturing community." Because of this, Canada had remained British during the nineteenth and early twentieth centuries. Despite "free trade," it continued to be primarily an "exporter of staples to a progressively industrialized mother country."[27]

Two decades after Innis, J.M.S. Careless further examined the systems of transportation and communication that "could transfer immigrants, ideas, and impulses" from distant centres of power "into the heart of the continent."[28] The frontier is, he said, "developed by a metropolitan centre of dominance which supplies its capital, organizes its communications and transport, and markets its products." Like Innis, he connected the staples economy to politics and culture.[29] "The frontier's culture, too, originally stems from a metropolitan community; at root, learning and ideas radiate from there – and thus is Turner answered." In short, trade and culture went "hand in hand, as newspapers, books, and men of education spread from the centre."[30] Careless studied distant imperial centres of power as well as regional ones, such as Montreal and Toronto. "London and New York are of course the classic examples of modern metropolitanism," he explained. "But the metropolitan relationship is a chain, almost a feudal chain of vassalage, wherein one city may stand tributary to a bigger center and yet be the metropolis of a sizable region of its own."[31] He thus demonstrated how the Northwest could be a "colony" of central Canada at the same time that the country as a whole was a hinterland of Europe and the U.S. In arguing this, Careless did not claim that Canadian history was unique. Just the opposite. Canadian scholars had arrived at a new framework, one that "pays heed both to the distinctive features of the history of this country and to a notable modern phenomenon, the rise of metropolitanism all around the world."[32]

To make his point, that the global "rise of metropolitanism is the other side of the coin to frontier expansion," Careless cited an American historian, W.P. Webb, who had recently written several articles on the "Age of the Great Frontier." Careless argued that the modern era "might just as well be called the 'Age of the Great Metropolis,' when western Europe in general, by spreading out its system of communications and commerce, organized the world about itself."[33] This is the most intriguing aspect of comparing Canadian and American theories of the frontier and the West. Canadian historiography is not unique in its "metropolitan" emphasis. Americans and Canadians both came to metropolitan conclusions, and have drawn on each other's work. But metropolitan thinking never captured the imagination of American scholars, let alone the popular culture, in the way that metropolitan and staples narratives did in Canada.[34] Nor did the frontier thesis take hold in Canada to the same degree it did in the U.S. Americans seem much less likely than Canadians to imagine themselves as ever having been hewers of wood and drawers of water. This makes sense. The U.S. has evolved from a frontier hinterland of Europe to a metropolitan superpower, while Canada, despite its first-world standard of living and culture, arguably remains a semi-periphery dependent on the U.S. economically.[35]

"North" and "West"

For Innis, the staples thesis was more than a theory to explain the evolution of Canada's political economy. His was a "northern vision," one rooted in a self-conscious desire to create a mythic basis for Canadian identity. This vision grew out of his dissatisfaction with the idea that Confederation and the building of the Canadian Pacific Railway had gone against geography, that Canada thus was an unnatural entity destined for continental integration with the U.S.[36] Like many Canadians in the 1920s, in the arts and literature, he dreamed of a Canada defined not by its relationship to the U.S. or Britain, but on its own terms.[37] After publishing his first book in 1923, *A History of the Canadian Pacific Railway*, Innis turned to the fur trade in Canada. Over the next decade, in 1924, 1926, 1929, and 1930, he travelled widely in the Canadian Northwest, by canoe, railroad, and steamboat, to pursue his northern vision, further his research, and inspire his teaching. This intellectual and personal journey inspired *The Fur Trade in Canada*. The book was a hard-headed analysis of the frontier economy, as we have seen. But it also was suffused with the romantic notion that the "wildness" of the North had given the Dominion its distinctive, vital character. Like Turner before him, and like countless Canadian and American writers in the nineteenth century, Innis "treated national history as a narrative of geographic transcendence."[38]

The idea that geography and climate determine a people's character and the identification of the West with paradise can be traced back to the ancient world. Such myths depicted "races" from Northern environments as savage, wild, and hardy, but deficient in culture and intellect. By contrast, warm climates produce high achievements in the arts, science, and philosophy, though hot climates could also produce sloth.[39] Like Americans who associated the West with pastoral, romantic ideals, Canadians who identified themselves as a Northern "race" often drew on British and European writers. Canada was "Lady of the Snows" for Kipling and "True North" for Tennyson. As Carl Berger has shown in his essay, "The True North Strong and Free," the new Dominion was "the 'Young giant nation of the North,' the 'Young scion of the Northern zone'; her people 'Our hardy northern race'; [and,] her location "Those stern Latitudes.'"[40] In the late nineteenth century, Canadian imperialists and nationalists turned these notions to their own uses.

The ideology of Canada as a Northern nation initially took coherent form in the Canada First movement of the 1860s and 1870s. A Fellow of the Royal Society of Northern Antiquaries of Copenhagen, Robert Grant Haliburton, asked rhetorically: "Can the generous flame of national spirit be kindled and blaze in the icy bosom of the frozen north?" Indeed it could. "*We are the Northmen of the New World*," he told the Montreal Literary Club in 1869.[41] At the time, such notions were taken seriously both as cultural descriptions and science; and, race, national character, and environment were identified with each other. Canada benefited doubly in such thinking. It shared with other Northern nations not barbarism but moral "strenuousness" and the "germ" of liberty. Better yet, Canada was a New World nation, with the boundless opportunities and open spaces of its Northwestern frontier. The Northern climate would produce a new people by blending the European "races" migrating to Canada into a homogenous society, claimed the physician William Hales Hingston in 1884. The future occupants of Dominion soil would be "taller, straighter, leaner people," with powerful physiques. To them would belong "the great privilege" of "aiding in erecting, in what was so lately a wilderness, a monument of liberty and civilization, broader, deeper, firmer, than has ever yet been raised by the hand of man."[42]

At the same time that it produced racial unity, overcoming even French-English divisions with "Northern blood," the frontier environment would distinguish Canada from the U.S. Along with its British heritage, which the foolish and unstable Americans had thrown off, the Northern climate would prevent Canada from falling into the indolence of American society. The racialist thread is evident here again, as "Southern races" would not be suited to Canadian life. Happily, the U.S. would provide a "safety valve" of sorts, because those who could not adapt to the rigours of the North would migrate South, leaving Canada free, prosperous, and well-ordered.[43] Only the "hearty" Northern races (from German and Norway, for example) would remain in Canada. This racialist rhetoric easily slipped into and justified social Darwinism, and it linked Canadian myth to imperialist ideologies and practices that explained and justified a world in which "Northern" races dominated those from the "South."

In addition to overtly political ideologies, this "Northern vision" also found expression in novels, artwork, travelogues, and scientific reports. Building on older images of fur traders and frontier pioneers going back to the French era in central Canada, the settlement and exploration of the Northwest at the turn-of-the-century provided new settings and stories: from H.A. Cody's life of the Anglican Bishop Bompas, *An Apostle of the North* (1905), to exploration accounts in J.W. Tyrell's *The New North* (1909) or Vilhjalmur Stefansson's *My Life with the Eskimo* (1913), and the stories of Ralph Connor. The Group of Seven inspired Canada's first national movement in the visual arts during the 1910s. Drawing on Scandinavian themes, in landscape paintings the Group depicted a Canada that was "a long, thin strip of civilization on the southern fringe of a vast expanse of immensely varied, virgin land, reaching into the remote north."[44] In the 1920s, the American-Canadian explorer Robert Flaherty created one of the first great documentary films, *Nanook of the North* (1922), which helped to define Canada for generations of Canadian elementary students.[45] The enduring power of this Northern vision can be seen in the historian W.L. Morton's book, *The Canadian Identity* (1960), where he restated, without the crude racialism or environmentalism of the past, the notion of Canada's "northern character," which he said was a product of the country's maritime heritage, its staples trades, and its seasonal rhythms of life.[46]

These themes suggest that in Canada the North has played a mythic role like that of the West in the U.S., as a frontier producing a "new world" people. Images and ideas associated with the "North" can be benign, humorous, or sublime, but also racist and imperialist, as they define the character and destiny of the nation. And, like the American West, the Canadian North is both a "place" and a "process." As a place, it is liminal, omnipresent, and elusive enough to provide a "North" for all parts of Canada. And, insofar as Canada is North of the U.S., "Northernness" is at least potentially a birthright of all Canadians, both native-born and immigrant. For this reason, the West and myths associated with the region play a different role in Canada than they do in the U.S. By itself, "West" is a regional and a continental identity, one that distinguishes the region from the rest of Canada or ties it to the U.S. in a common story of New World Western frontiers. Where it has contributed to national mythology, it has done so by adding stories and images to an older, more widespread Northern imagination. In the culture of Canadian nationhood, then, the West is "Northwest," West of the Old World and North of the U.S. The complex relationship between North and West in Canadian mythology signals that cultural myths can promote both national and regional, or "limited," identities, and have continental and international resonances.

"West" of What?

Distinctions between national, regional, and international identities break down on closer inspection, as all identities are "limited."[47] In *Imagined Communities*, a study of the origins and spread of nationalism, Benedict Anderson defines nations as *limited, imagined,* and *sovereign*.[48] They must establish and defend literal, geographic borders and imagined cultural boundaries, as well as determine who is included and excluded from the national community. Canada and the U.S. have shared much, continentally, as New World frontier societies defined against Old World Britain and Europe. But Canadians have at the same time always had to distinguish themselves from their neighbour to the South. As we have seen, Canadian myths met this need in visions of the "Mild West," a region of the mind in which the NWMP asserted Canadian sovereignty in a more peaceful, orderly, and just fashion than the U.S. had in its West. These observations suggest that no identity or myth is a perfect unity, a homogenous thing unto itself with a pristine essence. They always are defined and articulated in multiple, contending, and unpredictable contexts. For example, Canada and the U.S. each have a "West beyond the West." Neither British Columbia nor California easily or entirely fits common images of the West.[49] But if they are not Western, what are they? So the question is, "West" of what? West of Britain and Europe? West of Ontario and Quebec? "North" of what? North of Mexico? North of the so-called Third World? North of the U.S.? One way to address these questions is to think in terms of regional protest movements.[50]

In both the U.S. and Canada, popular protest movements have long flourished in the West, from farmer's alliances and cooperative movements at the turn-of-the-past-century to the "Sage Brush" rebels, Reform Party, and Canadian Alliance in the 1970s, 1980s, and 1990s. This pattern seems natural for hinterland regions that exist in unequal metropolitan relationships with distant centres of power. Whom have Western Canadians perceived as the greater threat? Whom have they defined themselves against? Classic Canadian Mild West myths suggest that the U.S. is the true threat to the "Canadian" West. But, remember that such nationalist myths of the West were created in the late nineteenth and early twentieth centuries, times of regular protest against established political and economic interests of central Canada. Did Western Canadians, perhaps, always participate in such myth-making uneasily? In the second half of the twentieth century, as an oil boom brought greater economic power and independence to a province such as Alberta, discontent flourished against Ottawa and its national oil policies, and against Toronto and its economic influence and cultural pretensions. Resentment grew even as American markets and investment capital transformed Alberta's economy. Ironically, or predictably, Canadian metropolitan centres in Toronto and Ottawa became the immediate threat for Albertans, while distant foreign ones in the U.S. seemed to offer greater independence and opportunity.[51] How Western Canadians defined themselves, and how being "Western" related to being "Canadian," or "American," became open questions. Many Albertans had cause to wonder whether states such as Colorado and Texas, and oilmen from American corporations, shared more with them than banks, oil-hungry politicians, and tax-collecting bureaucrats in Central and Eastern Canada. Even if especially common in the Canadian West, this pattern is not unique to the region. Indeed, it is commonplace today to observe that globalization has led to the reassertion of local and regional identities at the expense of national ones.[52] These remarks only scratch the surface of the political and cultural sources of "Western alienation" in Canada during the second half of the twentieth century, but they do point to the political and economic roots of its ideologies and myths.[53]

Similar concerns have shaped the politics of Western Americans who express antagonism against environmental regulations, public lands policies, and cultural attitudes that they perceive as defined by Washington, a distant federal government that seems at best marginally concerned with their needs. The crucial difference is that images of the frontier and mythic narratives of the West continue to represent something larger than a specific region, and still define key aspects of the "imagined" American nation.[54] The same does not seem to be true in Canada, where Western identities have become "limited" ones. Indeed, it is not clear that even Northern identities unify Canadians as they once did, however loosely and inconsistently. In part, this situation may be so because regional identities have weakened national visions even within English Canada. It may also reflect the effort of many Canadians (and their governments) to distance themselves from the negative aspects of classic myths of Northernness (e.g. racism and imperialism) by appealing to multicultural definitions of Canadian citizenship. Despite similar dynamics south of the border, classic Western frontier myths continue to play a powerful role in American popular culture and politics. The electoral success in the 1980s of Ronald Reagan, the cowboy president (and one of his successors in 2000, the cowboy-boot-wearing George W. Bush) exemplifies this trend. By contrast, despite efforts to shed the regional peculiarities of its origins in the Reform Party, the Canadian Alliance never had success outside the West.

Conclusions

"Perhaps the most striking thing about Canada is that it is not part of the United States," remarked J.B. Brebner in the opening sentence of his history of Canada.[55] The broad similarities that we have seen in Western, Northern, and frontier themes in the U.S. and Canada exemplify his point. Nonetheless, it does neglect the "limited," contradictory character of myths and identities, and the "small differences" and antagonisms that shape societies and cultures. This is especially true when it comes to the North American West. The imagined West plays a distinctive role in the structure of American and Canadian myths, whatever their similarities and small differences. This is so partly because of the competing resonance of the North in Canada, but it also reflects the opposing tendencies in American and Canadian forms of the frontier thesis. Canadians have been much more likely to imagine their frontiers and national life as controlled by outside forces. And, even when they have asserted a New World mission for Canada, typically they have done so by claiming to fulfill an Old World destiny. By contrast, frontier-Western destinies in the United States have depended on successfully leaving the past behind.

Leslie Fiedler once noted that as soon as they were invented, myths of the West, "like all myths, passed into the public domain: that region of waking dreams which knows no linguistic or national boundaries."[56] The success of German pulp fiction writers and Italian movie directors in creating epics set in the American West reveals this, as does the poetry of the Canadian Robert Service. But were Europeans more free than Canadians to remake Western frontiers in ways that reflected their own cultural sensibilities, because of their greater geographic and cultural distance from the U.S.?[57] This is likely, because while Canadians could always partake in the commercial-popular culture of the American West, they also had to reckon with their own West, Canadian myths of the frontier, the West and the North, and their close, one-sided political and economic relationship with the U.S. As Robert Service's poetry indicates, there was a simultaneity to the importation of American myth, the invention of Canadian myth, and the experience of history in the Northwest itself. Culturally, Canadians could hardly avoid living on both sides of the border.

In other words, Western myths do indeed cross borders, and in more than one direction. But like staples economies, they do not do so with the same resonances or to the same effect. It ought not to be a great surprise, then, that Ronald Reagan's favourite frontier poet was an English-Canadian who spun "American" tales set in the Canadian Northwest.

Questions to Ponder

1. How does Katerberg view Canada's relationship with Europe versus that of the United States? What is the significance of this difference in relationships?
2. How does the North play a mythic role in the development of Canada?
3. Is the North Canada's version of the United States West?
4. How do racial ideas play into regional definitions?
5. How do regions shape politics?

Must Reads

Francis, Daniel. *National Dreams: Myth, Memory, and Canadian History*. Vancouver: Arsenal Pulp Press, 1997.

Milner, Clyde et al, eds. *The Oxford History of the American West*. New York: Oxford University Press, 1994.

Owram, Doug. *Promise of Eden: The Canadian Expansionist Movement and the Idea of the West 1856–1900*. Toronto: University of Toronto Press, 1980.

Smith, Allan. *Canada – An American Nation? Essays on Continentalism, Identity, and the Canadian Frame of Mind*. Montreal: McGill-Queen's University Press, 1994.

Vanderhaeghe, Guy. *The Englishman's Boy: A Novel*. New York: Picador USA, 1996.

Notes

1. Daniel Francis, *National Dreams: Myth, Memory, and Canadian History* (Vancouver: Arsenal Pulp Press, 1997), p. 158. On Robert Service, see Carl F. Klink, *Robert Service, A Biography* (Toronto: McGraw Hill Ryerson, 1976).
2. Service, "The Shooting of Dan McGrew," first published in *Songs of a Sourdough* (1906), and later in *The Spell of the Yukon and Other Verses* (1907); with corrections, from "The Original Home Page of Robert Service" (2 May 2000; the home page address is www.ude.net/service; the poem can be found at www.ude.net/verse/ The%20Spell%20of%20the%20Yukon.html#13).
3. On this theme, see Dick Harrison, ed., *Crossing Frontiers: Papers in American and Canadian Western Literature* (Edmonton: University of Alberta Press, 1979), especially Leslie Fiedler's essay, "Canada and the Invention of the Western: A Meditation on the Other Side of the Border" (pp. 89–98), which includes a discussion of Robert Service's poetry.
4. Francis, *National Dreams*, ch. 2.
5. In addition to Francis, cited above, see Michael Dawson, *The Mountie from Dime Novel to Disney* (Toronto: Between the Lines, 1998).

6   Philip Goldring, "The Cypress Hills Massacre – A Century's Retrospect," *Saskatchewan History* 26, no. 3 (1973): 81–102.
7   Examples of Heritage Minutes related to the NWMP include "Steele of the Mounties" (on the Yukon) and "Sitting Bull." They can be found on the VHS tape "The CRB Foundation Heritage Project" (Montreal: The Heritage Project, 1998). For more on the series and related projects see the website: <www.histori.ca/minutes/default.do>.
8   For a useful introduction to violence in the American West, see Richard Maxwell Brown, "Violence," in *The Oxford History of the American West*, ed. Clyde Milner II et al. (New York: Oxford University Press, 1994).
9   Anna-Maria Mavromichalis, "Tar and Feathers: The Mounted Police and Frontier Justice," *Alberta History* 43, no. 2 (Spring 1995): 16–24.
10 John Phillip Reid, "The Hudson's Bay Company and Retaliation in Kind Against Indian Offenders in New Caledonia," *Montana: The Magazine of Western History* 43, no. 4 (Winter 1993): 5–17.
11 For a comparative history, see Roger L. Nichols, *Indians in the United States and Canada: A Comparative History* (Lincoln: University of Nebraska Press, 1998).
12 I refer here to the common notion that the Canadian government was much more proactive in shaping the course of Western development, through its "National Policies," than was the U.S. For an example of Canadian borrowing from U.S. policies, note homesteading policies. On these issues, see essays/bibliographies in *The Oxford History of the American West*: Walter Nugent, "Comparing Wests and Frontiers," and Carl Abbott, "The Federal Presence." Richard White uses this as an organizing theme in his synthesis of Western American history, *"Its Your Misfortune and None of My Own"* (Norman: University of Oklahoma Press, 1991). On themes of survival in Canadian literature, see Margaret Atwood, *Survival* (Concord, ON: Anansi, 1972). On ethnicity in the West, the classic distinction is between the Canadian "mosaic" and the American "melting pot." For the complexities of this question in the Canadian West, see Francis, *National Dreams*, ch. 3. Finally, note Arnold Davidson, *Coyote Country: Fictions of the Canadian West* (Durham, NC: Duke University Press, 1994).
13 On development, see Donald Worster, "Two Faces West: The Development Myth in Canada and the United States," in Paul W. Hirt, ed., *Terra Pacifica: People and Place in the Northwest States and Western Canada* (Pullman, Washington: Washington State University Press, 1998). On the myth of the desert and subsequent re-evaluation of the West, see Douglas Owram, *Promise of Eden: The Canadian Expansionist Movement and the Idea of the West, 1856–1900* (Toronto: University of Toronto Press, 1980); R. Douglas Francis, *Images of the West: Changing Perceptions of the Canadian Prairies* (Saskatoon: Western Producer Prairie Books, 1989); and Henry Nash Smith, *Virgin Land: The American West as Symbol and Myth* (Cambridge, MA: Harvard University Press, 1950).
14 Classic studies include: Carl Berger, *The Sense of Power: Studies in the Ideas of Canadian Imperialism, 1867–1914* (Toronto: University of Toronto Press, 1970); Owram, *Promise of Eden*; and Reginald Horsman, *Race and Manifest Destiny: The Origins of American Racial Anglo-Saxonism* (Cambridge, MA: Harvard University Press, 1981).
15 This is my own statement of these themes, but I have adapted the material from Berger, *The Sense of Power*; especially chs. 5 and 9; and Owram, *Promise of Eden*, especially ch. 5.

16 The concept of the "narcissism of small differences" goes back to Freud; see *Group Psychology and the Analysis of the Ego*, trans. James Strachey (London: International Psycho-Analytical Press, 1922), pp. 52–59; *Civilization and Its Discontents* (London: Hogarth Press, 1963), pp. 51–52.

17 For the notion of "myth-history," see William McNeill, *Mythhistory and Other Essays* (Chicago: University of Chicago Press, 1986). For a useful frontier example, see Richard White's comparison of Frederick Jackson Turner and Buffalo Bill Cody, in James R. Grossman, ed., *The Frontier in American Culture* (Berkeley: University of California Press, 1994).

18 Turner, "The Significance of the Frontier in American History," reprinted in *Rereading Frederick Jackson Turner: "The Significance of the Frontier in American History" and Other Essays* (New Haven, CT: Yale University Press, 1994), pp. 31–33. On him, see Allan Bogue, *Frederick Jackson Turner: Strange Roads Going Down* (Norman: University of Oklahoma Press, 1998); and Kerwin Lee Klein, *Frontiers of Historical Imagination: Narrating the European Conquest of Native America, 1890–1990* (Berkeley: University of California Press, 1999).

19 Turner, "Significance of the Frontier ," p. 59.

20 For more on the culture associated with the frontier and the West, see the relevant essays and bibliographies in *The Oxford History of the American West*.

21 Arthur R.M. Lower, *Colony to Nation* (Toronto: Longmans, Green, 1946), p. 49. For a useful one-volume collection that surveys the Canadian literature to 1970, see Michael S. Cross, ed., *The Frontier Thesis and the Canadas: The Debate on the Impact of the Canadian Environment* (Toronto: Copp Clark, 1970).

22 The first articulation of the Canadian staples thesis was also indebted to Turner; see W.A. Mackintosh, "Economic Factors in Canadian History," *Canadian Historical Review* 4 (1923): 12–25. On Innis, see ch. 4 in Carl Berger, *The Writing of Canadian History: Aspects of English-Canadian History Writing since 1900*, 2nd ed. (Toronto: University of Toronto Press, 1986); and Donald Creighton, *Harold Adams Innis: Portrait of a Scholar* (Toronto: University of Toronto Press, 1957).

23 Innis, *The Fur Trade in Canada*, rev. ed. (Toronto: University of Toronto Press, 1956; originally pub. 1930), p. 383. Innis was a poor writer, whose analysis typically was buried under mountains of relatively undigested material. This chapter was the most succinct statement of his thesis. Its significance is evidenced by the frequency with which it is excerpted.

24 Ibid, p. 383.

25 Ibid, pp. 383–84.

26 Ibid, pp. 384–85.

27 Ibid, p. 385.

28 J.M.S. Careless, "Frontierism, Metropolitanism, and Canadian History," *Canadian Historical Review* 35 (1954): 16. Note also his more recent book-length treatment, *Frontier and Metropolis: Regions, Cities, and Identity in Canada before 1914* (Toronto: University of Toronto Press, 1989).

29 Innis made these connections in his work on the pulp and paper industry, and the newspaper industry, and extended them further in theoretical work on communications. See Innis, *The Bias of Communication* (Toronto: University of Toronto Press, 1951); *Empire and Communications*, rev. by Mary Q. Innis (Toronto: University of Toronto Press, 1972; orig. pub. 1950); and "The Newspaper in Economic Development," *Journal of Economic History* 2, Supplement: The Tasks of Economic History (1942): 1–33. On Innis and com-

munications, see William Melody et al., eds., *Culture, Communication, and Dependency: The Tradition from H.A. Innis* (Norwood, NJ: Ablex Publishing); Charles R. Acland and William J. Buxton, eds., *Harold Innis in the New Century* (Montreal: McGill-Queen's University Press, 1999).

30   Careless, "Frontierism," p. 18.
31   Ibid, p. 17.
32   Ibid, p. 21.
33   Ibid, p. 18. Of Webb's writings, see "Ended: 400 Year Boom – Reflections on the Age of the Frontier," *Harper's Magazine* 203 (October 1951): 25–33; and "Windfalls of the Frontier," *Harper's Magazine* 203 (November 1951): 71–77. Webb also published *The Great Frontier* (Boston: Houghton Mifflin, 1952). Note that Careless studied at Harvard University with Arthur Schlesinger, Sr., and took up the American critique of Turner. He also drew on the writings of N.S.B. Gras, the Canadian-born American scholar of urban development who first elaborated stages of metropolitan development in *An Introduction to Economic History* (New York, 1922). Note also the influence of Robert Park and other University of Chicago sociologists in the 1920s. On this, see Berger, *The Writing of Canadian History*, pp.123–24, 175–78.
34   This is true even of the New Western History. While it makes use of metropolitan and staples models, sometimes acknowledging Canadian scholarship, and while it has transformed how professional historians think, and even spawned vociferous public debates, New Western History has not transformed the prevailing popular culture, whether in movies, on TV, in pulp novels, or in documentaries by Ken Burns on the West and Lewis and Clark. On the NWH, see Patricia Limerick, *Legacy of Conquest* (New York: W.W. Norton, 1988); Limerick et al., eds., *Trails: Toward a New Western History* (Lawrence: University of Kansas Press, 1991); Forrest G. Robinson, ed., *The New Western History: The Territory Ahead* (Tucson: University of Arizona Press, 1997); and William Cronon et al., eds., *Under an Open Sky: Rethinking America's Western Past* (New York: W.W. Norton, 1992). For examples of Americans who cite Canadian scholarship, see William Cronon, *Nature's Metropolis: Chicago and the Great West* (New York: W.W. Norton, 1991); and William G. Robbins, *Colony and Empire: The Capitalist Transformation of the American West* (Lawrence: University Press of Kansas, 1994).
35   It is noteworthy that recent discussions of Canada's dependent relationship with the U.S. draw on Innis. A classic from the 1960s is Kari Levitt, *Silent Surrender* (Toronto: Macmillan, 1970). See Mel Watkins, "The Staples Theory Revisited," *Journal of Canadian Studies* 12 (1977): 83–95; Wallace Clement and Glen Williams, eds., *The New Canadian Political Economy* (Montreal and Kingston: McGill-Queen's University Press, 1989); Glen Williams, *Not for Export: The International Competitiveness of Canadian Manufacturing*, 3rd ed. (Toronto: McClelland & Stewart, 1994); and Mel Watkins, "Economic Development in Canada," in Immanuel Wallerstein, ed., *World Inequality: Origins and Perspectives on the World System* (Montreal: Black Rose Books, 1975).
36   On this issue, see Matthew Evenden, "The Northern Vision of Harold Innis," *Journal of Canadian Studies* 34, no. 3 (Autumn 1999): 162–86.
37   On this issue, see Creighton, *Harold Adams Innis*, ch. 2, especially pp. 56–61; and Evenden, "The Northern Vision of Harold Innis," pp. 163–66. In addition to the literature cited

in Evenden, see Mary Vipond, "National Consciousness in English-Speaking Canada in the 1920s: Seven Studies" (PhD diss., University of Toronto, 1974); and Daniel Francis, *National Dreams*.

38 Evenden, "The Northern Vision of Harold Innis," p. 178.

39 See Loren Baritz, "The Idea of the West," *American Historical Review* 66 (1961): 618–40. While it romanticizes paleolithic peoples and ways of life, Max Oelschlaeger's *The Idea of Wilderness: From Prehistory to the Age of Ecology* (New Haven, CT: Yale University Press, 1991), usefully fleshes out the larger intellectual context of ancient ideas about the wilderness. Note also Leo Marx, *The Machine in the Garden: Technology and the Pastoral Ideal in America* (New York: Oxford University Press, 1964); and J.W. Johnson, "Of Differing Ages and Climes," *Journal of the History of Ideas* 21, no. 4 (October–December 1960): 465–80.

40 Carl Berger, "True North Strong and Free," in Peter Russell, ed., *Nationalism in Canada* (Toronto: McGraw-Hill Ryerson, 1966), pp. 4–5.

41 Ibid, pp. 5, 6.

42 Ibid, p. 11.

43 Ibid, pp. 13–15.

44 Ibid, p. 21.

45 On Flaherty and the film itself, see Sherrill Grace, "Exploration as Construction: Robert Flaherty and Nanook of the North," *Essays on Canadian Writing* 59 (Fall 1996): pp. 123–46.

46 Berger, "True North Strong and Free," p. 23.

47 Ramsay Cook first called Canadian scholars to focus on "limited identities"(regional) rather than national identity; see "Canadian Centennial Celebrations," *International Journal* 22 (1967): 659–63. The phrase is often identified as originating with J.M.S. Careless, for the influence of his essay, "'Limited Identities' in Canada," *Canadian Historical Review* 50, no.1 (1969): 1–10. For a recent re-evaluation, see Cook, "Identities Are Not Like Hats," *Canadian Historical Review* 81, no. 2 (2000): 260–65. For application of the term to the Canadian West, see Theodore Binnema, "'A Feudal Chain of Vassalage': Limited Identities in the Prairie West, 1870–1896," *Prairie Forum* 20, no. 1 (1995): 1–18. For a rejection of limited identities and metropolitanism in conceptualizing Western identities, because they subordinate regional identities (as protests) to national ones, rather than treat them as independent forms of consciousness, see Robert Irwin, "Breaking the Shackles of the Metropolitan Thesis: Prairie History, the Environment and Layered Identities," *Journal of Canadian Studies* 32, no. 3 (1997): 98–118.

48 Anderson, *Imagined Communities: On the Origin and Spread of Nationalism*, rev. ed. (London: Verso, 1991), pp. 5–7.

49 On this, see Jean Barman, *The West Beyond the West*, rev. ed. (Toronto: University of Toronto Press, 1996); and Walter Nugent, "Where is the American West?" *Montana: The Magazine of Western History* 42 (Summer 1992): 2–23.

50 Robert Irwin, in "Breaking the Shackles of the Metropolitan Thesis," argues that Western identities need to be understood on their own terms, rather than in relation to national ones. My view is that such a separation is possible only in abstraction. "We" can define who "we" are only by seeing what makes "us" alike in relation to "others" who are different. This is true of national, regional, and continental identities, and those of race, gender, sexuality, and religion.

51 See Allen Smith, "The Ideology of Regionalism: the West Against Ottawa in the 1970s," in *Canada: An American Nation?* (Montreal and Kingston: McGill-Queen's University Press, 1994).
52 For example, see Robert Kaplan's essay, which focuses on the Pacific West in the U.S., but also discusses Vancouver: "Travels Into America's Future," *The Atlantic Monthly* 282, no. 2 (August 1998): 37–61. Note also the larger book, *An Empire Wilderness: Travels in America's Future* (New York: Random House, 1998). His argument is often one-dimensional in its relentless assertion that the U.S. has always been a fundamentally liberal, individualistic culture, with no alternative or competing moral, cultural, mythic, and political visions. But he does well to highlight the political economic sources of local and regional interests and identities, as well as the fragmentation of national ones, as a result of globalization. For a more theoretical view of the relationship between localization and globalization, see Mike Featherstone's work, notably *Undoing Culture: Globalization, Postmodernity, and Identity* (London: Sage, 1995).
53 For example, on the Reform Party, and tensions in its political, economic, religious, and cultural roots, see Trevor Harrison, *Of Passionate Intensity: Right-wing Populism and the Reform Party of Canada* (Toronto: University of Press, 1995). For an interesting discussion of the "naturalness" of regional and national borders by a journalist, see Joel Garreau, *The Nine Nations of North America* (Boston: Houghton Mifflin, 1981).
54 It is also worth noting that the U.S. federal government continues to play a much larger role in supporting the economy of the West than the Canadian federal government: see Carl Abbott, "The Federal Presence," in *The Oxford History of the American West*.
55 Quoted in Cole Harris, "The Myth of the Land in Canadian Nationalism," in Russell, *Nationalism in Canada*, p. 28; cf. Brebner, *Canada* (Ann Arbor: University of Michigan Press, 1960), p. ix.
56 Fiedler, "Canada and the Invention of the Western," p. 91.
57 I am referring here to the novels of Karl May and the movies of Sergio Leone. On Europeans and the American West, see Loetz P. Kroepnick, "Unsettling America: German Westerns and Modernity," *Modernism/Modernity* 2, no. 3 (1995): 1–22; Christopher Frayling, *Spaghetti Westerns: Cowboys and Europeans from Karl May to Sergio Leone* (London: Routledge and Kegan Paul, 1981); Frayling, *Sergio Leone: Something to do with Death* (London: Faber and Faber, 2000); Richard Cracoft, "The American West of Karl May," *American Quarterly* 19 (1967): 249–58; and, Ray Allen Billington, *Land of Savagery/Land of Promise: The European Image of the American Frontier in the Nineteenth Century* (New York: W.W. Norton, 1981). Also, remember that European ideas and intuitions helped to create the myth of the West, in the nineteenth century, in the form of Romanticism, through travel literature, painting, and scientific reports.

Thanks to the organizers of the conferences "One West, Two Myths: Comparing Canadian and American Perspectives," Gerry Conaty, Carol Higham, and Bob Thacker. I am grateful to Fran Kaye and Alice Kehoe for comments on an earlier draft. Thanks also to Charlene Porsild and Jodie Foley of the Montana Historical Society Research Center. Michel Hogue assisted me with research on Fanny Kelly.

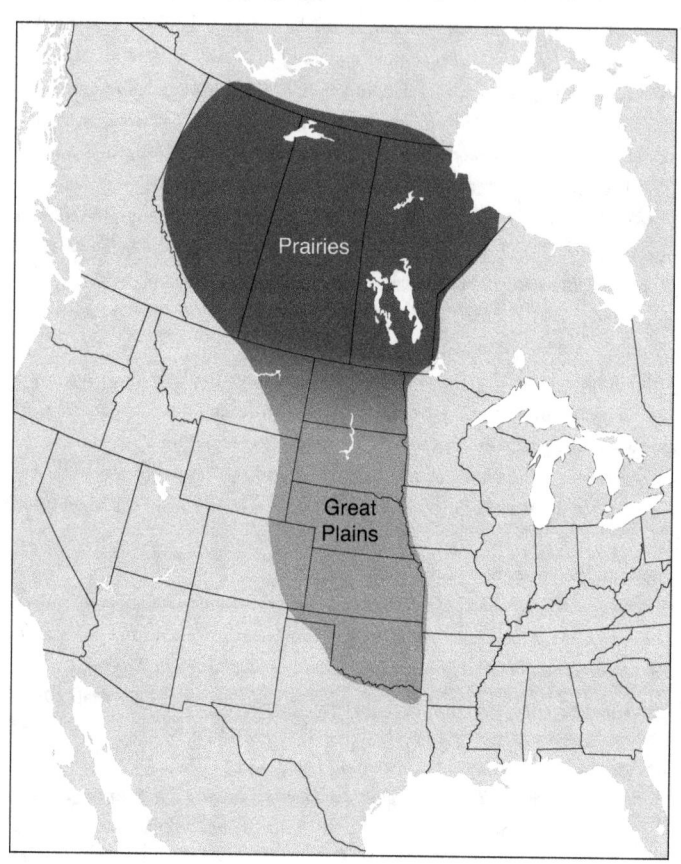

The Great Plains of the Unitied States and the Prairies of Canada

chapter five

Transnational Perspectives on the History of Great Plains Women: Gender, Race, Nations, and the Forty-ninth Parallel

Sarah Carter, University of Alberta

"History is sadly truncated if national historians travel without passports and stop investigating when the subject reaches the 49th parallel," writes Jan Noel in her introduction to a recent collection of articles that focus on race and gender in the intertwined histories of the border colonies of seventeenth- and eighteenth-century eastern North America.[1] There is enormous potential for similar work on cross-border history in the regions to the west of the colonies of the Noel collection. The modest goal of this article is to create interest in transnational approaches to the northern Great Plains region of the Canadian and U.S. Wests by drawing on examples from my past, present, and future areas of research that focus on Aboriginal and non-Aboriginal women's and gender history within the context of imperialism of the late nineteenth to early twentieth centuries. "Transnational" histories question the nation-centred focus of history, and they encompass and blend diverse approaches and perspectives, including comparative and borderlands history, analysis of boundary-crossing people, ideas and institutions, and examination of the ways in which national borders were ignored, contested, and manipulated.[2] A transnational approach to the Great Plains permits fresh perspectives on the history of colonized and co-lonial women and on gendered and racial dimensions of nation-making. Many recent studies have shown that the gendering of imperialism took different forms in different parts of the world, although there were also shared features.³ The Great Plains provides a unique opportunity to examine a region in which two nations' institutionalization of gender and race difference, which limited and legitimized peoples' access to the resources of the nation-state, took divergent forms, while sharing some features, in the *same* part of the world, although one bisected by a border.

The field of Aboriginal women's history cannot be narrowly grounded in the nation-state. The territory of many Aboriginal nations, including the Plains Cree, Blackfoot, Assiniboine, Dakota, Lakota, and Ojibway, spanned the forty-ninth parallel. Yet most historians, as Beth LaDow has commented, "tend to divide the American story from the Canadian along this boundary, as if it split the past as neatly as a meat cleaver."⁴ Aboriginal people are neatly categorized as "Canadian" or "American," and are dropped from each nation's narrative once they cross the line, skewing understanding of experiences and identities that pre-date, transcend and ignore the border. One of the most prominent of the women of the mid-nineteenth-century Great Plains, Natoyist-Siksina', Holy Snake (known in her lifetime and since to English speakers as Natawista) has been relegated to a realm outside of history because of her Aboriginal and transnational status. She is virtually unknown today in non-Aboriginal Canada, although she is one of few women to have an entry in the *Dictionary of Canadian Biography*.⁵ While much of her life was spent in the American West, she was born in what became Canada in 1825, lived there for the last twenty years of her life, died on the Blood Reserve in 1893, and is buried at Stand Off, Alberta. Natoyist-Siksina' was a Kainai (Blood) woman who was born, likely near Lethbridge, Alberta, to Two Suns, chief of the Fish Eaters band, and Red Deer Woman.⁶ At the age of fifteen she married Alexander Culbertson, chief trader for the Upper Missouri Outfit of the American Fur Company. A description of this marriage was written by anthropologist Lewis Henry Morgan, who met the couple in 1862 and noted in his journal that "When Culbertson obtained his Blackfoot wife he sent 9 horses to his wife's eldest brother. He told his men to hitch them at his lodge and to ask for the girl as his wife. She was sent to him the next day the brother returned nine other horses as a present to Culbertson. It is customary for the brother to distribute the presents among the relatives, and for the relatives to return presents to the groom. In this case the marriage was one which gave great satisfaction to the girl's family, and hence the manner in which it was acknowledged."⁷

Along with her husband, Natoyist-Siksina' was at the centre of fur and robe trade operations on the Upper Missouri for nearly three decades and this is partly why she so often emerges in the documentary. Other reasons for her frequent mention have to do with her dynamic, energetic personality, her knowledge, skills, and her appearance, which captivated numerous observers. She is consistently depicted as strong, independent, and outspoken. Like many of the Aboriginal women described in Sylvia Van Kirk's *Many Tender Ties*, Natoyist-Siksina' played an important role as an intermediary between her people and her husband's, as a diplomat and as a translator.[8] She worked to establish the foundation for a world in which Aboriginal and non-Aboriginal people could peacefully co-exist, and she exemplified this co-existence in her family, her diplomatic work, and even in her own appearance, as she loved fine clothing and jewellery from both cultures. She was from a prominent, influential family in the mid-nineteenth-century West, and her position likely helped her husband as well as her Kainai relatives to gain influence. Her brother Seen-From-Afar was a head chief of the Kainai, and her cousin Little Dog was head chief of the Peigan. Her nephew was Red Crow, head chief of the Kainai at the time of the making of Treaty 7 in 1877.[9]

With her husband, Natoyist-Siksina' established Fort Benton on the Upper Missouri as the centre of a trade that reached far to the north into British territory. During her Fort Benton years Natoyist-Siksina' assisted in a number of delicate negotiations between the Blackfoot[10] and American authorities. In 1853 she was present at meetings between the Blackfoot and the Governor of Washington Territory, Isaac Stevens, when the route for the Pacific railroad was surveyed through Blackfoot land. Governor Stevens found her assistance to be of great value, writing that "I soon perceived the advantage to be derived from Mrs. Culbertson's presence. She was in constant intercourse with the Indians, and inspired them with perfect confidence...."[11] When Stevens heard shrieks of laughter coming from the women who visited Natoyist-Siksina's tent, he was informed that she was regaling them with tales and descriptions of the White ladies in St. Louis. She had visited the city several times and she often entertained her friends with carefully mimicked stories of her adventures.[12] In 1855 Natoyist-Siksina' assisted in the negotiations of the Lame Bull Treaty, a treaty that was to permit the building of railroads and roads in return for a recognition of the territory of the Blackfoot and assistance toward the establishment of agriculture. In 1868 it was reported in the *Montana Post* that the terms of a treaty with the Bloods and Blackfoot near Fort Benton were explained by Culbertson and his wife.[13]

Natoyist-Siksina' was an important informant to many of the visitors to her territory who were gathering information on the people, resources, and environment. Naturalist and artist John James Audubon was very taken with Natoyist-Siksina' during his visit to Fort Union in 1843. He admired much about her, including her appearance, her artistic work such as a parfleche she decorated with porcupine quills and a necklace she made for him of red berries, and her amazing range of skills, such as her ability to swim, catch mallards, and ride a horse at breakneck speed. Audubon described a sham buffalo hunt that the Culbertsons put on to entertain their guests:

> The Ladies had their hair loose and flying in the breeze and then mounted on horses with Indian saddles and trappings. Mrs. Culbertson and her maid rode astride like men and all rode a furious race, under whip the whole way, for more than a mile on the prairie; how amazed would have been any European lady, or some of our modern belles who boast their equestrian skill, at seeing the magnificent riding of this Indian princess, for that is Mrs. Culbertson's rank. Mr. Culbertson rode with them, the horses running as if wild, with these extraordinary Indian riders, Mrs. Culbertson's magnificent black hair floating like a banner behind her.[14]

In 1862 Natoyist-Siksina' provided anthropologist Lewis Henry Morgan with detailed information on Blackfoot and Gros Ventre kinship systems and acted as his interpreter.[15]

Audubon painted portraits of Natoyist-Siksina' and her husband, and artist John Mix Stanley painted Natoyist-Siksina' several times. Stanley accompanied Governor Stevens' party in 1853, mentioned above. She was his model for his paintings *A Family Group* and *The Last of Their Race*, originally owned by the Culbertsons and displayed in their Peoria, Illinois mansion,[16] Swiss artist Rudolph Friederich Kurz was also very taken with Natoyist-Siksina', writing during his 1851 visit that "If Mr. Culbertson's Indian wife had not received news of her younger brother having been shot by the Assiniboin, I should have had the chance to study one of the most beautiful Indian women. In token of her grief she had her long lustrous black hair cut short. She would be an excellent model for a Venus, ideal woman of the primitive race; a perfect 'little wife.'"[17] Kurz's comments, as well as those of many others who met Natoyist-Siksina,' indicate that while she lived in the world of the trading post, she also retained the ceremonies, observances, and beliefs of her own people, and was not at all concerned if these might offend the sensibilities of her visitors. Audubon wrote that "I lost the head of my first buffalo bull because I forgot to tell Mrs. Culbertson that I wished to save it, and the princess had its skull broken open to enjoy its brains. Handsome and really courteous and refined in many ways, I cannot reconcile myself to the fact that she partakes of raw animal food with such relish."[18]

Natoyist-Siksina' and Alexander Culbertson together made a substantial fortune on the Upper Missouri, and in 1858 they retired to Peoria along with their five children. A year later they were married according to the rites of the Catholic Church. Their mansion became one of Peoria's showplaces.[19] It was surrounded by three acres of grounds, designed by an English gardener. A corral on the property was stocked with antelope, elk, and buffalo. There were also stables with the finest carriage horses. Yet it was reported in the local paper that in the summer months, Natoyist-Siksina' preferred to live in a tipi which she put up on the grounds of her estate. Natoyist-Siksina' and her husband also travelled back to Blackfoot country frequently following their move to Peoria. The life of luxury was over by the late 1860s, however, when the fortune was spent. Creditors demanded payment and their possessions were auctioned off, among them Stanley's painting *The Last of Their Race*. Other belongings, including a cup from Isaac Stevens inscribed "To the Second Pocahontas," burned in a warehouse fire.[20]

The Culbertsons moved back to Fort Benton in 1869, but Natoyist-Siksina' stayed there only briefly and then left Culbertson forever, returning to the Kainai and to British territory to the north, despite at least two visits that Culbertson and their youngest son Joe made to persuade her to return. "Natawista," age forty-five, is listed in the 1870 census of Benton City along with her husband (sixty-one), daughter Fanny (twenty), son Joseph (twelve) and nephew Robert Culbertson (twenty-seven).[21] The last evidence of her presence at Fort Benton is a record that she purchased "3 Bottles of Eau D Cologne" from T.C. Powers in May 1870.[22] The reasons why she left can only be guessed at. She may have been thoroughly angered and disillusioned at the disintegration of any hopes for a world in which Aboriginal and non-Aboriginal accommodated each other.

At the treaty she had participated in the year before, the Blackfoot had protested against the agency being located at Fort Benton because of the "abuse and insults" of certain Whites.[23] 1869 was a momentous year as smallpox took a huge toll, and her brother Seen-From-Afar was one of the victims.[24] The years 1865–70 were also characterized by intensive warfare waged on the Blackfoot in the U.S. West, culminating in the notorious "Baker Massacre" in January 1870, when four companies of cavalry and two infantry troops slaughtered nearly two hundred Peigan, including women and children. Most of the survivors of this incident left for the north, taking up permanent residence on the Canadian side of the border.

Natoyist-Siksina' may have been with her people in present-day Lethbridge in late October 1870 when the last major battle took place between the Cree and the Blackfoot. On the first day of that battle the Cree killed one of her nephews, a brother of Red Crow.[25] Blackfoot women displayed great courage during this battle and perhaps Natoyist-Siksina' was one of these. According to one Kainai account of the battle, "Some of the Blackfoot women swam across the [St. Mary] river to the main camp to summon aid. One of these women showed remarkable bravery by slaying four Cree warriors with her only weapon, a tomahawk, during the first part of the hostilities."[26] The majority of the casualties were Cree (approximately two hundred), and about forty Blackfoot were killed and fifty wounded.[27] Perhaps Natoyist-Siksina' remained with the Kainai to assist those who lost family during this battle. Perhaps the border now had meaning for her and she had resolved to remain to the north.

Natoyist-Siksina was married briefly to American whisky trader Henry Alfred (Fred) Kanouse, who set up his operations on the British side of "Whoop-Up" country, as the territory became known that included southern Alberta, the Cypress Hills region of Saskatchewan, and south to Fort Benton. She emerges again from time to time in the documentary record mainly because of her unique history and often extraordinary appearance. In an 1875 letter North-West Mounted Police surgeon Richard B. Nevitt described Natoyist-Siksina' as she arrived to attend races at Fort Macleod:

> The ladies came on horseback; only one, however, had a saddle and this was Madame Kanouse. You should have seen her dress. It was the Dolly Varden style, a large figured chintz just short enough to display the gorgeous stripes of balmoral petticoat which in turn was also just short enough to show two

very small feet clad in moccasins and the end of a pair of leggings beautifully worked in beads. She also had on a heavy black velvet loose-fitting overcoat, and over this, a most brilliant striped shawl, the striped being about three inches broad and alternatively red, blue, green and red, with a narrow line of yellow between each color. Her head gear consisted of a small plaid shawl. The other titled aristocrats were also dressed in gorgeous array, but perforce they yielded the palm to Madame.[28]

Natoyist-Siksina' moved to the Blood reserve following the making of Treaty 7. She was no longer married to Kanouse at the time of the establishment of the Blood reserve; if she had still been with him, she would not have been permitted to live on the reserve. *Toronto Mail* reporter George Ham encountered her in 1885, writing that she lived frugally but still had some of her fine clothing and silverware. Ham found hers "a strange history, not the strangest part of which is, that she prefers the wild freedom of the plains to the conventionalities of society."[29] She continued to make visits to the south, across what had become, in 1874, a surveyed border between the U.S. and Canada. Her son Joe lived on the Fort Peck reservation and she visited him there. Other children lived farther away. Her daughter Fanny lived in El Paso, Texas and was married to lawyer L.S. Irvine, although they later moved to Great Falls, Montana. Daughter Julia lived in Orleans, Nebraska. She was also married to a lawyer, George Roberts, the first elected attorney general of that state.[30] Alexander Culbertson was staying with Julia and her family when he died in 1879.

In 1891 Natoyist-Siksina' was living on the Blood reserve with her nephew, Chief Old Moon, when she wrote a letter to her daughter Fanny and her husband, with the assistance of the agency clerk, complaining about her rations and housing, and saying that she wished for a house of her own.[31] Indian agent William Pocklington sent a terse reply when he received a letter from Irvine concerning his mother-in-law's living conditions, which indicates the sort of control government employees now exercised over reserve residents. The agent did not intend to address the problem of Natoyist-Siksina's living conditions but rather promised that "You can rest assured that no such letter will ever be sent from this office again."[32] Pocklington wrote that the agency clerk should not have assisted to send such a letter, that "as a rule I write all letters my Indians desire to send," and that Mrs. Culbertson "draws the regular rations here, which is considered ample, and resides in her nephew's 'Chief Old Moon's' house, a log building, shingled roof and partitioned. I fancy she wishes for a house of her own, which is only natural, but unfortunately I have none to give her, nor the material for one." Natoyist-Siksina' died in March 1893, and is buried in an unmarked grave in the Catholic cemetery at Stand Off, Alberta.

While the forty-ninth parallel had little meaning for Natoyist-Siksina' and Aboriginal women of her generation for most of their lives, this began to change by the late nineteenth century. Regimes of government administration that were introduced in both nations in the late nineteenth century had much in common. The imposition of European gender norms was central to the assimilation program of both nations. Patriarchal family units were to be the cornerstone of re-fashioned communities in which men engaged in farming or other trades and women were to be transformed into submissive housewives. In both nations, residential schools trained students in these gender norms, with girls educated for domesticity.

Along with these similarities, however, there were also crucial differences in government policies in both nations that had a significant impact on the lives of Great Plains Aboriginal women and that warrant careful consideration. Aboriginal women on both sides of the border had less access to rights and resources than newly arrived White women. This is a complex history with many dimensions that can only be hinted at in this paper, but once again the perspective of an individual story can assist in understanding some of the differences. In the spring of 1895 Mary Aspdin and her children were not granted permission to return across the border to their home in Moose Jaw, after visiting relatives in South Dakota.[33] It required several months of correspondence between her husband Thomas Aspdin, and officials in Ottawa and Washington, before the necessary permission was acquired. Mary Aspdin was a Lakota woman, who had been living north of the forty-ninth parallel for nearly twenty years. She was the daughter of distinguished Lakota chief Black Moon, Sitting Bull's uncle, and her family was among the Lakota who moved north of the border in 1876, following the battle of the Little Big Horn, which Mary witnessed at age sixteen. The Lakota hoped to remain in Canada, claiming that they were allies of the British and that present-day southern Saskatchewan was within their territory. While most of the Lakota were persuaded to leave Canada, not all did so, and in 1911 a fragment of

Sitting Bull's band camped around Moose Jaw were granted a reserve at Wood Mountain. Mary married Thomas Aspdin while he was a policeman posted at Wood Mountain. He left the force and by 1890 had been appointed an Indian Affairs agent overseeing the Lakota of Moose Jaw, and the Aspdins lived there with their three daughters.[34]

Mary and her daughters were detained by the Indian agent at Cherry Creek, Cheyenne River Agency, South Dakota. They had travelled there in 1894 with a party of Lakota from Moose Jaw that had been persuaded to move there.[35] While in the U.S., Mary Aspdin was treated by officials as a Lakota woman, subject, like others, to the orders of the Indian agent. Her status in Canada was quite different and complicated. In Canada she was not legally considered "Indian" at all because she was married to a White man. Although she was not a treaty Indian (as the Lakota and Dakota in Canada were not included in the treaties), before her marriage she nonetheless had "Indian status," which meant that the federal Indian Act applied to her and under that Act, once she married Thomas, she lost that status and became legally "White." She and her husband would have had no right to live on the reserve that was eventually granted the Lakota, although there were many such couples on her relatives' reservations across the line. The Aspdin's children were also not entitled to benefits such as annuities because they were not legally recognized as Indian. Aspdin himself remarked on these differences when he travelled to South Dakota in 1895 to retrieve his wife and family, writing that "a feature about all the Sioux Reserves is the number of white men living there, being married to the Indian women. Some of them are very well off. Their wives and children draw rations and annuities."[36] He likely commented at length because he knew none of this was possible in Canada, whereas in the U.S. there was no legislation that dissolved a woman's status upon marriage to a White man.

When the Aspdins returned north across the border they were briefly detained once again, this time by the North-West Mounted Police at Estevan, as Mary was made to pay duty on all of her belongings because she had been across the border for over a year. This was despite the fact that her belongings had all originally been brought from Moose Jaw, and that she had been detained against her will for that length of time.[37] White women moved much more seamlessly across the border. Violet Pearl Sykes, for example, was born in Montana in 1892 and as a young teenager she and relatives effortlessly and often travelled back and forth across the border to work on ranches on either side of the line.[38] By contrast, Peigan elder Cecile Many Guns described the inauguration of a regime that severely restricted the movement of her people.[39] She recalled that the Peigan had once occupied a vast territory spanning the international boundary. After the 1877 Treaty 7 their ability to travel to draw on the resources of the land was sharply curtailed:

> In my girlhood days I remember there were no fences. This country was wide open ... there were no fences, no houses, no white people from the Porcupine Hills, the Crow Lodge Creek to the Belly Buttes. We thought all this space was ours. My belief was that this land was our principal natural asset. Suddenly it was surveyed and fenced and it was small and we were told to stay in this corral.... When we left the reserve we had to have a paper and if we did not have it, we had to pay a fine, or go to jail if we didn't have any money.

Mary Aspdin's later years also provide insight into some of the key differences between U.S. and Canadian policy that had an impact on the lives of Aboriginal women. In 1913, then a widow, Mary Aspdin moved to the Cheyenne River reservation where she and her daughters were allotted land.[40] Together they went into the cattle business. Although such an enterprise was not typical of Native American women on reservations, this access to land and such a business opportunity would have been virtually impossible for a woman on a Canadian Indian reserve. A brief digression into a complex area of Indian policy is necessary to understand these differences. The U.S. Dawes Severalty Act, passed in 1887 and implemented over the next several decades, divided reservation land into allotments. The rationale was that this would further remake Indian society by embedding Euro-American gender roles and instill property values. The Act also resulted in massive losses of reservation land as unallotted land was sold to settlers and railroads. The implementation process was complicated, and it varied from one reservation to another, but in most cases single women, including those with children, and widows, received allotments.[41] In the Canadian West there was no direct parallel to the Dawes Act, although on many fertile reserves beginning in the late 1880s, the land was surveyed in severalty and a system of "location tickets" was devised.[42] Administrators hoped this would encourage Indian males to enfranchise, giving up their Indian status in order to eventually receive title to an allotment.

In Western Canada there was no means through which women could acquire location tickets, or individual rights to any land on reserves, except through strictly monitored cases of inheritance. Under the Indian Act a widow could inherit her husband's property only if, in the view of administrators, she had led a "moral" life.

Another potential area of investigation relates to gender, nation building, and ideas of nation. It has become commonplace to say that Canadian nation-builders carefully nurtured an identity as a peaceable, tranquil, orderly dominion that was dependent on representations of the United States as the antithesis, as turbulent, aggressive, and violent. But the gendered dimensions of the social and cultural constructs of Canadian regional and national identities, forged in opposition to an imagined American identity, have not been as fully explored. Some of the gendered dimensions important to understanding the history of the two Wests emerged at the recent two meetings of the conference "One West, Two Myths: Comparing Canadian and American Perspectives."[43] When considering dominant myths and symbols, the two Wests appear to have much in common, as overwhelmingly masculine imagery prevails. At the first session at Cody, Wyoming's Buffalo Bill Historical Center, conference coordinator Carol Higham asked participants to call out the dominant mythic images and symbols of the two Wests that sprang to mind, and aside from a few icons such as "madonna of the plains," and "prostitute with a heart of gold" there was little that related to women among the Indian chiefs, fur traders, explorers, Mounties, cowboys, soldiers, miners, farmers, and railroad barons. As John Herd Thompson reminded us in his presentation, these are not precisely the same masculine ideals.[44] The Canadian West cherishes the courteous, affable Mountie (Dudley Do Right) as opposed to the whisky-guzzling, gun-toting cowboy (John Wayne) of the American West, but for both a particular, gendered Western identity is celebrated. The myth of the West as manly space is present in both Wests.

In "No Place for a Woman: Engendering Western Canadian Settlement," Catherine Cavanaugh explored the expansionist and settlement discourse that "perpetuated the myth of the West as a 'manly' space, assigning to it a moral and political force that underwrote elite Anglo-Canadian men's hegemony in the territories."[45] Cavanaugh found that there were striking parallels with American expansionist discourse, as for both nations the West was "a source of national regeneration and spiritual renewal through a reinvigorated manhood."[46] Yet the cultural constructions of the West as manly space were not fixed and stable, rather they fluctuated and varied depending on the needs of the nation. While the manly West may have eventually predominated, there was a time in the late nineteenth to the early twentieth centuries, when a feminine Canadian West, which drew its inspiration and identity partly in opposition to the image of an unsavoury, salacious masculine United States, was a useful and popular image. The Canadian West was young, pure, pristine, virginal, and a little naive and vulnerable, so in need of a strong protector. The masculine U.S. was base, rapacious, debauched and menacing, poised to possess, dominate and ravish the Canadian West's untapped resources. This imagery was evident in Canadian political cartoons of the day. The forerunner of the Canadian West, Red River (Winnipeg) was depicted in a January 1870 issue of the *Canadian Illustrated News* (Montreal), as the young, vulnerable "Miss Red River," dressed as Red Riding Hood complete with basket. She must choose between the "U.S. Hotel" and "Hotel Canada." As John H. Thompson wrote in his caption describing this cartoon in his book *Forging the Prairie West*, "A leering, whittling, smoking Uncle Sam lounges in front of the former, while the respectable Mrs. Britannia keeps the latter. Victorian readers accustomed to such artistic conventions would have had no doubt about the fate that awaited 'Miss Red River' inside the U.S. Hotel."[47] A guardian and protector was required in the form of the "Mother" country and a strong, centralized, paternal Canadian government to prevent the maiden from falling into the hands of this base male.

The "beautiful, wholesome, hopeful maiden" imagery was applied not just to the new Western region; "Miss Canada" was a popular representation of the entire nation. As historian Christina Burr wrote in a recent article "In Western culture, woman, as a national symbol, was the guardian of the continuity and immutability of the nation and the embodiment of its respectability."[48] "Miss Canada" was often depicted as the young offspring of another strong feminine icon, Mother Britannia. The imminent danger to the purity and virtue of the young, fair Miss Canada posed by the U.S. was depicted in an 1891 Conservative party campaign poster which made the rape metaphor quite explicit.[49] Miss Canada is running from a group of men that Uncle Sam instructs to "Seize her fellows! Now's your chance! Ah ha! Miss Canada, you shall not escape." Boldly entitled "Miss Canada's Rescuer," the young woman is saved by Sir John A. Macdonald (the prime minister running for re-election), who sends the Americans away saying "I think you had better call another day gentlemen." The demure Miss Canada stands behind her protector Sir John, her hand on the head of a (British) lion.

The Canadian West was frequently depicted as a young woman. The illustration on the front page of *The Globe* (Toronto) of September 2, 1905, bore the caption "Fair Alberta Makes Her Bow." A young woman rides a frisky horse, but demurely, on a sidesaddle. It was declared that "The great sisterhood of Provinces received an addition today by the admission of the promising young maiden Province of Alberta." The feminine imagery associated with the West, however, ultimately served and enhanced the idea that here was a land with limitless possibilities for manly pursuits, and that man was the missing quantity. And not just any men of course, but preferably White men of the British stock, for as the author of *The New West* wrote in 1888, "in this fair land there are countless thousands of leagues of territory on which the foot of man has never trod, lying tenantless and silent, only awaiting the advent of the Anglo-Saxon race to be transformed into a prosperous and thriving country.... The virgin soil, the primeval forest, and the teeming seas and lakes and rivers all possess undeveloped riches. Man alone is apparently the missing quantity, and his energy, industry and capital are the required elements...."[50] As Anne McClintock has written, "The myth of the virgin land is also the myth of the empty land, involving both a gender and a racial dispossession.... Within colonial narratives, the eroticizing of 'virgin' space also effects a territorial appropriation, for if the land is virgin, colonized people cannot claim aboriginal territorial rights and white male patrimony is violently assured as the sexual and military insemination of an interior void."[51]

The ideas expressed in the political cartoons and posters, of a virtuous but vulnerable feminine Canada as opposed to a corrupt and threatening masculine U.S., may have been reflected in the attitudes of Western Canadians, and is a topic worthy of further investigation. Certainly British traveller Bessie Pullen-Burry found this to be so during her 1912 visit across Canada.[52] In Manitoba she was told that women in solitary districts had to become skilled in the use of firearms, particularly if they lived close to the international border. A woman on a farm informed her that "We live close to the international boundary, and queer characters are sometimes seen prowling round our neighbourhood; but they think twice about attacking a woman if they know she has firearms in the house, and will use them without hesitation if necessary."[53] Pullen-Burry further wrote about the threat posed to innocent, inexperienced Western Canadian girls from Americans lurking about Winnipeg who were connected to "a hideous traffic south of the line, the result...of an insufficient supply to meet the demands of the immoral men of cities like Chicago, which send well-dressed females as well as male emissaries into Canada to entrap the unwary and ignorant into life-long bondage."[54] Fears of young girls being enticed into "white slavery" and other reminders of the threats supposedly posed by unscrupulous Americans functioned to reinforce Canada's self-image as a superior nation and haven for a virtuous, wholesome and pure femininity.

The gendered dimensions of American views of Western Canada could be compared to their northern counterparts. There is some evidence that the tropes of a bold and aggressive Uncle Sam and a frail Miss Canada, one day to be united, were popular representations in American political cartoons. An 1880 *Puck Magazine* (New York) cartoon depicts Uncle Sam using a magnet labelled "Business Interests" to attract Miss Canada, who has been swept off her feet but is tethered to a dilapidated post which bears the features of Sir John A. Macdonald, with the aid of a strap labelled "Conservative Party."[55] The caption reads "'It's only a question of time:' Old fogeyism may hold her back for a while, but she is bound to come to us." Uncle Sam lacks the debauched and menacing characteristics of the Canadian representations, as here he has a magnetic charm, but the outcome of their imminent future union is made just as clear. In the 1910 *New York Herald* cartoon, "Irresistible," a charming, rather than a menacing American farmer "casts sheeps eyes at the Canadian West".[56]

There is evidence that American travel writers who visited Western Canada also depicted the land as feminine, as virgin and pristine, and thus a new arena for manly American pursuits. In his account of his visit published in 1888 as *Daylight Land*, W.H.H. Murray described his delight at the landscapes, the sunsets, storms, quietude, and especially the wildlife, "the reason why the great area north of us is to be commended to the American sportsman...."[57] Here there were, Murray wrote, "great possibilities for healthy men and happy homes lying far to the north of present settlements...millions on millions of acres that only wait for the plough and the seed, the sower's hand and the harvester's sickle...."[58] Another genre of American literature, by those who had not travelled to Western Canada (described as "not-travel" literature by historian Adele Perry[59]) touted the grandiose accomplishments of the American men who were transforming the Canadian West, showing an example to their effete Canadian counterparts, and convincing them of the virtues of annexation. English travel writer A.G. Bradley described these accounts as "absurd" in his 1905 *Canada in the Twentieth Century*. "Men who scarcely know wheat from oats, who have never crossed the Canadian border, draw upon their vivid imagination for a forecast of what the American settler will do and how they will sap the loyalty of the Canadians.... The Manitoban wheat farmer is pictured by these cockney scribblers in New York or Chicago as a sort of French habitant, standing amazed at the American farmer who is bursting on his vision with a two-storied frame house and a brand-new self binder, and the blessings of annexation to be thrown in some day when he is 'educated up to it.'"[60] Bradley had also read a "perfectly serious" column in a Southern American newspaper which described the half a million "dead shots" in Canada "all with their secret orders for a prompt invasion of the United States in case of war, and that the slaughter they would create would make the South African War seem child's play."[61] The entire population of Canada was depicted as absorbed in rifle shooting in anticipation of such a conflict, according to the article. Bradley concluded "That all these things can be gravely printed are evidence of the extraordinary darkness of the average American concerning Canada and everything in it."

In Canada, the idea that young, wholesome Canadian women had much to fear from the rapacious, violent, masculine American West was made vividly clear through the Canadian editions of a popular captivity account, Fanny Kelly's *Narrative of My Captivity Among the Sioux Indians*.[62] In May 1864 Fanny Kelly was with a party travelling by covered-wagon train from Kansas through Wyoming when they were attacked by Oglala Lakota. Kelly was a captive for five months until her ordeal ended at Fort Sully, Dakota Territory. Her book was first published in 1871 and a Canadian edition appeared one year later, followed by three more with a fourth Canadian edition appearing in 1878. Canadian publishers were not in the habit of publishing editions of the numerous captivity narratives to emerge from the American West, but were moved to do so in this case because Fanny Kelly was originally from Orillia, Ontario, having moved to Kansas at the age of twelve. Not only would her account be of interest to Canadian readers because of her background, but it would provide a good opportunity to impart some important lessons, including that Canada was a superior nation, that the Canadian West was peaceful and orderly compared to the events Kelly described, that such a "tenderly reared" White Canadian woman would never be subject to such outrageous treatment in the Canadian West, and that it would be best for all but especially White women to avoid the American West. For American readers Kelly would symbolize the helpless White woman victimized by savage assailants. The captivity narrative was a popular form of writing in the U.S., and while they were diverse, they generally functioned to whip up anti-Indian sentiments.[63] But for Canadian readers, Kelly's story would be put to other uses. It engendered anti-American sentiments in order to demonstrate that Canada was a safer and better place for Aboriginal people and White women.

In Canadian editions of *Narrative of My Captivity Among the Sioux Indians*, the original introduction is followed by a "Preface to the Canadian Edition." The author of this preface is not named, and it is not in Kelly's voice. The purpose of the preface was to point out that because of the superior form of government in Canada, it would be unheard of for a situation to arise such as the one that embroiled Fanny Kelly. Readers should be thankful to live in Canada. Here there was greater equality among people. The author asked readers to imagine how the heroic authoress must have longed for her Canadian home during her trials among the "loathsome, sickening, debasing life of the wildest savages:"

> Imagine her longing, mourning retrospect during those dreary months-cold, in a starving condition; her dreams of a happy childhood, and joyous youth on the romantic shores of Lake Simcoe, where under the best form of government now in existence, she had doubtless mingled with the Indians who dwell there on an equal footing with all other nationalities, creed and colors, 'no one daring to make them afraid' and be thankful that the lines have fallen to you in pleasanter places.[64]

In an explanatory note at the end of Chapter One in the Canadian editions, written in Kelly's voice, American Indian policy is harshly criticized and unfavourably compared with the kindness and benevolence of the Canadian system. It was no wonder that such a fate should befall Kelly because of the "steady exterminating policy of the Americans towards the Indians, the cold-blooded butcheries perpetrated upon them by soldiers, settlers, trappers and adventurers...."[65] By contrast, Canadians could expect military assistance from their Aboriginal residents. The footnote continues that "here it may not be inappropriate to mark the contrast between our system and theirs. Although our Dominion is greater in extent that the 'Great Republic,' with large numbers of Indians in every quarter, yet there is not a tribe, perhaps, in the whole vast dominion that would not freely take up arms in our cause, should we ever, unfortunately, be dragged into war by our restless cousins." The most immediate prospect for a "bloody war," also mentioned in the footnote, was the San Juan Island dispute. This was a controversy between the U.S. and Great Britain over the boundary between the U.S. and British Columbia that came to focus on the issue of ownership of San Juan and other islands.[66] It was finally settled in 1872 when the San Juan archipelago was given to the U.S., and until that year there were soldiers of both powers on the island with the potential for conflict. At one point in the dispute an American settler on San Juan Island killed a pig owned by the Hudson's Bay Company, and the settler was threatened with the prospect of having to appear before British authorities in Victoria for the crime. Although he never was taken to court, Americans "were roused to the highest pitch of wrath at the thought of a United States citizen being arrested on American soil and taken to a British port to await a British trial."[67] Similarly, Canadian editions of Kelly's narrative were intended to rouse fury at the indignities a Canadian woman had to endure in the American West.

The message that Canada was a vastly superior place was highlighted even further in the fourth Canadian edition of Kelly's narrative. By this edition Kelly had become a Canadian heroine to the Sioux, who wished her to live among them, teach and govern them. The fourth edition featured a new caption accompanying the likeness of the author: "THE QUEEN OF THE SIOUX: A cultured Canadian Lady, once their captive drudge, now their idol."[68] In a new and greatly extended introduction, written by an anonymous "Washington correspondent" it was explained how in 1877 Fanny Kelly met a Sioux delegation in Washington. There was indeed a delegation that year of twenty-three Lakota led by Red Cloud and Spotted Tail who were anxious to confer with President Rutherford Hayes. Fanny Kelly, working in the Patent Office in Washington at that time, did, in fact, meet with the delegation. In the Washington *Evening Star* of September 25, 1877, it was noted that the delegation was visited "by a large number of persons, among them being Mrs Kelley [*sic*], who for five months was among them as a captive." It is not clear, however, just how much of the introduction to the fourth edition was embroidered and embellished from there. It was claimed that Kelly met the Lakota at the train station and that they were overjoyed to see her. Kelly allegedly "saluted one of them in a strangely outlandish tongue for one who seemed to represent so thoroughly the refined type of American civilization. An exclamation of surprise and pleasure, a deep quick gutteral note that called the whole band together, and Mrs. Fanny Kelly, a lady born at Orillia, Ontario, stood once more among the savages who had once held her a prisoner, but now surrounded her with an enthusiasm of delight akin to reverence."[69]

It was further emphasized in the introduction how the Lakota admired Kelly, that she taught them and sang to them. They wished her to return to teach them and to govern them, according to this introduction. Kelly was quoted as saying that "they really do wish me to go out there and be their big chief. Not twenty-four hours ago one of their head men wept because I declined, in a kind and respectful way, to go to the theatre with him." The correspondent asked her if she returned whether they would not again "lord it over you and treat you harshly at times." Like the good Canadian that she was at heart, Fanny Kelly replied:

> I do not have any idea that they would. I really think the Indians have been in many instances treated unjustly and cruelly by the whites, and one reason you cannot believe an Indian is because the Indian has learned that he cannot believe a white man.[70]

In the conclusion to the introduction it was noted that the Indians who wished her to return promised Kelly that they would give her "horses, honours and lands, and make her "Queen of the Sioux."

Additions to the Canadian editions, that expressed criticism of the American military and Indian policy, and that indicated the Lakota leaders were kind and considerate in their treatment of a White woman captive, did not appear in the numerous American editions of Kelly's narrative. In the later 1870s, following the 1876 Battle of the Little Big Horn, it was vital in the U.S. to keep more negative images of the Lakota before the public. In the U.S., Kelly needed to be cast as the White woman captive of savage Indians. At the same time in Canada, however, smugness over the superiority of Canadian policy toward Aboriginal people was pronounced as groups such as the Lakota and the Nez Percé sought refuge across the border. In Canada Kelly could be presented as the beloved heroine and friend of the Lakota. A few short years later, in 1885, this sense of superiority about the contentment of Aboriginal people was severely challenged through the events known as the North-West Resistance or Riel Rebellion. Suddenly soldiers, warfare, White women captives, and hangings of convicted Aboriginal men appeared in the Canadian West. The two White women captives who garnered the most attention, Theresa Delaney and Theresa Gowanlock, who were with the Cree for two months, published their narrative of events together as *Two Months in the Camp of Big Bear*.[71] In this book they were presented, not as the beloved heroines or Queens of the Cree, but rather as women subjected to indignities and sufferings, in order to galvanize troops and inspire public support for the war effort.

Despite the differences, a message common to both Fanny Kelly's Canadian editions and the Gowanlock and Delaney volume, was that Canada was home to and nurturer of the purest and most virtuous White women. This ideal, and a determination to keep women in a dependent position, and deliberately not to permit opportunities allowed in the U.S., was deeply embedded in Canadian law and public policy. Ideals of appropriate behavior for Canadian women and for the Canadian family were fashioned to some extent in opposition to what was seen as American. "American" once again meant all that was debauched and depraved in contrast to the virtuous Canada. The more lenient American divorce laws were regularly condemned, and as James Snell has argued, the prolonged rigidity of Canadian divorce law was influenced in part by a perceived need to remain a land of respectability in contrast to a degenerate, decadent U.S.[72] After reporting the story of an American woman married seven times, an 1869 *Montreal Evening Star* editorial declared that "There can be no surer sign of the degeneracy of a country than the fact that the virtue of the women has become so loose that the stringency of the marriage law has to be relaxed for their benefit."[73]

One of the most pronounced differences between the Canadian and American Wests relates to issues of gender and land policy. As Anne McClintock has written, "All nations depend on powerful constructions of gender. Despite many nationalists' ideological investment in the idea of popular *unity*, nations have historically amounted to the sanctioned institutionalization of gender *difference*. No nation in the world gives women and men the same access to the rights and resources of the nation-state ... nations are contested systems of cultural representation that limit and legitimize peoples' access to the resources of the nation state."[74] Canada and the U.S. adopted startlingly different approaches to the institutionalization of gender difference in the allocation of resources. Dimensions of race are also involved, as mentioned here earlier, as in neither nation were the Aboriginal inhabitants permitted the same access as newly arrived White people to the rights and resources of the nation-state.

The forty-ninth parallel mattered a great deal to single White female immigrants who wanted to farm. In the spring of 1902, Scottish remittance woman Jessie de Prado MacMillan arrived in southeastern New Mexico to begin a career as a homesteader.[75] Given her background, she might have been more "at home" in Western Canada, but she was steered instead to the U.S. because there she could obtain a homestead, an opportunity single women were denied in Canada. When MacMillan arrived, single women had the legal right to homestead in the U.S. for thirty-five years, a privilege Canadian single women would not be granted for nearly another thirty years, by which there was virtually no homestead land available. MacMillan's farming endeavours proved successful; by 1907 she had received title to her land and owned what she described as "the most flourishing homestead in the canyon."[76]

By contrast, in 1905, Georgina Binnie-Clark, from England, settled in Saskatchewan intent on farming. Her efforts were beset with difficulties and challenges, but she did become a successful grain grower, establishing a farm called the Union Jack Farm Settlement on the outskirts of Fort Qu'Appelle that she ran with her sister Ethel until sometime in the late 1930s.[77] Her early years to 1908 are chronicled in her remarkable book *Wheat and Woman*, which was her assembled lessons for women hoping to earn their living by agriculture in Western Canada. Binnie-Clark was at an immediate disadvantage compared to her male farmer neighbours as she had to purchase her farm because, as a woman, she was not eligible for the homestead of 160 acres. Nor was she eligible to expand her holdings under other provisions of the Dominion Lands Act that permitted expansion of farms. Her experiences compelled Binnie-Clark to become a determined spokesperson for a "homesteads-for-women" movement. Her book demonstrated that agriculture could provide a profitable means of wealth and independence for women, but in Western Canada they were denied a "fair start."

But on every side my neighbours had obtained their land as a gift from the Government, or at least one hundred and sixty acres of it, and a further hundred and sixty had been added on the condition of preemption, which is by payment of three dollars an acre in addition to the performance of homestead duties; in this way a farm in every way equal to the one which had cost me five thousand dollars was to be obtained by any man for nine hundred and seventy dollars. So that even allowing that a woman farmer is at a slight disadvantage in working out a farm proposition, she has the killing weight of extra payment thrust on her at the very outset. She may be the best farmer in Canada, she may buy land, work it, take prizes for seed and stock, but she is denied the right to claim from the Government the hundred and sixty acres of land held out as a bait to every man.[78]

The homestead regulations of the two Wests are in many respects precisely the same. Indeed, the Canadian Dominion Lands Act of 1872 was to a great extent modelled on the American Homestead Act of 1862. Both awarded 160 acres of land (one quarter section) to a head of household who would register a claim, and "prove up" (for five years in the U.S. and three years in Canada) by building a home and planting crops. But in 1867 the U.S. Homestead Act was amended to include single women over the age of twenty-one. The Canadian Dominion Lands Act provided that "every person who is the sole head of a family" could apply for homestead, and any male eighteen years of age or older. The Act permitted three categories of women to apply as a heads of households: widows, divorcees, and in certain cases separated or deserted wives. But in all of these categories they had to have children under the age of eighteen dependent on them for support. Unlike in the U.S. then, a widow could not apply for homestead unless she had minor children. Having young children would have limited a mother's capacity to devote her attention to farming.

In Canada the eligibility of each woman applicant was carefully scrutinized. An 1895 Justice Department ruling set out the categories under which women were and were not eligible for homestead privileges.[79] Not eligible were "Spinsters without anyone related or otherwise dependent upon them." "Spinsters with servants or employees dependent upon them." "Spinsters with brothers and sisters dependent upon them." "Unmarried women with illegitimate children depending upon her." "An unmarried woman with adopted children depending upon her." In the last three categories, however, notes were made to the effect that there might be some window of eligibility in certain cases. Under the category of spinsters with dependent siblings, for example, the Justice Department official wrote: "I do not think such spinsters are eligible as a matter of law unless perhaps where by virtue of a will or other instrument, or by a competent court, they are given the right to custody or control of the other children." Similar comments were made with regard to women with adopted children. Mothers of "illegitimate" children "may sometimes be eligible as it has been held that a mother has a natural right to the custody of young children. I think, however, that every case of this kind should be decided upon its own merits, it being impossible to lay down any satisfactory general rule." Department of the Interior officials were concerned about the possibility of single women adopting children in order to be able to qualify for homesteading. Minister of the Interior Frank Oliver wrote in a 1910 memo that a widow with an adopted minor child might be considered "in cases where the adoption was made a sufficiently long time prior to the application for entry to satisfy the Department that such adoption was not made for the mere purpose of making her eligible for homestead entry as the sole head of a family."[80]

There were other ways in which the Canadian Dominion Lands Act discriminated against single women and families with daughters. A male homesteader could expand his own holdings through clauses of the Act that at various times permitted second homesteads and the right to pre-emption, described by Binnie-Clark above, which allowed the purchase of adjoining land for a modest sum. Homesteaders with sons could expand their holdings as sons could file on adjoining land, while those with daughters were denied this opportunity.

Appeals to have the legislation changed to permit single women homesteaders were unsuccessful despite the efforts of Binnie-Clark, Isabel Beaton Graham (woman's editor of the *Grain Grower's Guide*) and other supporters. The matter was raised in the House of Commons in 1910 when a Member of Parliament asked Frank Oliver to consider allowing women to homestead as it might encourage men with families of girls to move west, and would "afford the male members of the population an opportunity to find helpmeets."[81] A letter was read into the record from a Rev. R.W. Beveridge, of Watrous, Saskatchewan, who described a meeting with a Toronto father of four daughters who, when asked why he did not move west, stated "'Oh, if my girls were only boys I would have been west long ago....' Now, I ask you why that man had not just as much right to homestead and get a quarter section for each of those girls as the man who happened to have four grown-up boys?" The reverend also wrote that "in the Dakotas and Minnesota, there are many men with large families of fine, strong, healthy girls, who would come to Canada if their girls could homestead, but because they cannot they are moving on down into the new country in Montana, where they have the privilege."

Oliver's reply was that "our experience is entirely against the idea of women homesteading." In order to make a homestead productive there should be "not a single woman upon it, nor even a single man, but there should be both the man and the woman in order that the homestead may be made fully advantageous to the country. The idea of giving homesteads to single women would tend directly against that idea." It was the job of the single man "to get the woman, and for the woman who wants to settle on land in the Northwest to get the man, rather than that she shall have land of her own...." A 1913 petition of over 11,000 electors (that is, men) from the West and the support of many influential organizations was also ignored.[82] In 1930, when the Prairie Provinces assumed control of their own public lands from the federal government, the homestead right was abrogated entirely. In Alberta, where a little homestead land was still available, the provincial government drew up its own regulations which permitted "every person" to enter for homestead who was over the age of seventeen, had resided in the province for three years, and was or declared the intention to become a British subject.[83]

Not surprisingly there were few farms owned and operated by women in western Canada. By contrast, the U.S. West offered women the very real prospect of land ownership, and thousands of single women claimed homesteads.[84] There was some variation in the administration of public land in the different states of the West, but generally for a woman to file a homestead claim in the U.S. she had to be twenty-one and single, divorced, separated, widowed, or otherwise considered the head of the household. This was regardless of whether they had minor children. Married women, however (not deserted or separated), could not file for homestead, as in Canada. Women homesteaders "proved up" and established farms, but many sold their claims, using the income for their education or to establish themselves in business. As historian Dee Garceau has observed, for many women it was the "*sale of the claim* that earned them economic independence. In this respect, homesteading presented a unique opportunity for single women, since investment in land could yield more cash than most occupations open to women at that time."[85] A genre of popular literature in the U.S. in the early twentieth century featured women homesteaders and celebrated individualistic and egalitarian values. But many homesteading women were not as independent as this literature suggested, rather they were part of cooperative ventures, filing claims adjacent to a parent, brother or fiancé, thus combining forces to accumulate property. And not all women homesteaders were successful at "proving up" or selling their claim. The U.S. laws which permitted single women to homestead however meant that in that nation there were a host of complex legal issues that had no parallel in Canada regarding women's rights if she married, for example, after filing but before "proving up." Marriage could result in the loss of a claim, and some women postponed marriage to retain their land, or bent and distorted the rules.[86] Newspapers in the U.S. West sensationalized the extent to which these rules were manipulated. In the December 15, 1916 issue of *The Ronan Pioneer*, the story was told of a frugal married couple who divorced, in order that the woman could locate on a homestead of her own. When she "proved up," the couple was remarried.

Single women homesteaders, women filing to expand family holdings and women selling their land for education and business opportunities, all have no parallel in the Canadian West. That this was recognized at the time is hinted at in the appendix to H. Elaine Lindgren's *Land in Her Own Name: Woman as Homesteaders in North Dakota*, which indicates that a number of women from Canada went to the U.S. West to homestead. Etta Smalley (Bangs) was a teacher in Edmonton, Alberta in 1910 when she went with friend Sadie Woods, from a nearby farm, to Inverness, Montana, where they both took out homesteads.[87] She continued to teach school in Alberta and then in Montana while she proved up. She married and raised a family on her homestead, which her son inherited. Ida Robert (Hewitt) was a teacher in rural Saskatchewan in 1914 when she went to Glasgow, Montana to file for a homestead adjoining that of her husband-to-be, also from Saskatchewan.[88] They persisted on their combined holdings until 1923, when they sold out and moved to Wisconsin, where Ida was originally from. How widespread was the phenomenon of single women moving from Canada to the U.S. to homestead? It would be intriguing to know whether, as suggested by Rev. Beveridge, immigrant families made decisions about homesteading in the U.S. or Canada based on the sex of their children. Should the fact that single women could homestead in the U.S. be added to the list of reasons that Canadian historians routinely cite when accounting for the attractiveness of the U.S. West over Western Canada before 1900? These questions are the subject of my future research.

There are many similarities in the histories of the Canadian and American Wests. As Donald Worster has stressed, in the late nineteenth century, the U.S. and Canada set off on similar paths to make their Wests over into lands of economic opportunity.[89] Canada's blueprint or "National Policy" for the development of their West was borrowed from the U.S., and both were dictated by the international logic of capitalist development, according to Worster. The two Wests shared administration from a distant and often insensitive federal government, powerful railroad interests, the confinement of Aboriginal people to reserves, the survey of the land into the same grid pattern, despoilment of the environment, technologies, politics, and religion. They shared blizzards, dust, weeds, and baseball. Attention to race and gender reveals a much more complex stratigraphy of similarities and differences essential to understanding our shared continent. A transnational approach, that includes comparison but moves beyond a fixation with similarities and differences, will also enrich understanding of our shared past.

Questions to Ponder

1. What is a transnational history?
2. What is the significance of Natoyist?
3. How did the differences in Canadian and United States policy affect Native women?
4. How is the West a masculine construct? How is it a feminine one?
5. In what ways were women treated differently in the two Wests?

Must Reads

Bennet, John W., and Seena B. Kohl, *Settling the Canadian-American West, 1890–1915*. Lincoln: University of Nebraska Press, 1995.

Carter, Sarah. *Capturing Women: The Manipulation of Cultural Imagery in Canada's Prairie West*. Montreal: McGill-Queen's Press, 1997.

Higham, Carol, and Robert Thacker, eds. *One West, Two Myths: A Comparative Reader.* Calgary: University of Calgary Press, 2004.

LaDow, Beth. *The Medicine Line: Life and Death on a North American Borderland.* New York: Routledge, 2001.

Wischmann, Lesley. *Frontier Diplomats: The Life and Times of Alexander Culbertson and Natoyist-Siksina.'* Spokane: Arthur H. Clark, 2000.

Notes

1 Jan Noel, ed., *Race and Gender in the Northern Colonies* (Toronto: Canadian Scholars' Press, 2000), p. 2.

2 David Thelen, "The Nation and Beyond: Transnational Perspectives on United States History," *Journal of American History,* "The Nation and Beyond: A Special Issue," (December 1999): 972–73.

3 See, for example, Claire Midgley, ed., *Gender and Imperialism,* (Manchester: Manchester University Press, 1998); Ruth Roach Pierson and Nupur Chaudhuri, eds., *Nation, Empire, Colony: Historicizing Gender and Race* (Bloomington: Indiana University Press, 1998); Caroline B. Brettell and Carolyn F. Sargent, *Gender in Cross-Cultural Perspective,* 2nd ed. (Upper Saddle River, NJ: Prentice-Hall, 1997).

4 Beth LaDow, *The Medicine Line: Life and Death on a North American Borderland* (New York: Routledge, 2001), p. 1. Notable exceptions to the tendency to divide the past along the border include Paul Sharp, *Whoop-Up Country: The Canadian-American West, 1865–1885* (1955: rpt., Norman: University of Oklahoma Press, 1978). A new generation of cross-border historians is represented in the work of Carol Higham, *Noble, Wretched and Redeemable: Protestant Missionaries to the Indians in Canada and the United States, 1820–1900* (Albuquerque: University of New Mexico Press, 2000); Michel Hogue, "Crossing the Line: The Plains Cree in the Canada-United States Borderlands, 1870–1900," M.A. thesis, Department of History, University of Calgary, July 2002; David G. McCrady, "Living with Strangers: The Nineteenth-Century Sioux and the Canadian-American Borderlands," Ph.D. diss., Department of History, University of Manitoba, 1998; Sheila McManus, "The line which separates: Race, Gender and the Alberta-Montana Borderlands, 1862–1892," Ph.D. diss., Department of History, York University, 2001; Sheila McManus, "'Their Own Country:' Race, Gender, Landscape and Colonization around the 49th Parallel, 1862–1900," *Agricultural History* 73, no. 2 (Spring 1999): 168–82; Molly Rozum, "Grasslands Grown: A Twentieth-Century Sense of Place on North America's Northern Prairies and Plains," Ph.D. diss., Department of History, The University of North Carolina at Chapel Hill, 2001; Molly Rozum, "Indelible Grasslands: Recent Understandings of North America's Western Region," in Robert Wardhaugh, ed., *Toward Defining the Prairies: Region, Culture, and History* (Winnipeg: University of Manitoba Press, 2001), pp. 119–35; Jill St. Germain, *Indian Treaty-Making Policy in the United States and Canada, 1867–1877* (Lincoln: University of Nebraska Press, 2001).

5   Hugh A. Dempsey, "Natawista" in F. Halpenny, ed., *Dictionary of Canadian Biography* 12 (1891–1900) (Toronto: University of Toronto Press, 1984), p. 778. See also Hugh A. Dempsey, *Red Crow: Warrior Chief* (Lincoln: University of Nebraska Press, 1980).
6   Lesley Wischmann, *Frontier Diplomats: The Life and Times of Alexander Culbertson and Natoyist-Siksina'* (Spokane: Arthur H. Clark, 2000), p. 86.
7   Lewis Henry Morgan, *The Indian Journals 1859–62*, ed. and introduction Leslie A. White (Ann Arbor: University of Michigan Press, 1959), p. 144.
8   Sylvia Van Kirk, *"Many Tender Ties:" Women in Fur-Trade Society, 1670–1870* (Winnipeg: Watson and Dwyer, 1980).
9   See Dempsey, p. 778 and Wischmann, pp. 91–93.
10 Editors' note: Throughout this work, we have allowed author's to choose the protocol for the use of Blackfoot versus Blackfeet. There are at least three variations of which we are aware: Canadian versus United States designations, tribal versus individual identifications, and Confederacy versus individual tribe. Each author chose the variation that best suits his or her purposes.
11 Quoted in Mildred Walker Schemm, "The Major's Lady: Natawista," *Montana Magazine of History* 11 (January 1952): 11.
12 Many years later Stevens held a reception for Natoyist-Siksina' in St. Louis, Missouri, as she was there to visit her daughter Frances, who was attending Maplewood, a select school for girls. Stevens presented her with a "loving cup" inscribed "To the Second Pocahontas." Montana Historical Society Archives, Culbertson Family Folder, "Last Surviving Daughter of Major Culbertson Dies," *Bainville Democrat*, 27 February 1939.
13 *Montana Post*, 11 September 1868. Extract in Joel F. Overholser Research Center, Fort Benton, Montana (extracts from Montana newspapers binders).
14 Quoted in Schemm, p. 8.
15 Morgan, pp. 142, 144, 165.
16 Wischmann, p. 276. "The Last of Their Race," is in the Buffalo Bill Historical Center, Cody, Wyoming, and "A Family Group" (now called "Barter for a Bride") hangs in the Diplomatic Reception Rooms at the United States Department of State (Wischmann, p. 241).
17 Quoted in Schemm, p. 6.
18 Quoted in Schemm, p. 9.
19 Montana Historical Society Archives, Culbertson Family Folder, clippings from *Bainville Democrat*, 27 February 1939 ("Last Surviving Daughter of Major Culbertson Dies,"); *Peoria Journal Transcript*, 19 February 1939 ("Colorful Story of Early Peoria is Recalled By Woman's Death in West").
20 Ibid., *Bainville Democrat*.
21 Binder of Fort Benton notes kept by Joel F. Overholser, Overholser Research Center, Fort Benton, Montana.
22 Wischmann, p. 336.
23 *Montana Post*, 11 September 1868, Overholser Research Center, binder of newspaper extracts.
24 Wischmann, p. 335.
25 Carlton R. Stewart, ed., *The Last Great Inter-Tribal Indian Battle* (Lethbridge, AB: Lethbridge Historical Society, 1997), p. 10.
26 Ibid., p. 17.

27 Ibid., p. 13.
28 Hugh Dempsey, ed., R.B. Nevitt, *A Winter at Fort Macleod* (Calgary: Glenbow-Alberta Institute, 1974), p. 83.
29 *Daily Manitoban*, 30 September 1885.
30 Wischmann, p. 352.
31 Montana Historical Society, William Pocklington to L.S. Irvine, 21 December 1891, Indian Service/ Blood Agency, SC 514 (Blood Agency documents originally obtained from Hugh A. Dempsey.)
32 Ibid.
33 National Archives of Canada (NA), Record Group 10 (RG10), Records of the Department of Indian Affairs, vol. 3599, file 1564, pt. B.
34 Maggie Siggins, *Revenge of the Land: A Century of Greed, Tragedy and Murder on a Saskatchewan Farm* (Toronto: McClelland & Stewart, 1991), p. 94.
35 NA, RG10, vol. 3599, file 1564, Thomas Aspdin to U.S. Indian Commissioner, Washington, D.C., 23 April 1895.
36 Ibid., Aspdin to the Indian Commissioner, Regina, N.W.T., 26 September 1895.
37 Ibid., Aspdin to the assistant Indian Commissioner, Regina, 22 November 1895.
38 Provincial Archives of Alberta, Violet Pearl Sykes Ladouceur, "Memoirs of a Cowboy's Wife."
39 Saskatchewan Archives Board, Indian History Film Project. Cecile Many Guns transcript (IH 236).
40 Siggins, p. 110. According to Siggins, who interviewed family members, Mary Black Moon Aspdin lived until 1944.
41 Wendy Wall, "Gender and the 'Citizen Indian,'" in Elizabeth Jameson and Susan Armitage, eds., *Writing the Range: Race, Class and Culture in the Women's West* (Norman: University of Oklahoma Press, 1997), pp. 207–8. See also Frederick E. Hoxie, *A Final Promise: The Campaign to Assimilate the Indians, 1880–1920* (Cambridge: Cambridge University Press, 1984), p. 78.
42 Sarah Carter, *Lost Harvests: Prairie Indian Reserve Farmers and Government Policy*, (Montreal and Kingston: McGill-Queen's University Press, 1990), pp. 193–202.
43 "One West, Two Myths: Comparing Canadian and American Perspectives" held 16–18 May 2002, Buffalo Bill Historical Center, Cody, Wyoming, and 4–5 October 2002, Rosza Centre, University of Calgary, Alberta.
44 John Herd Thompson, "'Manifest Duty:' Myths of the Canadian West," paper presented at "One West, Two Myths" conference, Buffalo Bill Historical Center, 16–18 May 2002.
45 Catherine A. Cavanaugh, "'No Place for Woman:' Engendering Western Canadian Settlement," *Western Historical Quarterly* 28 (Winter 1997): 494.
46 Ibid., p. 496.
47 John Herd Thompson, *Forging the Prairie West* (Toronto: Oxford University Press, 1998), p. 40.
48 Christina Burr, "Gender, Sexuality and Nationalism in J.W. Bengough's Verses and Political Cartoons," *Canadian Historical Review* 83, no. 4 (December 2002): 36.
49 "Miss Canada's Rescuer, " Conservative Party Campaign Poster, 1891, National Archives of Canada.

50   *The New West: Extending From the Great Lakes Across Plain and Mountain to the Golden Shores of the Pacific* (Winnipeg: Canadian Historical Publishing, 1888), preface, n.p.
51   Anne McClintock, *Imperial Leather: Race, Gender and Sexuality in the Colonial Contest* (New York: Routledge, 1995), p. 30.
52   B. Pullen-Burry, *From Halifax to Vancouver* (Toronto: Bell and Cockburn, 1912), pp. 218–19.
53   Ibid.
54   Ibid., p. 220.
55   "'It's Only A Question of Time: Old Fogeyism may hold her back for a while, but she is bound to come to us'," 1880 *Puck Magazine* (New York), National Archives of Canada.
56   *Manitoba Free Press*, 18 April 1910 (from the *New York Herald*).
57   W.H.H. Murray, *Daylight Land* (Boston: Cupples and Hurd, 1888), p. 164.
58   Ibid., p. 168.
59   Adele Perry, *On the Edge of Empire: Gender, Race and the Making of British Columbia, 1849–1871* (Toronto: University of Toronto Press, 2001), p. 135.
60   A.G. Bradley, *Canada in the Twentieth Century*, (Toronto: Morang and Co., 1905), p. 312.
61   Ibid., pp. 612–13.
62   Fanny Kelly, *Narrative of My Captivity Among the Sioux Indians*, (Toronto: Maclear, 1872). For more on Fanny Kelly see Sarah Carter, *Capturing Women: The Manipulation of Cultural Imagery in Canada's Prairie West* (Montreal and Kingston: McGill-Queen's Press, 1997).
63   Literature on "Indian captivity" narratives in the United States is lengthy and growing. A comprehensive analysis is provided in June Namias, *White Captives: Gender and Ethnicity on the American Frontier* (Chapel Hill: University of North Carolina Press, 1993).
64   Kelly, *Narrative*, p. viii.
65   Ibid., p. 23.
66   W.H. New, "The Centre of Somewhere Else: The Pig War and the English," in W.H. New, *Borderlands: How We Talk About Canada* (Vancouver: UBC Press, 1998), pp. 69–102.
67   *The San Juan Dispute: A Thrilling Period in U.S. History, 1852–1872*, n.a., n.p., p. 10.
68   Kelly, *Narrative*, 4th Canadian ed. (Toronto: Maclear, 1878), frontispiece.
69   Ibid., p. iii.
70   Ibid., p. viii.
71   Theresa Delaney and Theresa Gowanlock, *Two Months in the Camp of Big Bear: The Life and Adventures of Theresa Gowanlock and Theresa Delaney*, introduction Sarah Carter (Parkdale: Times Office, 1885; rpt.: Regina: Canadian Plains Research Centre, 1999).
72   James Snell, *In the Shadow of the Law: Divorce in Canada, 1900–1939* (Toronto: University of Toronto Press, 1991).
73   *The Evening Star* (Montreal), 5 April 1869.
74   McClintock, p. 353.
75   Sandra Varney MacMahon, "Fine Hands for Sowing: The Homesteading Experiences of Remittance Woman Jessie de Prado MacMillan," *New Mexico Historical Review* 74, no. 3 (July 1999): 271–94.
76   Ibid., p. 286.
77   Georgina Binnie-Clark, *Wheat and Woman*, introduction Susan Jackel (1914; rpt.: Toronto: University of Toronto Press, 1979), p. xii.
78   Ibid., p. xx.

79 NA, RG13, Department of Justice Records, vol. 2108, rulings of the Department of Justice re: right of women to make homestead entries. Commissioner's letter, 19 April 1895, p. 53, ruling no. 167.
80 Quoted in Susan Jackel, introduction to Binnie-Clark, p. xxv.
81 Canada. *House of Commons Debates*. 30 April 1910, pp. 8488–90.
82 Jackel, introduction, p. xxviii.
83 Ibid., p. xxxi.
84 Elizabeth Jameson, "Foreword" to H. Elaine Lindgren, *Land in Her Own Name: Women as Homesteaders in North Dakota* (Norman: University of Oklahoma Press, 1996, 1991), p. vi.
85 Dee Garceau, *"The Important Things of Life" Women, Work and Family in Sweetwater County, Wyoming, 1880–1929* (Lincoln: University of Nebraska Press, 1997), p. 117.
86 Ibid., pp. 76–77.
87 Montana Historical Society, Mrs. Will Bangs, "My Homesteading Days," Small Collection 116.
88 Ibid., Ida Hewitt, "Homesteading Memories."
89 Don Worster, "Two Faces West," unpublished paper presented to the Canadian Historical Association Annual Meeting, Calgary, June 1994.

chapter six

Myths and Realities in American-Canadian Studies: Challenges to Comparing Native Peoples' Experiences

Roger L. Nichols, University of Arizona

From the start it is clear that several myths surround the comparative study of historical issues in America and Canada. First, the assumption is that such work will be welcomed with enthusiasm. Certainly in the U.S. many historians speak glowingly about the need for and the benefits from comparative history. Participants at major national conferences, however, often find rather different responses. Sparse attendance at the few comparative sessions is common. Even more striking is the glazed look received when trying to discuss ideas and projects. Listeners often glance furtively around the book display hoping to find a friend they can use as an excuse to break away from what is obviously a boring conversation.[1]

My experience with Canadian academics is somewhat more limited. At first glance they seem to have somewhat more interest in doing parallel studies of related issues in the two nations. To an outsider it appears that a higher percentage of Canadian historians do some cross-border work than do so in the U.S. However, there is little welcome for such work done by scholars south of the border. Rather, Canadian cross-border scholarship seems to be treated in two ways, both negative. Much of it receives little attention, often being overlooked in citations and bibliographies when it probably deserves a place. Second, comparative studies often are reviewed more harshly than in the U.S.

American academic reviewers tend to look at comparative work as having made a basic scholarly contribution, and tend to focus on the broad, general themes being considered. Canadian reviewers tend to criticize the same project for what it lacks and for minor factual errors or omissions. This certainly inhibits or even discourages some from serious consideration of comparative work.[2]

If such a transnational interest is actually wishful thinking by a small number of scholars, how does this apply to studies of Indian/First Nations people? In the past decade a few studies of tribal groups and their experiences with the two nation states have appeared. But, like comparative history in general, they seem not to have made a significant impact in either country. Here too, myths confuse the issues. One depicts society in the U.S. as highly individualistic while that in Canada is seen as more group oriented. The latter is described as an ethnic mosaic while the U.S. is a melting pot. How American society can be more individualistic than Canada when distinct ethnic identities are vanishing in the U.S. is not explained, nor is any attention given to the Enfranchisement Act of 1869 that set the Dominion government on the path of individualism for First Nations people when in the U.S. policies still dealt with tribes as units.

A myth related directly to Native Studies is that the U.S. used wars to reduce its Indian population, but Canadian officials let starvation and disease do the job.[3] It seems to me that even a brief look at our two histories demonstrates that such claims are false. First, Canada's relatively peaceful frontier dealings with its tribal groups lasted only until it sent Mounted Policemen west. Just over a decade after the Mounties marched onto the Plains, the 1885 fighting broke out. At the same time, bungling caused widespread starvation and disease tolls in the U.S. as well.

Although the obvious need to get past such widely held myths, and the chance to enter rather uncharted waters, helped attract me to comparative study, other factors helped too. Family stories of pioneer settlement caught my interest, and led to my obtaining a Ph.D. in American frontier history at the University of Wisconsin. At Madison my training focused on the actions of the settlers in creating new communities and the experiences of the Native Americans as they dealt with their unwelcome neighbors. The History Department at Wisconsin had a sought-after British Commonwealth Chair, and prominent scholars such as A.L. Rouse from Britain, and Max Crawford from Australia lectured frequently. At some point William L. Morton, then from the University of Manitoba, directed my attention to things Canadian. The seeds he sowed that semester lay fallow for years, but eventually they led to my efforts to compare experiences in the two countries.

In 1969, the year I went to the University of Arizona, two books appeared that whetted my appetite for comparing the experiences of North American Indians. The first, Vine Deloria, Jr.'s *Custer Died for Your Sins*, launched a scathing attack on the U.S. government, American society, and academics for the continued mistreatment of American Indians throughout the nation's history.[4] Witty, hard-hitting, caustic, and to the point, it rose to the bestseller lists quickly. Its companion, Harold Cardinal's *The Unjust Society*, leveled similar blasts at Canadian treatment of Native peoples.[5] Clearly, here was something worth investigating, but other interests and commitments kept me away from that project for more than a decade. In the early 1980s, after completing a narrow monograph about the eight-year career of Major Stephen Long as an explorer, I decided that it was time for something larger. Little did I realize that to study how two diverse societies dealt with aboriginal peoples over four centuries would keep me busy for almost fifteen years.

Having spent that much time and effort on the project, I find it easy to point out some challenges faced while doing comparative history. For me, living only about sixty miles from the border with the Mexican state of Sonora, it is almost impossible to escape the overwhelming interest in things Latin American. At the same time, a corresponding lack of enthusiasm for anything north of the forty-ninth parallel makes it difficult to get much serious attention in my home state. Certainly Arizona is a part of NAFTA, and people there have serious interests in borders, frontiers, and comparative study. Still, somehow, events and issues in Canada are a long way away, and those people hardly seem foreign – after all most of them do speak English.

Once that sort of generic bias was overcome, practical issues intruded. Twenty years ago they included beginning my work with only modest library holdings. The University of Arizona Library is undoubtedly a good one. At the time it ranked as high as seventeenth among American research libraries. But, the faculty offered almost no courses related to Canada. As a result, when I sought published material that went beyond *The Canadian Historical Review* and a few of the provincial journals, I found only modest holdings. That meant a heavy dependence on interlibrary loan, and the need for extended off-campus travel. For historians, research and travel support are often in short supply and, in fact, on our campus one technically cannot use state money for foreign travel. Closely related to that is the difficulty in getting grants when one has no track record as a comparative scholar. Obviously that can both complicate and slow one's efforts.

A host of academic and intellectual obstacles loom beyond these practical obstacles. First, twenty years ago scholars spoke glowingly about the benefits of comparative history, but few had tried their hand at it. Little comparative historical literature about the two societies existed; the field was new. That was exciting, but daunting too. From the start the question of scope became central. Should one apply the broad strokes of a macro-study, or would it be more valuable, and wiser, to confine the project to monographic limits? On the U.S. side the amount and variety of monographic literature on American Indian issues can be overwhelming. That is not yet the case for Canada. Despite that, to me the situation called for a broad study. I had just finished a short monograph. But, more importantly, a tightly focused study seemed to have less chance of encouraging others to try their hand at comparative history. If I could present broad generalizations that incorporated existing scholarship, my work could offer a foundation on which to build, or even a target others could use. After reading some of the reviews it is clear that I produced a good target. In either case the result might encourage others to try comparative work. Responses during the past few years show that is happening to a limited degree.

While choosing the macro approach in terms of chronology, my focus on Native people in the two countries left the study with distinct challenges. A scholar needs to spend only a single day at the National Archives of Canada in Ottawa or the National Archives in Washington to recognize the extent of historical materials available. Thousands of reels of microfilm, banks of file cabinets filled with microfiche cards, as well as tons of archival materials line the shelves of such institutions. In addition, these places hold thousands of relevant manuscripts and published items. Somewhere during the project, in a fit of despair, I remarked to a friend that if my entire department was employed for a century we would not even be able to touch all of the material, much less read and analyze it effectively. Clearly, the issue of selectivity is central. One has to consider what questions can and should be raised and how much detail will be needed for the project.

Another question relates to the differing historiographies of dealing with Native peoples in each country. In the U.S., policy studies dominated for decades. Often they focused on the motivations and actions of the federal government as it sought to impose its will on inter-ethnic relationships. Tribal histories, often little more than focused policy studies, line the stacks in American libraries. Canadian historians have written fewer of these, perhaps to their credit. A second category of literature concerning Native Americans before the mid-1970s is really intellectual history. That is, it analyzes American ideas about and attitudes toward the tribal groups. In neither of these two categories do many "real" – that is, individual – Indians appear. Again, Canadian scholars have produced fewer studies of this kind.

The scholarship diverges in several other ways too. For decades frontier studies in the two nations took distinctly different approaches. In the U.S., much of the writing applied some aspects of Frederick Jackson Turner's ideas.[6] That is, the frontier basically moved from east to west as Europeans and Anglo-Americans brought civilization across the continent. In Canada, historians paid little attention to this approach. Rather they depicted the East as a metropolitan region and the West as its hinterland. Therefore American settlement brought pioneers west to stay and develop the region. In Canada the historical narrative focused more on great distance, isolation, and a tiny resident population.[7] Also Canadian scholars avoided the intellectual turmoil and debates during the 1980s resulting from the "New Western History" that swept American academic circles. While this oversimplifies the ideas and the nature of the scholarship, it demonstrates substantial distinctions between how frontier and the West have been depicted on both sides of the border. In turn, these intellectual differences complicate any comparative study of topics related to the Aboriginal peoples of North America.

Turning from these general issues to more specific ones makes the challenges to across the border scholarship clear in other ways. The physical geography of each nation differs substantially. Canada is considerably larger than the U.S. While size, in and of itself, isn't crucial, it has played different roles in each country. In Canada, given the small population, the vastness of the land certainly inhibited some population movement. Other geographic factors brought major differences in development too. The St. Lawrence River, one of Canada's largest streams, flowed east into the Atlantic, and became a major avenue of commerce and travel. No eastern stream played the same role in American development until the 1820s, when New York State opened its Erie Canal to overcome that lack. The nearly thousand-mile-wide Laurentian shield separated most of the Canadian population from the West until the last third of the nineteenth century. In the U.S., by contrast, the central plains made westering appear inviting.

Differing population densities as well had a direct impact on Indian policies in the two nations. Long before American independence, the thirteen colonies had substantially more people than did New France and later British North America, and throughout history that gap continued to widen. The number of pioneers, the speed with which they moved into areas occupied by the Native people, and the size of the tribal populations all differed substantially. More and larger tribes claimed the land and its resources in the U.S. Backed by a government that encouraged rapid settlement, American pioneers brought much violence and disruption to their frontiers. With a smaller population, more difficulty in moving west, and dealing with a central government that hesitated to anger the Indians lest it bring war and unwanted expenses, Canada saw relatively less violence.

The nature of government also differed widely. Between 1763 and 1867 the Canadian colonies had to look to Britain for oversight of Indian policy making and implementation. For much of that time the small colonial population might object to imperial policies, but it could exert little direct leverage on the European policy makers. Then, too, from 1670 to 1870 almost the entire Canadian North and West remained under the control of the Hudson's Bay Company. As a mercantile and trading institution, the Company had no interest in promoting settlement. Indeed, for most of its history it actively opposed pioneer activities not tied directly to the fur trade. This separation of authority from the wishes of the population differed significantly from the frontier situation in the U.S. There, pioneers' incursions onto tribal lands affected nearly all aspects of American Indian policy during the nineteenth century. However, at the same time Canadian provinces had considerably more autonomy when dealing with their federal government than did the American states. This encouraged provincial leaders in British Columbia to ignore the Indian policies of the Dominion government. That in turn set of a series of disputes between the two that stretched down to the near present. In the U.S. some states may have wanted to set their own policies, but they never could.

The issue of contrasting national chronologies is important, too. The U.S. gained its independence nearly a century before Confederation tied the geographically disparate Canadian provinces together. This meant that tribes from all parts of the nation had plenty of experience in dealing with the pioneers and their government. To the north, both the Shield and the Prairies separated Ontario from British Columbia by well over a thousand miles. For all practical purposes, this meant that peoples on the Pacific coast ignored national policies for managing tribal affairs.

By the late nineteenth century the new central government had little meaning for the First Nations peoples on the northern Plains, at least until railroad construction and treaty negotiations strengthened Canadian influence there. Certainly officials in Ottawa had some decades of experience in dealing with the Native Americans in the East, but they avoided the inter-ethnic difficulties the U.S. had endured until well after similar events took place in the American West. Except for British Columbia and much later the Yukon, mining rushes had brought few people to the Canadian West. Professional buffalo hunters active in the U.S. played little role in destroying the dwindling buffalo herds in Canada. Likewise, homestead settlement by farmers on the plains occurred later and in much smaller numbers north of the border.

Because of the vast area and the limited number of pioneers in much of the Canadian West, that region escaped most of the repeated warfare that kept the U.S. in turmoil for decades in the nineteenth century. There, the smaller and somewhat less aggressive plains tribes had few targets for their anger and frustration. Unlike the U.S., which dotted much of the West with small army garrisons, the young Confederation government lacked a military force until 1874, when it sent the newly created North West Mounted Police to the region. Even then, by the time that group saw any extended action in 1885, the last of the Indian wars had nearly ended in Arizona and the Southwest. So, while on the surface the events share some similarities, the social and economic situations on opposite sides of the border often differed substantially. This makes the task of comparative scholarship difficult at best.

Since the 1830s the legal position of American Indians in the two societies differed too. The most significant contrasts result from definitions of "Indianness" and the positions of Native groups in each of the two societies. Taking the second issue first, court pronouncements during the 1830s placed tribal groups in exactly opposite relationships to their respective societies. In his celebrated 1831 *Cherokee Nation v. Georgia* decision, Chief Justice John Marshall ruled that the tribes were "domestic dependent nations." As clearly defined wards of the federal government in the U.S., they remained outside the general society and population. Just eight years later, in 1839, Chief Justice James Macaulay of the United Canadas ruled that Indians there had no claims to any separate nationality. Rather, they were Canadians. So, from the 1830s on, the tribal groups faced their legal, constitutional futures from a vastly different starting point.

Even though such rulings laid out the broad outlines for locating the tribal peoples within the two societies, specific laws and policies often had as much or even more impact. By the middle of the nineteenth century each government had established both biological and social criteria for identifying just what it took to be an Indian. The 1846, *U.S. v. Rogers* decision called for some Indian blood and acceptance by others in the tribe. Just four years later, Canadian legislation added another standard – people who had been adopted into the group. The Canadian law also demanded that the individuals in any of the three categories needed to be living with the rest of the tribe. In 1869 the Lands and Properties Act further differentiated Indians in Canada from those in the U.S. It ignored tribal practices and defined Indian families as being headed by an Indian male. As a result, women who married Euro-Americans lost their tribal membership. This happened in the U.S., but in general it has not been a central issue.

The legacy of the 1869 legislation in Canada remains at the centre of who the government considers is an Indian. Under this act, women who were 100 per cent Indian but married non-Indians lost their legal standing in their tribe/nation. This left Canada with the peculiar situation of having Native people in several distinct categories. The status or registered Indians have full legal standing for government programs and tribal benefits. People in the other category, non-status or non-registered, may be as fully Native by blood and culture as the others, but they are ineligible for benefits. The position of these people in Canada contrasts sharply with their situation in the U.S. A study of the situation on the Pacific coast at the beginning of the twentieth century shows this clearly. In British Columbia over 90 per cent of the mixed-race individuals there live as part of the general population. By contrast, in Washington state directly to the south, virtually all such people are considered Indians.[8]

In both countries, descendants of early fur trade intermarriages have received different treatment. The Métis, or descendants of French-Canadian traders and Indian women, and the Country Born, children of Hudson's Bay Company employees, are recognized as a distinct group in Canada. They are neither First Nations people nor simply Canadians. Having played a brief but significant role in Canada's westward expansion, they have had some reserves laid out for them. At present, they also take part in multi-ethnic discussions with the federal government. In the U.S. the situation differs. During the 1830s there were several brief attempts to create what they called "half-breed" reservations at the time. These failed. Today, unless they choose otherwise, nearly all mixed-race people are tribal members and receive whatever benefits come to their particular group.

For Indians in the U.S. there is still plenty of confusion, but this usually results from group membership rather than the race of the male head of family. As the nation spread westward many small bands and remnant groups slipped "under the radar" of the general society. The removal policy of the 1820–40 era led eastern Indians to fade into the countryside whenever possible. The descendants of such people remained in New England, throughout the Southeast, and in a few other places. Over the years some of these "lost" tribes had tried to acquire tribal status from the federal government. Occasionally a sympathetic member of Congress pushed legislation that brought them tribal recognition. During the upsurge in ethnic pride that swept through American society in the 1960s, the situation changed dramatically. Many groups of Native people asked Congress to accept their claims.

Unwilling to handle a flood of individual bills, and worried that large numbers of "wannabees," or non-legitimate claimants, might slip through, the legislators asked the Bureau of Indian Affairs to confront this issue. So, in 1978, the present Federal Acknowledgement Program began its task of deciding who were actual Indians. At first it faced only modest numbers of applicants, but by the 1990s some two hundred groups stood in line asking for tribal recognition. The process is slow and cumbersome, and riddled with political infighting. Some existing tribes object to adding others to the federal roles because they fear that will reduce their share of benefits. Others complain that the applicants are not really Indians at all. Thus far about 50 per cent of the groups seeking tribal recognition are turned down. Already twenty-five years old, the process of approving tribal status for groups not currently having it has become increasingly bureaucratic and appears likely to last for decades more.[9] Whatever their difficulties with status and Métis issues, Canada has been spared some of the bitter infighting the U.S. now faces over this matter.

While American tribal groups and the government bicker over who is a "real" Indian, in 1999 Canada moved in a new direction by establishing the new Territory of Nunavut, giving control of a region that includes thousands of square miles of territory to a group of First Nations people, the Inuit. In the U.S., particular tribes occasionally regain control of small religious sites, but the idea of ceding any large land area to tribal groups has no public support, and most likely would encounter substantial opposition, In fact, despite the 1975 doctrine of "self determination," and substantial economic gains by many tribes, assimilationist thought remains strong in the United States.

To conclude, the treatment of Native peoples in Canada and the U.S. has been significantly different. While the two societies often faced similar issues, their motivations, policies, and actions differed repeatedly. Yet, there are also many similarities in the position of American Indians in the two countries, demonstrating that comparative analysis of relations with the Native peoples is difficult at best. It seems likely that this particular field will continue to be one of the more challenging areas for those to write comparative North American history.

Questions to Ponder

1. What is the difference between transnational and comparative history?
2. What practical problems does a comparative historian face?
3. What historiographic differences between Canada and the United States?
4. How might the United States historians' focus on Turner and the Canadian historians' focus on metropolitanism shape the study of Native peoples?
5. How was the government of Native peoples different and/or similar in Canada and the United States?

Notes

1 The dearth of comparative U.S.–Canadian studies seems to support this contention.
2 This comment is based on an informal survey of major U.S. and Canadian historical journals for the past decade.

3   C.E.S. Franks, "Rights and Self-Government for Canada's Aboriginal Peoples," in Curtis Cook and Juan D. Lindau, eds., *Aboriginal Rights and Self-Government* (Montreal: McGill-Queen's University Press, 2000), pp. 221–63.
4   Vine Deloria, Jr., *Custer Died for Your Sins* (New York: Macmillan, 1969).
5   Harold Cardinal, *The Unjust Society* (Edmonton: Hurtig, 1969).
6   F.J. Turner, "The Significance of the Frontier in American History," in *The Frontier In American History* (New York: Henry Holt, 1920.)
7   See, for example, works by H.A. Innes and Donald Creighton.
8   Jean Barman, "What a Difference a Border Makes: Aboriginal Racial Inter-Mixture in the Pacific Northwest," *Journal of the West* 38, no. 3 (July 1999): 14–24.
9   Mark E. Miller, "Ambiguous Tribalism: Unrecognized Indians and the Federal Acknowledgement Process," Ph.D. dissertation, University of Arizona, 2001.

chapter seven

Prairies and Plains: The Levelling of Difference in Stegner's *Wolf Willow*

David L. Williams, University of Manitoba

If there is any place where citizens of Canada and the United States should come close to being one people, that place would be the unbroken reaches of the plains states and Prairie Provinces. For these prairies and plains were settled at roughly the same historical moment by a similar class of people who share to this day a pioneering culture. The question is whether this one region has been divided by a political myth – on the one hand, by a myth of the western frontier, based on a mystical faith in the deculturating effects of "wildness"; on the other hand, by a myth of the northern frontier, based on the continuity of Nordic culture carried overseas and by inland waterways. The first myth, associated with the American historian Frederick Jackson Turner, is continentalist, predicated upon an Emersonian view of nature; the second, associated with the Canadian historian W.L. Morton, is trans-Atlantic, predicated upon a view of northern culture as shaped by a long succession of "Viking frontiersmen, ... Bristol traders, and Norman fishermen."[1] From this latter perspective, the idea of "One West" already begs the question of regional unity by effacing the geographical term "Northwest," an historical marker for Morton of "a distinct and even an unique human endeavour, the civilization of the northern and arctic lands."[2] From this standpoint, then, prairies and plains would not be synonyms for the same geographical space, but opposing signs for distinct forms of cultural memory.

Wallace Stegner's *Wolf Willow* (1962) is an ideal text through which to explore this cultural question, since it was written by a western American novelist at the height of his powers after visiting his boyhood home on the prairies – Eastend, Saskatchewan, near the northern border of Montana – where he spent six formative years from 1914 to 1920. Better yet, Stegner admits that his historical sense came late, making him almost wholly a product of his natural environment, one of those "prime sufferers from discontinuity," like all children who "grow up in a newly settled country."[3] I intend to show, however, that Stegner unwittingly imports a western frontier myth that tends to forget French exploration and settlement in the Northwest, and thus is oblivious to Norman influence in the region. And so the noble attempt of *Wolf Willow* to negotiate the distance between prairies and plains largely fails to read the differing cultural memories encoded in these two signs.

From the outset, Stegner is keenly aware of the ambivalence of his attempt to straddle two cultures, somewhat in the manner of a lake he mentions in the Cypress Hills which has two outlets, one flowing south toward the Gulf, the other north toward the Bay. At first, it seems that because the place itself is "so ambiguous in its affiliations ... we felt as uncertain as the drainage about which way to flow."[4] And yet the boy already understands that there are horizons in time, as well as space, that can shape one's destiny, that there may even be watersheds of culture that force us into one affiliation or another:

> In winter, in the town on the Whitemud, we were almost totally Canadian. The textbooks we used in school were published in Toronto and made by Canadians or Englishmen; the geography we studied was focused on the Empire and the Dominion.... But if winter and town made Canadians of us, summer and the homestead restored us to something nearly, if not quite, American.... Our plowshares bit into Montana sod every time we made the turn at the south end of the field.... Our summer holidays were the Fourth of July and Labor Day.... We learned in summer to call a McLaughlin a Buick.[5]

Recognizing different words for the same thing suggests the likelihood of finding differing histories of the same thing. In a long history section, "Preparation for a Civilization," particularly in two chapters entitled "The Medicine Line" and "Law in a Red Coat," Stegner shows how the forty-ninth parallel has indeed been policed by myths and stereotypes. To the child sitting in the Weyburn customhouse in 1914, or to "the Plains hostiles" sitting on reserves in 1885, "One of the most visible aspects of the international boundary was that it was a color line: blue below, red above, blue for treachery and unkept promises, red for protection and the straight tongue. That is not quite the way a scrupulous historian would report it," he concludes, as "Canada in red coats hunted down its hostiles in 1885 just as the blue-coated Long Knives had used to do."⁶ So, in "The Medicine Line," the scrupulous historian tells of nameless heroes in the Joint Boundary Commission who also "surveyed the limits of endurance"⁷ in an epic of neighbourly cooperation.

A heroic story of cooperation is likewise adapted to fiction in "Genesis," the long novella which spans the middle of the book. Rusty Cullen, an English boy, arrives on the Prairies just before the dreadful blizzard of 1906, but comes of age in finding that "he knew enough not to want to distinguish himself by heroic deeds: singlehanded walks to the North Pole, incredible journeys, rescues, what not. Given his way, he did not think that he would ever want to do anything alone again, not in this country. Even a trip to the privy was something a man might want to take in company."⁸ Whether he rejects the romantic hero out of Robert Louis Stevenson, or the self-reliant hero out of Ralph Waldo Emerson, Rusty learns the lesson spelled out in Stegner's epilogue – that what had begun "in individual effort" on the Canadian Prairies "remained – *if* it remained – to cooperate," a process that took "its inevitable course to political flowering in a society militantly cooperative, even socialist. It is so because the country tolerated settlement on no other terms."⁹

Here, Stegner is almost heroic himself, expressing sympathy for a prairie culture of cooperative socialism so soon after the McCarthy era. And yet his grasp of this political form is also distorted by a western myth which continues to shape his experience. "The lateness of my frontier," he writes initially, "and the fact that it lay in Canada intensified the…dichotomy between American and European that exists to some extent in all of us [and which] exists most drastically in people reared on frontiers, for frontiers provide not only the rawest forms of deculturation but the most slavish respect for borrowed elegances."¹⁰ For all his concern to demythologize the myths of history, this story of his boyhood can easily slip into the frontier myth of baptism into the "wildness" of Emersonian nature.

To the child, "[W]e were junior Boones and Bumppos," he writes of his former playmates, meaning that "we were self-reliant individualists with nothing between us and the lightnings except our own unparted hair."[11] To the man, it is the smell of wolf willow that returns him to this scene of childhood, reassuring him that "The sensuous little savage that I once was is still intact inside me."[12] At first, Proust would seem to preside over this recovery of lost time: "For here, pungent and pervasive, is the smell that has always meant my childhood. I have never smelled it anywhere else, and it is as evocative as Proust's madeleine and tea."[13] Symptomatically, however, the narrator admits that "It is wolf willow, and not the town or anyone in it, that brings me home."[14] Typically, the recovery of lost time is tied to wild nature, not to a social artefact, betraying an Emersonian desire to "enjoy an original relation to the universe."[15] Emerson's "Nature," in fact, helps to explain the man's response to the scent of wolf willow: "The sun illuminates only the eye of the man," Emerson writes, "but shines into the eye and heart of the child. The lover of nature is he whose inward and outward senses are still truly adjusted to each other; who has retained the spirit of infancy even into the era of manhood."[16] The man who recovers the spirit of childhood in a whiff of wolf willow is ultimately a man who believes in the power of wild nature to renew and redeem the world.

In another figure of this Transcendental/Turnerian self, the frontier myth is soon writ large over the face of a whole continent: "I can see the river," Stegner muses, "where it shallows and crawls southeastward across the prairie toward the Milk, the Missouri, and the Gulf, and I toy with the notion that a man is like the river or the clouds, that he can be constantly moving and yet steadily renewed. The sensuous little savage, at any rate, has not been rubbed away or dissolved; he is as solid a part of me as my skeleton."[17] The persistence of a sense of "wildness" at the core of the self is crucial to the whole enterprise of *Wolf Willow*. For, "How does one know in his bones what this continent has meant to Western man unless he has, though briefly and in the midst of failure, belatedly and in the wrong place, made trails and paths on an untouched country and built human living places, however transitory, at the edge of a field that he helped break from prairie sod?"[18]

The failure of the frontier myth still marks a climax in *Wolf Willow*, as the Stegner family pulls up stakes again to head south of the Line, quite unaware that they have been victims of the "myth of the Garden West. Franklin and

Jefferson had formulated it, politicians and speculators and railroads had promoted it, the ignorant faith of hundreds of thousands of home-seekers had kept it alive well into the industrial age and out into the dry country where it had little chance of coming true."[19] In such a judgment, Stegner is clearly indebted to Henry Nash Smith, who a decade earlier had already articulated the contradictions at the heart of the western frontier myth. On the one hand, Smith notes, the men of the "'Western World' turned their backs upon the Atlantic Ocean, and with a grim energy and self-reliance began to build up a society free from the dominance of ancient forms."[20] On the other hand, Turner's "theory of civilization implied that America in general, and the West *a fortiori*, were meaningless except in so far as they managed to reproduce the achievements of Europe."[21] The myth of the frontier might then be impossible, yet it is contradictorily coherent. For America must become/not be Europe by subordinating history to nature for it to be truly American history.

In spite of his own early brush with failure or contradiction in the frontier myth, the adult historian gives new life to it in his history of the Lewis and Clark expedition of 1805, particularly in the "First Look" by Europeans at this "unknown" part of the continent: "They came watchfully, for they were the first. They came stiffened with resolution and alert with wonder. Beyond the bottoms with their cutbanks and their half-flooded willow-grown bars was the wide disk of the Plains, the same Plains they had known, wintering among the Mandans, that extended and extended beyond expectation and beyond credulity, unknown to every horizon and past it."[22] This myth of origins, hardly original to Stegner, duly authorizes possession of the territory by erasing all memory of precursors, including the La Vérendrye expedition that crossed and re-crossed the Missouri in 1742 on its way through North Dakota, Montana, Wyoming, Colorado, Nebraska, and South Dakota. That Stegner should succumb to this myth is hardly surprising. For if it is truly America's destiny to replace Europe, then it must be the American, not the representative of *l'ancien régime*, who is reborn in the wilderness.

More telling still is the way in which *Wolf Willow* manages to translate the cultural space of the Canadian Prairies into the language of "the American grain."[23] Typically, the book opens with the term *Plains* – more commonly used in the U.S. than in Canada – in order to make it virtually interchangeable with *Prairies*. Stegner admits that

It is the place where I spent my childhood. It is also the place where the *Plains*, as an ecology, as a native Indian culture, and as a process of white settlement, came to their climax and their end. Viewed personally and historically, that almost featureless *prairie* glows with more color than it reveals to the appalled and misdirected tourist. As memory, as experience, those *Plains* are unforgettable; as history, they have the lurid explosiveness of a *prairie* fire, quickly dangerous, swiftly over.[24]

This might be nothing more than a courtesy of translation for American readers drawn into the book through its cartographic first sentence: "An ordinary road map of the United States, one that for courtesy's sake includes the first hundred miles on the Canadian side of the Line, will show two roads, graded but not paved, reaching up into western Saskatchewan to link U.S. 2 with Canada 1, the Trans-Canada Highway."[25] And yet it is hardly a courtesy, hundreds of pages later, to be using both terms interchangeably to describe those who "found the semi-arid Plains a place where no man and no family could do it alone. I have seen those who tried – red-necked Swedes and Norwegians half crazy with hard work and loneliness who came riding or driving down to our shack on the prairie and could hardly bring themselves to leave again."[26] In fact, *prairies* are yoked together with *Plains* on almost every page, a pairing that is surprisingly revealing.

The Oxford English Dictionary records the word *prairie* as entering the language in 1773, a year before the Quebec Act, two years before the outbreak of revolution in the Thirteen Colonies. What the OED fails to say is that this word *prairie* was also a pretext for revolution. The Quebec Act of 1774 proved utterly intolerable to land speculators because it encircled the Thirteen Colonies with a French presence that limited westward expansion as sharply as the old network of French forts had done before the Conquest. When "the government in 1774 transferred all of the country north of the Ohio to the Province of Quebec," it did so because it was "the only one of the Colonies unhampered by the private designs on the Indians' lands."[27] Indeed, the private interests of George Washington were suddenly menaced, like thousands of others, by the Quebec Act:

In 1763 Washington owned 9,581 acres of plantation lands east of the mountains but, not to fall behind in the new wave of speculation, he joined with forty-nine other men in forming the Mississippi Company which aimed at a grant large enough to give 50,000 acres to each shareholder. By 1773, through his interest in the older Ohio Company, Washington achieved a total of 32,885 acres.[28]

It was these *prairies* west of the Allegheny and north of the Ohio Rivers which would be up for grabs in 1773 when the Quebec bill was introduced, then debated for a year in Parliament, since the Bill proposed to restore the Ohio prairies to the administration of "the ancient Catholic fur-trading colony on the St. Lawrence.... To the rebellious minds to the south, especially in New England where religious prejudice was second nature, the Quebec Act seemed an intolerable insult."[29] To land speculators in Virginia and Pennsylvania, however, the Quebec Act made their land grants virtually worthless, and so rendered the British as dangerous a foe as the former French empire.

Even before the Quebec bill had been introduced in 1773, Benjamin Franklin had "suggested that a Congress of all the Colonies be held. This plan however was doomed to failure because it was premature. At that time intercolonial rivalries and jealousies still operated too powerfully as centrifugal forces to make the project possible of realization."[30] A scant month after the news of the passage of the Quebec Act reached New York, however, the First Continental Congress was assembled in Philadelphia in September 1774. Suddenly, what had been an alien word a year before was a flashpoint for revolution. The British were giving back the *prairies*, both in name and thing, to French Catholics. From a European perspective, it might look like "a great piece of statesmanship"[31]; but the rights of Americans – life, liberty, and the pursuit of prairie – were ultimately the right to possess a continent. Here was the germ of a myth in which the prairies must be levelled into plains, and plains into prairies. For here was the space in which the American soul could lose itself in its born-again identity with the place.

Such levelling of difference is largely implicit in *Wolf Willow*, where it seeks a metaphysical justification: "It is not hills and mountains which we should call eternal," says Stegner. "Nature abhors an elevation as much as it abhors a vacuum; a hill is no sooner elevated than the forces of erosion begin tearing it down. These prairies are quiescent; close to static; looked at for any length of time, they begin to impose their awful perfection on the observer's mind. Eternity is a peneplain."[32] And yet this metaphysical conclusion can also obscure a political truth, for it is not just landscape which imposes on the observer, but the observer who imposes an "awful perfection" of universals on the landscape.

If "these prairies" are "quiescent," they appear so only to the eye bent on reducing them to a "plain," to a continentalist historiography that by definition flattens them into "sameness." What then occurs in this levelling of prairies into plains is an overwriting of French history by a version of Anglo-American history and culture. Although the French word remains, its historical content has been largely evaporated, much as the journeys of La Vérendrye have been evaporated into the mist of Lewis and Clark's "First Look." No wonder one hears the constant reminder in Canada's other official language, *Je me souviens*.

So what does it mean to remember the journals of Pierre Gaultier de Varennes et Sieur de la Vérendrye, the first European to give the Canadian prairies their name? In his journal of 1738–39, addressed to the Governor General of New France, La Vérendrye notes

> the orderly fashion in which the Assiniboines march to guard against surprise attacks, marching always in the prairies, through hillsides and valleys from the first mountain onwards, which is rather tiring as you climb and descend quite often throughout the day. There are magnificent plains which stretch out for three or four leagues. The march of the Assiniboine villages, especially when they are in great numbers, is done in three columns, with scouts in front and on the wings and a good rear guard. The elderly and the infirm march in the middle, which is the centre. I had all the French keep together as much as possible.[33]

Speaking for once of "des plaines" in the same breath as "des prairies" – his more usual term is "prairie" – the eighteenth-century explorer notes a pleasing variety in the landscape, as well as a pleasing harmony in the organization of society.

Indeed, as Denis Combet points out in his lavishly illustrated, newly translated bilingual text, "What stands out in [La Vérendrye's] writings is a dialogue between the two peoples. The explorer and his sons always tried to create harmonious bonds with the first inhabitants of the land. This method of respecting the customs of Aboriginals in order to better establish commercial relations was not new. In fact, it was a part of a policy going back to the first days of New France."[34] To this end, "La Vérendrye was quite ready to have his sons adopted by local tribes; he took part in their ceremonies; he lamented the dead [including his own son Jean-Baptiste] and chanted war songs with them."[35] At the same time, this man who built a network of forts reaching from Lake of the Woods to Lake Manitoba to the Saskatchewan River was a trader as well as an explorer. As such, he is a typical representative of the northern maritime frontier in which commerce and government precede settlement in this separately organized, northern hinterland of Montreal.

For those of us who associate La Vérende with the continuing presence of French culture in the word *prairie*, the French name typifies something else about our frontier. As Morton points out, this "northern frontier was much more a maritime than a land frontier," giving it "its own northern economy...an extensive and a gathering economy, dependent on new lands, new seaways, and the transport the seas and rivers afforded."[36] Indeed, the form of transport is one of the hallmarks of our northern frontier. For the canoe, in contrast to the wagon trains that settled a Turnerian frontier, is based not on European technology but on the buoyancy and portability of birch bark. In other words, our history in the Northwest has a profoundly different orientation to native culture than is evident in the image of the wagon-wheel riding roughshod over the Plains Indians.

The ultimate test of our differing orientation to Native culture, of course, is the willingness of French traders and explorers to take Native wives. "In one century the Métis nation grew on the banks of the Red River into a unique and distinct society."[37] This merging of European and Native cultures may not be what Jefferson or Turner had in mind in their Western myth of born-again agrarians. And yet it was a "new nation" of Métis who ultimately shaped the imaginative boundaries of the West and the Northwest, when Louis Riel chose to lead Manitoba into Canadian Confederation in 1870, rather than to negotiate with American annexationists. To Morton, Métis history refutes any historiography that would try to make the Canadian West "a northern extension of the agricultural frontier of the United States."[38] But long before the Métis, La Vérendrye had confirmed an existing boundary between "the Prairie Sioux" and Crees and Assiniboines by allying himself with northerners in opposition to warriors from the South.

To the question, then, of whether there is any real difference between the West of *prairies* and *plains*, it is under the infrared light of history that distinctions show most clearly. And under this light, it does seem to matter which track we choose to follow: the iron wheel-ruts of the western frontier, or the silver wake of the northern maritime frontier.

References

Berger, Carl. *The Writing of Canadian History: Aspects of English-Canadian Historical Writing since 1900*. 2nd ed. Toronto: University of Toronto Press, 1986.

Combet, Denis, ed. *In Search of the Western Sea: Selected Journals of La Vérendrye. À la Recherche de la mer de l'ouest: mémoires choisis de La Vérendrye*. Winnipeg: Great Plains Publications & Les éditions du blé, 2001.

Emerson, Ralph Waldo. "Nature." *Selections from Ralph Waldo Emerson*, ed. Stephen E. Whicher. Boston: Houghton Mifflin, 1957, pp. 21–56.

Metzger, Charles H. *The Quebec Act: A Primary Cause of the American Revolution*. New York: United States Catholic Historical Society, 1936.

Morton, W.L. *The Canadian Identity*. Toronto: University of Toronto Press, 1961.

Smith, Henry Nash. *Virgin Land: The American West as Symbol and Myth*. 1950. New York: Vintage, n.d.

Stegner, Wallace. *Wolf Willow: A History, a Story and a Memory of the Last Prairie Frontier*. 1962. Toronto: MacMillan, 1977.

Turner, Frederick Jackson. "The Significance of the Frontier in American History." *The Frontier Thesis and the Canadas: The Debate on the Impact of the Canadian Environment*, ed. Michael S. Cross. Toronto: Copp Clark, 1970.

Van Alstyne, Richard. *Empire and Independence: The International History of the American Revolution*. New York: John Wiley & Sons, 1967.

Williams, William Carlos. *In the American Grain*. 1925. New York: New Directions, 1956.

Questions to Ponder

1. What role does the border play for Stegner and Williams?
2. What are the plains and prairies: regions, places, concepts, or all of those? How so?
3. How does Williams use Turner to understand *Wolf Willow*?
4. What makes the French important to the plains and prairies?
5. Are there differences between the plains and prairies?

Must Reads

Friesen, Gerald. *The Canadian Prairies: A History*. Toronto: University of Toronto Press, 1984.

Sieur de la Vérendrye, Pierre Gaultier de Varennes. *In Search of the Western Sea: Selected Journals of La Vérendrye. À la recherche de la mer de l'ouest: mémoires choisis de La Vérendrye*. Ed. and trans. Denis Combet. Winnipeg: Great Plains Publications & Les éditions du blé, 2001.

Roy, Gabrielle. *La Route d'Altamount*. Trans. Joyce Marshall. *The Road Past Altamont*. Toronto: New Canadian Library, 1966.

Vanderhaeghe, Guy. *The Englishman's Boy*. Toronto: McClelland & Stewart, 1996.

Williams, David. *The River Horsemen*. Toronto: Anansi, 1981.

Notes

1. W. L. Morton, *The Canadian Identity* (Toronto: University of Toronto Press, 1961), 92.
2. Ibid., 93.
3. Wallace Stegner, *Wolf Willow: A History, a Story and a Memory of the Last Prairie Frontier* (1962; Toronto: MacMillan, 1977), 111.
4. Ibid., 8.
5. Ibid., 81–84.
6. Ibid., 101–2.
7. Ibid., 90.
8. Ibid., 219.
9. Ibid., 300–301.
10. Ibid., 22–23.
11. Ibid., 292.
12. Ibid., 19.
13. Ibid., 18.
14. Ibid., 19.
15. Stephen E. Whicher, ed., *Selections from Ralph Waldo Emerson* (Boston: Houghton Mifflin, 1957), 21.
16. Ibid., 23.
17. Stegner, *Wolf Willow*, 19.
18. Ibid., 281–82.
19. Ibid., 255.
20. Henry Nash Smith, *Virgin Land: The American West as Symbol and Myth* (1950; New York: Vintage, n.d.), 304.
21. Ibid., 305.
22. Stegner, *Wolf Willow*, 39.
23. William Carlos Williams, *In the American Grain* (1925; New York: New Directions, 1956).

24 Stegner, *Wolf Willow*, 3–4 (my italics).
25 Ibid., 3.
26 Ibid., 300.
27 Richard Van Alstyne, *Empire and Independence: The International History of the American Revolution* (New York: John Wiley & Sons, 1967), 19.
28 Ibid., 16.
29 Ibid., 19–20.
30 Charles H. Metzger, *The Quebec Act: A Primary Cause of the American Revolution* (New York: United States Catholic Historical Society, 1936), 146.
31 Van Alstyne, *Empire and Independence*, 37.
32 Stegner, *Wolf Willow*, 7.
33 Denis Combet, ed., *In Search of the Western Sea: Selected Journals of La Vérendrye. À la Recherche de la mer de l'ouest: mémoires choisis de La Vérendrye* (Winnipeg: Great Plains Publications & Les èditions du blè, *2001)*, 105.
34 Ibid., 165.
35 Ibid., 167.
36 W. L. Morton, *The Canadian Identity*, 91.
37 Denis Combet, ed., *In Search of the Western Sea*, 167.
38 Carl Berger, *The Writing of Canadian History: Aspects of English-Canadian Historical Writing since 1900*, 2nd. ed. (Toronto: University of Toronto Press, 1986), 245.

chapter eight

Whose West Is It Anyway? Or, What's Myth Got to Do With It? The Role of "America" in the Creation of the Myth of the West

Lee Clark Mitchell, Princeton University

Little more than a year ago, I was sitting in a darkened cineplex on a Saturday afternoon with four small boys (two of them mine), munching popcorn and drinking cherry slushes, waiting to see *Shrek* for the third time. Suddenly, on the screen, appeared a trailer for an animated film due out last summer – a Dreamworks production called *Spirit: Stallion of the Cimarron*, directed by Kelly Asbury and Lorna Cook, with a screenplay by John Fusco, who has been credited with the retro Westerns *Young Guns* and *Young Guns II*. The trailer opens as a horse paws a cliff, before panning alongside an eagle flying over the plains, into steep canyons and mesas, finally tracking alongside a herd of wild horses running freely (with John Williams'-style music on the soundtrack). That's all the context we're given, with a voice-over reminding us of the countless stories told of how the West was won, though never a story from the horse's point of view. "I remember when the horses ran free ... this is that story." As the film's official website states: "The movie features photorealistic horses set against panoramic vistas and very little dialogue. The whole story will be told from the viewpoint of the horse, with his thoughts heard as narrative."[1] The producers were reputed to have searched far and wide for the supposedly perfect horse "voice," finally settling on Matt Damon for his airy exuberance and innocent tone, though the site helpfully reminds us that horses don't actually talk, they "just whine and make horse noises." Here is the rest of the website's description:

> *Spirit: Stallion of the Cimarron* follows the adventures of a wild and rambunctious mustang stallion as he journeys through the untamed American frontier. Encountering man for the first time, Spirit defies being broken, even as he develops a remarkable friendship with a young Lakota brave. The courageous young stallion also finds love with a beautiful paint mare named Rain on his way to becoming one of the greatest unsung heroes of the Old West. Through the eyes of Spirit, we follow the story of the westward movement, as the mustang runs free across the American countryside and sees his life changed by the slow but inexorable push of civilization in the wild. The film first introduces Spirit in the freedom of the wild, only to have him caught by the cavalry and trained to be a war horse.

However grim this may seem as cartoon, the film offers only the most recent version of a recognizably American "myth of the West," incorporating the idea of free land and spectacular landscapes; of a wild, untamed spirit resisting the encroachments and suasions of civilization; and finally, of lost freedom as civilization advances and the claims of responsible citizenry are made. And while nothing about the materials *per se* precludes their being Canadian or Mexican, or for that matter Australian, Brazilian, or South African, something about the myth requires American citizens to imagine it *as* intrinsically American.

In short, a recognizable "myth of the West" exists for America but not for Canada or Mexico; while I am not an expert, the proximate causes for this are not hard to find, beginning with the fact that Canada continued much longer as a colonial dependency, as part of the British Empire. Or that the "garden" image of the *American* West was more suitable for mythic appropriation, unlike the far bleaker, more severe, more "terrifying" landscapes of Mexico and Canada. Or that (notwithstanding the Spanish rodeo and the Calgary "stampede") neither Mexico nor Canada had much experience of the nineteenth-century cattle trade, with those "western" activities that helped transform the cowboy into a mythic figure: the roundup and long drive, the battles with farmers and Indians, the drunken escapades and deadly confrontations in cow towns and trail heads. Popular culture has celebrated the cowboy, the mythic descendant of American frontiersmen, as an independent labourer posed against the industrial working stiff, ever a stranger to the factory floor, unsupervised during the working day, free to roam on horseback with a six-gun at his hip (the only worker actually allowed to do so). One might press interesting implications out of the contrast between the most recognized symbol of the Canadian West on the one hand, the law-enforcing North West Mounted Policeman who "always gets his man," and on the other, the footloose, asocial American cowboy who occasionally was the "man" the Mounties "got." Yet whatever history is invoked to explain why the American myth of the West did *not* extend much above the forty-ninth parallel or below the forty-second and the Rio Grande – whether broad imperialist aspirations, or the quality of prairie soil, or even more immediate resonances of the cattle trade – these are rarely touted as the explanation for what makes the overall Western myth so powerful that for countless people it would define Americans *as* American. The image that *is* always invoked is the land itself, and the implications of that image in the construction of the myth of the American West are what concern me here. For it is the very capacity of the American western landscape to become metaphorized that contrasts with the Mexican South's and Canadian North's apparent resistance to this process, and thereby helps to explain the role of myth in making the West American.

The first grand architect of the Western American myth was notoriously Frederick Jackson Turner (though, of course, he never used the word "myth"). And it's worth pausing again over his simple yet daring assertion that "the significance of the frontier in American history" was due to the availability of "free land," the settlement of which constituted an almost mystical process transforming individuals *into* Americans. "To the frontier the American intellect owes its striking characteristics," Turner stoutly asserted at the end of his celebrated paper in 1893:

> That coarseness and strength combined with acuteness and inquisitiveness; that practical, inventive turn of mind, quick to find expedients; that masterful grasp of material things, lacking in the artistic but powerful to effect great ends; that restless, nervous energy; that dominant individualism, working for good and for evil, and withal that buoyancy and exuberance which comes with freedom, these are traits of the frontier, or traits called out elsewhere because of the existence of the frontier. Since the days when the fleet of Columbus sailed

into the waters of the New World, America has been another name for opportunity, and the people of the United States have taken their tone from the incessant expansion which has not only been open but has even been forced upon them.[2]

There's something a bit quaint in this listing that recalls a period when people actually believed in dominant national characteristics. Even by that standard, however, Turner was extraordinarily reductive, attributing to the Western frontier not only egalitarian social processes and democratic political institutions, but whatever was intrinsically American about the nation's population. As he reiterated, "the wilderness masters the colonist," allowing Turner to ignore completely a whole series of other, equally powerful influences: the Puritan sense of mission as a "chosen people," for instance, or the legacy of civil religion and republican institutions (what Louis Hartz famously termed the "liberal tradition"), or the profound effect of the South's "peculiar institution" of slavery on American history, or the shifting impact of a polyglot, immigrant population.[3] Each of these has been advanced at various times to help explain the special historical configuration of the United States, and Turner blithely ignored each one of them. He even ignored the idea of the American West as a particular place, identified by a set of mapped coordinates, choosing instead to define the frontier as a "process" – a definition that invariably makes historians edgy (as Patricia Nelson Limerick first observed in her pointed critique of Turner, "conceive of the West as a place and not a process, and Western American history has a new look").[4] More generally, the New Western Historians of the past fifteen years have dismantled Turner, arguing persuasively that his thesis ignores Native Americans, Hispanics, Chinese, African Americans, women, even that group of Anglo-Saxon males untransformed by Turner's mystical process, motivated as they were by far less admirable traits. Part of the problem may be that Turner was simply too "nice" a man, as the historian Richard Hofstadter was the first to speculate. He never credited the shameful side of the westward movement: the "riotous land speculation, vigilantism, the ruthless despoiling of the continent, the arrogance of American expansionism, the pathetic tale of the Indians, anti-Mexican and anti-Chinese nativism, the crudeness, even the near-savagery, to which men were reduced on some portions of the frontier."[5] The straightforward optimism and simplicity of Turner's thesis gave it a powerfully appealing edge, at the same time that it allowed people to disregard the salient fact that his claim for a "return to primitive conditions" in the American West must have occurred as well in the Mexican and Canadian Wests – indeed, wherever frontier environments exist – though without necessarily producing a similar national character. The question left unasked, and unanswered, is, of course, why not?

Still, numerous historians accepted Turner's Western version of the American myth, though it was curiously a non-historian who gave that myth its next major boost: Henry Nash Smith (and I've often whimsically thought that his three names serve to authenticate his descent in a line of influential Western thinkers, from Frederick Jackson Turner through Walter Prescott Webb, Herbert Eugene Bolton, and Ray Allen Billington, right down to Patricia Nelson Limerick; even the tri-syllabic Frederick Merk can sound a bit like three names). Donald Worster has claimed that "the first bonafide revisionist, in a sense the prophet of a new western history, was Henry Nash Smith, for it was he who first told us what was wrong with the old history and dared to call it myth."[6] Smith trumped Turner by turning analysis away from the historical fact of "free land," with all the political and economic implications that "free land" involved, to the richer, rhetorical metaphor of "virgin land," with resonances of the West as a blank slate, an unexplored region, an uncontested terrain open more to imaginative than to actual physical conquest. Smith believed, along with Turner, that an otherwise regional history had created a national consciousness. But he believed it in a special way: not that the *actual* experience of a relatively small number of Western pioneers had moulded a new national character, but rather that a much larger population of those residing in the East had projected *fantasy* views on the West that figured forth from afar the larger meaning of America. In short, he simply ignored Turner's idea of the frontier as an alleged *process* with immediate nationalizing effects, in order to concentrate instead on a set of distant expectations for the supposedly empty West, which had prompted Americans (so he claimed) to project their deepest desires onto the landscape. Whatever else his thesis may be, however true or false, it represents an interesting move: away from actual pioneers and settlers *in* the American West, undergoing whatever mystical process of transformation Turner assumed they underwent, to writers, politicians, businessmen, housewives, laborers, painters, photographers, all *looking* West from a largely eastern vantage.

Smith's 1950 book *Virgin Land*, subtitled *The American West as Symbol and Myth*, laid out three dominant images of the West that became part of its mythic state. The first image was as a route to Far Eastern empire, which evolved into appreciation of the West itself as centre for imperial fantasies. Passage to India became instead the power of the heartland, economically and morally, and ideas of Manifest Destiny were gradually associated with Western landscape as America *became* the empire whose location had so long been sought. The second image grew from actual historical figures like Daniel Boone and Kit Carson, who defined a Western type that came to be thought of as distinctively American: independent, self-reliant, rugged, a son of Nature freed from the trappings of civilization yet prompted by Christian ethics. The third dominant image was of the West not as Turner's "free land" but as either Edenic garden or wasted desert, the two alternative possibilities that fuelled public policy in the nineteenth century. Borrowing from Turner's notion of the American West's mystical powers, Smith explained the emergence of a belief in the idea that "rain follows the plow," that cultivation of what seems like barren desert will convert the West into a fruitful garden, in defiance of conventional meteorological understanding. These three very different images of the American West coalesced as a monolith, Smith argued, though, as with Turner, it is not quite clear why they never came to be characteristic of Mexican or even more obviously Canadian national myths.

What lends Smith's version of national myth a more compelling edge than Turner's is his concentration on beliefs clearly at odds with history, believed in *despite* all contrary evidence. The fact that gunslinging cowboys were a negligible portion of the population, and never representative, or that homesteading farmers rarely achieved their dreams, or that rain never followed the plow, only confirms how powerful the impulse needed to be, the deep desire to *convert* cowboys into epic heroes, or to get homesteaders to *keep* heading west, or to plow up vast acreage of dry land. To some considerable extent, in fact, nineteenth-century easterners created a myth of the American West for *eastern* consumption, pre-dating John Filson's elaborate fictionalization of Daniel Boone's career and continuing long after railroads glowingly advertised the West as garden to lure the tourist trade. Turner actually believed what he described was history, not myth, faithfully assuming that the West *was* a "safety valve" – something Smith was historian enough to realize had never actually occurred. The frontier had not in fact served as outlet for dissatisfied eastern labor, by any measurable standard, and the widely touted Homestead Act did nothing to alleviate unemployment in crowded eastern cities or to cure more general social problems.

Yet Smith's point was that, however misplaced, the *belief* in a "safety valve" had served a host of important interests, including the interests of industrial and political leaders who desired their own "safety" from the poor in some imagined Western alternative to the threat of eastern strikes and labor violence. Western boosters themselves encouraged the same idea of a "safety valve" in trying to foster more rapid development, and even humanitarian reformers succumbed out of desire to open up opportunities for the disadvantaged and exploited. Smith's important claim was that belief can alter behavior as much, even more than actual conditions, and that national myths do have considerable historical consequences. This is the point that Stephen Crane defined so well in his range of Western stories, and that John Ford explored in later films – the fictional emptiness of a sentimental myth of the West that was based on supposedly historical circumstances, and yet the strength of that myth in terms of people's belief nonetheless, leading them to act upon it and thus to *create* history. Or as Maxwell Scott, the newspaper editor in Ford's *Man Who Shot Liberty Valance*, notoriously intones: "When the legend becomes fact, print the legend."

Like Turner, Smith had a powerful influence on a generation of scholars, though few of these were trained as American historians. Most (perhaps understandably) came from departments of English literature – people like Leo Marx, John William Ward, and R.W.B. Lewis, Tony Tanner, and Alan Trachtenberg – and they turned their attention to American fiction to discover the "myths and symbols" that supposedly dominated the national consciousness, accepted as true by a broad swath of the population. Of course, historians pointed out that any such self-conscious separation of empirical fact and Western myths, of actual social and geological conditions on the one hand, and on the other hand beliefs *about* those conditions, was unworkable, if only because it's so hard to distinguish between what's true and what people believe. As the New Western historians have since delighted in telling us, moreover, the facts of the case seem to be that Western patterns of life differed little from eastern standards for racial, ethnic, and gender relations, in attitudes toward the environment and the workplace, in ideas about personal responsibility and institutional claims, in social conflict and political oppression, and so on. The journalist Richard Harding Davis already knew this, even by 1890, when he observed in his travelogue, *The West from a Car Window*:

> The ideas which the stay-at-home Eastern man obtains of the extreme borderland of Texas are gathered from various sources, principally from those who, as will all travellers, make as much of what they have seen as is possible, this much being generally to show the differences which exist between the places they have visited and their own home. Of the similarities they say nothing. Or he has read of the bandits and outlaws of the Garza revolution, and he has seen the Wild West show of the Hon. William F. Cody.[7]

The mention of that celebrated name, the man more than any other responsible for promulgating an authentic Western myth, gives me pause. I'm as skeptical as the next person about the supposed *truth* of the Western myth that first Turner, then Smith, described, and am more than convinced by their critics of the excesses in each man's pronouncements. But even if we grant that "free land" did not produce the national character described by Turner, or even were we to concede that Smith's dominant myths of the West don't really help us understand the actual ways history takes place *prospectively*, through contested agendas and warring interests: still, what continues to fascinate us is the retrospective allure of a unifying myth of the West. And that's been true from the beginning, as various ideas and images are imposed nostalgically on a landscape always altered from what it once was. The cowboy hero was invented only as his demise was being trumpeted (Owen Wister already claimed in 1900, "it is a vanished world");[8] Native Americans were celebrated only as they too were seen to fade away, becoming less of a threat; the frontiersman, the small farmer, the pocket miner were storied and sung only as memory began to dim. If myth most forcefully imposes itself on a landscape seen to be in a process of transformation, its prelapsarian virtues long lost, that may have more to do with the inner image we hold of ourselves as figures in a cultural drama already played out rather than in one yet to be written.

The myth of the West is something we'd like to believe but can't quite accommodate, though that very desire itself becomes, as already pointed out, part of a historical reality, and has done so from the get-go. The real, historical Daniel Boone, for instance, began in 1784 to model his own public pronouncements on those of his fictional archetype, the heroic Daniel Boone portrayed by the popular writer John Filson. And in the mid-nineteenth century, the effects of the publisher Erastus Beadle's dime westerns on a whole range of actual figures has itself been lampooned in countless Westerns (Clint Eastwood's *Unforgiven* is only a recent example). The most prolific of these famous writers of "blood-and-thunder romances" was Ned Buntline, whose pre-eminent creation was Buffalo Bill Cody himself, converted from obscure Army scout into the West's own celebrated hero, whose exploits were equal part fact and fiction, and whose later Wild West show has been credited as the beginning of the western rodeo. What was most extraordinary about Buffalo Bill's "true West" was that his shows convinced millions of Americans, and millions as well abroad, that the reality of the West exactly matched their own romantic imaginings, with daredevil, bareback cowboy riding, actual Indian figures like Sitting Bull and Geronimo, trick marksmen like Annie Oakley, and authentic historical pageants that depicted the West reconquered at Deadwood and Little Bighorn. And after the North-West Rebellion in 1885, Riel's military leader, Gabriel Dumont, worked for Cody, too.

To capture the effect of Cody's West, however, one needs to skip half-a-century to Leslie Fiedler's notorious description of the "Montana face," which came as revelation to a Brooklyn-born academic out West for his first university job. This is his 1950 account of arriving in Missoula as a newly-minted Ph.D. (in a Hollywood experience akin to mine last year with my popcorn-sated kids):

> The seediest moving-picture theater in town, I soon discovered, showed every Saturday the same kind of Western picture at which I had yelled and squirmed as a kid, clutching my box of jujubes; but in this context it was different. The children still eagerly attended, to be sure, but also the cowhands. In their run-over-at-the-heels boots and dirty jeans, they were apparently willing to invest a good part of their day off watching Gene and Roy, in carefully tailored togs, get the rustlers, save the ranch, and secure the Right; meanwhile making their own jobs, their everyday work into a symbol of the Natural Gentleman at home.

Then Fiedler goes on to interpret the scene:

> They *believed it all*, not only that the Good triumphs in the end, but that the authentic hero is the man who herds cattle. Unlike, for instance, the soldier at the war picture, they never snickered, but cheered at all the right places; and yet, going out from contemplating their idealized selves to get drunk or laid, they must somehow have felt the discrepancy, as failure or irony or God knows what. Certainly for the bystander watching the cowboy, a comic book under his arm, lounging beneath the bright poster of the latest Roy Rogers film, there is the sense of a joke on someone, and no one to laugh. It is nothing less than the total myth of the goodness of man in a state of nature that is at stake every Saturday after the show at the Rialto.... The real cowpuncher begins to emulate his Hollywood version....[9]

This is simply a more direct and colourful version of Smith's sober account of belief, which raises all the old questions. And yet there's a significant difference in Fiedler's view of cowboys who style themselves according to the Hollywood version they see on screen, and Smith's less ironic view of urban Easterners filled with hopeful ideals about the frontier West. The very exaggeration in Fiedler's "total myth of the goodness of man in a state of nature" undercuts any claim at serious belief, even as it confirms how fully, from the beginning, Westerners have occasionally adopted the myth and lived by it (if only in play), creating a situation worthy of Jorge Luis Borges.

What's most interesting about that aspiration to act as Westerners are supposed to act, playing the role, wearing the garb, walking the walk, is that it is a role deemed more "American" than that of urban Northeasterner or rural Southerner. Likewise, even though New Jersey blazons "Garden State" on every licence tag, it's the West that continues to aspire to exemplary garden status, with huge irrigating wheels spinning across vast counties, bringing the desert into bloom in a fashion that makes New Jersey seem merely a truck-gardening state. That collective aspiration suggests where the line between fact and myth tends to erode – not for the historian, who's always interested in what the facts tell us, nor for literary types, who are just as interested in myths as structured narratives, but for those living according to certain mythic Western norms that have become defined *as* American, willy-nilly. Those myths were endorsed by

John Filson and James Fenimore Cooper, by Erastus Beadle and Ned Buntline, by Teddy Roosevelt, Owen Wister, and Frederic Remington, Ronald Reagan and George W. Bush, all of whom created themselves or others as mythic *Western* figures, and by extension as distinctively *American* heroes. And from 1880s railroad advertisements through 1950s Marlboro commercials up to billboards for Stetson cologne and low-rider jeans, the image of stalwart independence, of assured self-reliance, of natural ease in the landscape has been promulgated as at once a regional and yet national model of character.

It should be clear, then, what might serve as answers to the two questions of my title, which some will recognize as take-offs on popular culture. The answer to "Whose West Is It Anyway?" is that the invention of *America*'s West wins in any myth sweepstakes. And it is precisely the imperializing aspect of the Western American myth that lends it a quality overwhelming the more nuanced, historically informed, attentive view of the West that both Mexican and Canadian writers have provided. Yet if the mythic American West is distinctly a version of Eastern Americans' own projective desires, by that same token the vision of America thus refracted *through* that myth is itself a version of the Far West, become the West's America, seen *as* distinctly American because representative of that region more than any other. Of course, myth tends to be transnational, even the myth of the West. As Donald Worster has written about Turner's most famous student, the Harvard historian Frederick Merk: "If we follow his reasoning, the West is to be found wherever there is optimism, a love of freedom and democracy, an indomitable will to overcome all obstacles, a determination to make things better for the future. That is, I will grant you, the state of Oregon he is describing, but it also might be Australia or Hong Kong."[10] Yet construed less abstractly, the myth of the West has less benign implications for understanding American history, helping to explain America's isolationist past (as Smith understands it), or its scale of violence and propensity toward imperialism (as Richard Slotkin's emphasis on "regeneration through violence" suggests).[11] Of course, what those of us who stand aside from mythic explanations tend to realize is that many other factors have played into America's historical isolationism, or its high rates of civil violence, or its imperial global inclinations – factors other than its Western geography and frontier past – all of which suggests a series of counter-narratives that reduce the so-called myth of the West to something less powerful and pervasive, less capable of explaining America. And that provides a mixed answer to the second question, "What's Myth Got to Do With It?," an answer that reduces, after all, to "not much, and everything." After all the various images, symbols, and myths have been duly reviewed and catalogued, we're left simply unclear about the relation between Americans' beliefs and their history, except to know that both their beliefs and their history *are* different from Mexico's and Canada's, despite shared borders, shared landscapes, even shared institutions.

Returning briefly to the film, *Spirit: Stallion of the Cimarron*, what I realize already is that the power of its story will probably have as much to do with certain universals about growing up and becoming more responsible as it does about any myth of the West. It will probably be as much about Freud's notion of accepting the discontents of civilization, with all the necessary learned repressions, as it has to do with anything distinctively American. Looked at from this perspective, one might well say that the myth of the West, of the frontier, *is* a dream of escape from just such repressions, and that the power of that myth lies in the way, as *apparent* history, it maps a nonetheless deeper, psychological paradigm. But that still doesn't explain why *Spirit* is set in the American, not the Canadian Rockies, and not in Mexico's rugged terrain, or why such films are pitched not to Smith's eastern audiences any more, but to viewers world-wide, of every national origin. The American myth of the West has become ever more ubiquitous even as it remains distinctively American.

Questions to Ponder

1. What purpose has the frontier served?
2. In what ways does the demise or fading of something (the cowboy, the Indian, etc.) insure its use in the myth of the West?
3. How do different groups view the West?
4. What makes westward expansion American versus other experiences? Is it really unique?
5. Why did the cowboy become the mythic figure of the West? Are there other mythic figures?

Must reads

Bold, Christine. *Selling the Wild West: Popular Western Fiction, 1860-1960*. Bloomington: Indiana University Press, 1987.

Buscombe, Edward, ed. *The BFI Companion to the Western*. New York: Atheneum, 1968.

Mitchell, Lee Clark. *Westerns: Making the Man in Fiction and Film*. Chicago: University of Chicago Press, 1996.

Smith, Henry Nash. *Virgin Land: The American West as Symbol and Myth*. Cambridge: Harvard University Press, 1950.

Wister, Owen. *The Virginian: A Horseman of the Plains*. New York: Macmillan, 1902.

Notes

1. www.dreamworks.com/spirit/main.html.
2. Frederick Jackson Turner, *The Significance of the Frontier in American History*, ed. Harold P. Simonson (New York: Frederick Ungar, 1963), pp. 27, 57. Future references are included parenthetically in the text.
3. See Louis Hartz, *The Liberal Tradition in America: An Interpretation of American Political Thought Since the Revolution* (New York: Harcourt, Brace, 1955), and Kenneth M. Stampp, *The Peculiar Institution: Slavery in the Ante-bellum South* (New York: Knopf, 1956).
4. Patricia Nelson Limerick, *The Legacy of Conquest: The Unbroken Past of the American West* (New York: Norton, 1987), p. 26.
5. Richard Hofstadter, *The Progressive Historians: Turner, Beard, Parrington* (New York: Knopf, 1968), pp. 103–4. Also cited by Donald Worster, *Under Western Skies: Nature and History in the American West* (New York: Oxford University Press, 1992), pp. 7–8.
6. Worster, *Under Western Skies*, p. 6.
7. Richard Harding Davis, *The West From a Car-Window* (1892; New York: Harper & Brothers, 1903), p. 6.
8. Owen Wister, *The Virginian: A Horseman of the Plains* (New York: Macmillan, 1902), p. viii.
9. Leslie Fiedler, "Montana: or The End of Jean-Jacques Rousseau," in *An End to Innocence: Essays on Culture and Politics* (Boston: Beacon, 1952), pp. 135–36.
10. Worster, *Under Western Skies*, p. 21.
11. Richard Slotkin, *Regeneration through Violence: The Mythology of the American Frontier, 1600-1860* (Middletown, CT: Wesleyan University Press, 1973).

chapter nine

Leading the Parade

Aritha van Herk, University of Calgary

The mythologies embedded in the West exert their own ironies and displacements, their own refusals and contingencies. In the short story that follows, I have set out to play with the master narrative of the much-mythologized Calgary Stampede, "The Greatest Show on Earth," and its most dangerous sport, the Chuckwagon Races. This liminal story rides at the edge of this frontier and its narration, beyond the action of the real races, real danger, and real mythology as it might be encountered in the body of a woman whose family has been in "wagon racing" for generations. This is a fiction, but the Chucks, for all their carefully orchestrated competition and spectatorship, are not. They gesture toward potential transgressions and confrontations that are deliciously ironic and yet perversely real in their dangerous enactment.

On Friday morning at nine, the official opening of the "Greatest Outdoor Show on Earth" (or so they like to think and so it is called), Tulip, the undisputed matriarch of the Pane family, will assume the honorary and honoured position of Parade Marshall and ride at the head of the string of cars and balloons and horses and floats and marching bands that signify the opening of the Calgary Stampede's ten days of drink and debauchery. This is not an imaginary event, but materially predictable, a hyperbolic re-imagining of the ranching era that lasted in southern Alberta only about thirty years, and is good and dead now, but that continues to repeat its own memorial, as regularly as any carnivale or yearly religious bloodletting, lottery, or harvest.

The parade furls its droopy tail always and undeviatingly on the same day, the first Friday of July after Canada Day. The Stampede itself follows the parade, until the Monday ten days later, sodden with sunrise Caesars and midnight corn dogs, nursing their blistered feet and denim-chafed thighs, bankers return to their counting houses and secretaries to their computers and lovelorn urban cowboys gas up their suburban assault vehicles and take down their portable gun racks, although the "I love Alberta beef" bumper stickers flag freeway traffic for the rest of the year. The red and white Stampede pennants along the main thoroughfares of Calgary ripple for a few weeks longer, their edges shredding in the western wind. By August they are tattered and slatternly, although the day when tickets for next year's Stampede go on sale will reawaken one more summer lineup fuelled by nostalgia about the dust and mud of the infield, the blood on the cowboys' hands, the all-night line dancing.

Tulip Pane, it is important to know, is not a tall woman, five foot two even with the heeled boots that she wears only for Stampede. She struggles into them at that time of year, but would rather be wearing her more comfortable Nikes. Faster, better grip, rubber sole. She prefers too her threadbare sweats, her GMC truck, and her Palm Pilot, but they aren't part of her mythopoeic image, and so she doesn't mention them, won't be caught dead using them until after the Stampede is over. No point upsetting the chuckwagon.

She will be, in fact, driving a chuckwagon at the head of this world-famous but commercially impelled parade, her bony ass perched on the hard and narrow driver's bench. Discomfort should not be necessary, but it is noble. As Parade Marshall, an honour usually reserved for politicians and hockey stars and opera singers, she has the right to ride in a red convertible, but Tulip knows how that abdication could play out. The journalists would start their calculations and add years to her age. If she were to sit on a stuffed leatherette seat with a driver aiming the nose of the rag top forward, they'd begin to predict the end of the Pane family as champion wagon racers of the west.

Tulip Pane knows that a chuckwagon is a synecdoche. And don't kid yourself, as she would say, she knows what a synecdoche is too, although she'll deny that knowledge vehemently, refuse to admit her own grasp of metaphor. She is not a myth and she is less than a metaphor, Tulip Pane, but as Parade Marshall, she makes a bargain that she'll live up to the protocol, and to the character she's been assigned in this half-baked and endlessly circular part of the annual Stampede carnivale. Within which she represents the part that is called the Rangeland Derby, the ten-day cumulative wagon race that is the *pièce de résistance* of the world's great chariot races. Which, although it is 2003, persist.

Tulip was surprised by her own surprise when they asked her, the white-hatted Stampede committee of oil men and big riggers, CEOs, and advertising executives who drove up to her slouchy ranch house in a delegation of big bellies and clean shirts and ten-dollar words. She thought they wanted to use the Pane name for another memorial trophy or something but after a lot of hemming and hawing (they do enjoy their parts in the drama), they out and asked her to be the Stampede Parade Marshall. She was so surprised she bolted into the kitchen, muttering something about tea, although she never makes tea. Doesn't drink the stuff. She drinks coffee or beer or water. End of choices.

Turned out they were afraid she'd say no but being asked to serve as Marshall of the Stampede parade is better than an Order of Canada or a Damehood, both of which just award you a sticky little lapel pin. Being Parade Marshall, by contrast, is first in line at the Greatest Show on Earth – the Parade Marshall is the lead act in the Greatest Show on Earth, and although Tulip knows better, that phrase stills gets her blood hot. So Tulip stood over the stained porcelain sink in the kitchen for a few minutes, noticing that the breakfast dishes were still waiting, and trying to figure out if they expected her to cry, and then she'd gone back out to her living room and said, "Thank you boys. I'd be proud." Here's looking at me, she thought to herself, gleefully. All these years of backing this outfit and at last I get to ride at the front.

She can trace her family, Tulip Pane can, back to the Burns family, even the Wares, through a line of side-kick Mounties all the way to the Davis family, early American whiskey entrepreneurs who adaptably changed their goods to suit their customers when the Mounties dragged themselves, "squinting and squitching," as Tulip is fond of saying, over the sagegrass hills from the east. Well, from the south, technically, from Montana where they'd detoured to find horses that could eat prairie wool after all their fine Toronto horses had died. They were a rag tag lot, starving and thirsty, but Tulip Pane's great granddaddy quickly deduced that selling them flour and beef would be more profitable and less contentious than thinned-out liquor. Tulip's family has been around that long, since before the Mounties showed up, and after, working for I.G. Baker out of Fort Benton, bull training oatmeal and bacon, tea and sugar, beans and pepper and potatoes north from Montana into Canada. If she were a man they'd call her an old timer, but because she's a woman they say she's feisty.

She'd like to bite them. It's a word that makes her sneer, Tulip Pane, born one of the Brandon sisters, just north of Pincher Creek, on a rough gut ranch where her father practised riding and roping more than he practised making a living. He, old Ronnie Brandon, was a circuit cowboy at the rodeos who made just enough money staying on bucking horses to keep trying to stay on them. The rest of the time he pretended to raise a few steers and worked at making a profit trading bad horses for better horses. So Tulip comes to her proud moment at the head of the Stampede parade, a parade that lasts more than three hours and that includes the prancing of more than a thousand thoroughbreds, honestly enough, if honesty counts. She is eighty, Tulip Pane, and she is connected to three of the main wagon-racing houses of royalty in Alberta. She is one of the Brandon sisters and she married a Pane, and one of her sons married a Winder girl. The house of Windsor has nothing on this gang.

Tulip claims that she married into the Pane family, hard-handed wagon-crazy racers who would rather sleep with horses than in houses, on straw than on mattresses, only by accident. Other people claim that Buell Pane needed someone to hold his team outside a bar one afternoon and Tulip was the only one who wasn't afraid to hang onto a pair of reins attached to four disobedient devils. She was small and scrawny but she was strong, and Buell noticed that about her. To her own pragmatic disappointment, Tulip very quickly figured out that she had married a myth; she knew then and she still knows that myths are no bargain, just hard work staying a few steps ahead of the bank.

Tulip and Buell had five sons, and four of them are still alive, no small feat considering their penchant for getting stepped on by wild horses and driving too fast and failing in school. After one good year, when Tulip and Buell managed to build a new house, with an indoor bathroom, Tulip taught them to put the seat on the toilet down and to wash their hands with soap before wiping them on the towel. They've married now and they have sons, and those boys are marrying too, bringing home western-garbed Barbie and Bambi lookalikes that they hope she'll approve of. She approves and disapproves, and solemnly declares to every one of those mascara-eyed ladies that horses are miserable creatures, not to be trusted. That scares them good, since they're not capable of high or low-grade humor and Tulip gets a quiet chuckle. Irony. They all want to believe in the story, want to be convinced of its durability and romance.

None of Tulip's sons will be riding with her. She's alone on the driver's seat, handling the reins of four of the calmer wagon horses, at the head of the parade. The father of those boys, old Buell, has been dead for twenty years. She can hardly remember what he looked like, although she can hear his voice as plain as day – he never stopped talking, that man, talking and talking to the horses, cursing and coaxing them in the track behind the windbreak. He'll be talking to her too, while she's driving the six kilometres of the parade route, "Watch that lead there, Tulip," or "that horse is wanting to bolt."

"Shut up," she'll say, under her breath. "Don't you think I know how to drive a team of horses by now?"

People make the mistake of believing that the Calgary Stampede is about cowboys and Indians, that it's a celebration of the west's history. "In a pig's ear," Tulip says, and if she has one beer too many, she'll tell something close to the truth. "It's about dressing up," she'll say. "Just like Hallowe'en."

That shocks them. There's an aura to this event, this west, these horses, this competition and its dust and speed and danger that makes everyone want to imagine the Stampede as a historic replication of something intangible but real. Nostalgia is as dangerous as wagon racing, but it's easier to live with.

Nobody believes her anyway.

Tulip doesn't quite believe herself. Five sons, and all of them twice as tall as she is, or so she claims. That's not quite true either. She is something over five feet and they are over six, but the difference is enough to make them tower, enough to emphasize her relative smallness. And their sons are even bigger, the family growing toward some ceiling that hasn't been marked out yet. She can't remember any of their names, doesn't even try. "You," is the nearest she uses to addressing them personally. But in the world of wagon-racing, they are kings, championship after championship, and if they come second in Calgary, they'll likely come first in Stettler or Ponoka, Meadow Lake or Medicine Hat, driving the World Professional Chuckwagon Association circuit, or the Canadian pros. So long as they win enough day money to feed the horses, they can feed their own story; maybe they can put gas in the truck, and buy two beers and a foot-long hot dog with relish and mustard. Even the food at rodeos is hyperbolic.

In fact, although Tulip will drive the chuckwagon between the postmodern skyscrapers of this brash and moneyed oil town, there hasn't been a professional woman driver yet. It's a man's sport, or as Tulip used to say, an idiot's sport. She's driving because of the family that trails behind her and because she is eighty, and wagon racing is the scariest and the sexiest spectacle in the west. Tulip Pane knows the difference between myth and reality, but she is wily and experienced enough to gamble one against the other and hope to win. So far, she hasn't done badly, and unlike Buell, she's still alive to test her own tale.

The old West is gone. It never existed in the first place, but here it is, the 80th year of the yearly Calgary Stampede, and Tulip Pane gets to be the Parade Marshall. She was born in 1923, the year Guy Weadick and the city decided to make this on ongoing event. She's been here every year since it began. What was her mother going to do but take the three-month old baby along, and in 1923 her father stayed on Whipstock and won the bucking contest, and Tulip has been coming to the Stampede ever since, even when she was pregnant. Watching her husbands and her sons and her grandsons wagon racing, pretending to be heroes, urging on the horses and aiming for the finish line.

Tulip knows very well, and the irony is not lost on her, that chuckwagon is a fancy word for a cookshack on wheels, first invented by an American cattleman called Charles Goodnight, who bought a Civil War army wagon and turned it into a rolling kitchen. He nailed a square box to the back for a pantry, added a water barrel and a tool chest, and then stretched a canvas tarp over the hooped metal frame. Threw together a sack of flour and a tin of lard, lots of dried beans and enough coffee to keep a cowboy or two awake and the pantry was stocked. Beef supplies were right there, on the hoof, and the cook didn't need much else to feed the cowboys, although cooks did a lot of fetching and carrying, and even gave haircuts.[1] Tulip used to buzz-shave all her boys' heads, but she isn't fond of cooking. She can grill a steak or deck out a baked potato with sour cream and bacon bits, but she is not one for pastry or salad. She would rather be pulling porcupine quills out of a dog's nose than cooking. She would rather ride fence than wash dishes. She doesn't mind laundry too much, but cleaning out a barn stall is more satisfying. Yet, behind her reputation is a fact she cannot confess. She loves horses but she hates riding, has always hated riding, and because of that, forced herself to ride and ride and ride, until she could ride the devil himself and never be thrown. It's not that she thinks the discomfort is romantic; it's just not as boring as housework. No choice there. But she would rather be drinking beer and dancing at the Twin Buttes community hall too, although the Brandon girls are notoriously heavy on their feet. She would rather be riding the roller coaster on the midway – now that gives her a real thrill. "Here's looking at you," she says when she raises her glass. It's all about looking. Look ahead down the track, look past the horses' heads, look up at the sky. Keep your eyes open and don't believe anything you see.

Tulip Pane does not know who Leslie Fiedler is; but if she did know his story about watching cowboy movies with other cowboys, if she heard his astonished and naive eastern exclamation that "*They believed it all!*" she would snort with laughter. And likely say, "Fooled you. *You* believed that they believed it all. You believed that their communal dream was coded by some version of *Midnight Cowboy*."[2] Tulip Pane is perfectly aware of all the people and theories that she is not supposed to know, and that's where what she doesn't know stops.

Tulip Pane is the Parade Marshall of the 2003 Calgary Stampede parade despite knowing that the new West is a performative space, costumed and ritualistic as any religious procession walking barefoot over cobblestoned streets, dragging chains and crosses. "Bring out your dead," she might be tempted to shout, there at the head of that extravagant kitetail of clowns and balloons and baton-wielding dancers and trumpeting marching bands. They are assembling behind her, forty-six marching bands, twelve Blackfoot tribal groups, floats in honour of the Calgary Association of Sikh taxi drivers, the Liberal party of Alberta, the Lake Sundance Community Association, and the Chinatown Restauranteurs. There are twenty-nine Tsuu T'ina riders, a pair of llamas leading the Dutch Calgarian Christian Reformed church, a giant and obscene wurst in honour of Columbus's Sausage Company, a blond and fishnet clad Venus on the half-shell to symbolize Shell oil, and forty-six Peigan warriors on motorcycles. The butchers and bakers and car dealerships have spent hours pinning plastic flowers to hay wagons. It's a serious business, so Tulip Pane won't make any plague jokes, not now when Toronto is still feeling bruised about SARS. She'll don her best hat, her snuggest jeans and a red-checkered shirt, and she'll even put some boot polish to those shit kickers that she saves for this time of year. For sure it'll rain – it always does, so she's prepared to drape a clear plastic poncho over the works and hope that it doesn't thunder. Although some lightning would be poetic justice. The Pane family wagon is painted with a streak of lightning, only there because Tulip was supposed to paint stripes along the side, and made a mess of the job, so the stripes turned into a lightning flash. Accidents will happen.

She gets to choose who rides in the back of the wagon. Her great-grandchildren pestered her to come but she's told them a flat no, it's her show. She's chosen three ghosts to ride along, although they'll be invisible to the crowds that line the sidewalks and the roadside bleachers, that will cheer and applaud her progress. "There's Tulip Pane," she'll hear them say. "Isn't she feisty? I heard she's eighty and look at her drive those horses. They're ready to bolt!" And she'll shake the reins at them, those spectators in sunglasses and sunblock, all duded up in the cowboy clothes that they put on once a year. Here's looking at you, she'll think. But you're looking at me. And I'm the Parade Marshall of the parade that launches the Greatest Show on Earth. Who cares about being famous in New York?

London is a fusty city, and Toronto doesn't know how to have a good time. This is Calgary, Alberta, bright as a copper penny, barely one hundred years old and hot with a tradition, that she, Tulip Pane, represents.

The three ghosts she has asked along will jounce and rattle and complain in the back of the wagon. She'll have to ignore them for the parade route, although she's fond of having extended conversations with them over drinks on the veranda of her house. One of them is Henry Longabaugh. He worked the Bar U south of Calgary in 1890, and when he got sick of the dust and the flies, he traded his spare saddle and bridle to Tulip's great-grandfather before he rode south, down into the States to join up with the Wild Bunch and become the Sundance Kid, investing in a larger audience and a more spectacular death, one that even got memorialized in the movies. The second ghost she's invited to ride along is an American movie man too, Clint Eastwood. Since he's not dead, he's not a total ghost, although his spirit does hang around Calgary more than people from California might expect. Tulip met him (the flesh and blood man impersonating Clint Eastwood the movie star) at Sushi Bar Miki in the old Bowness end of Calgary where they sat and drank Kirin beer and ate raw tuna and pretended that they weren't in any West, real or imaginary, at all. The whole four months that he was filming *Unforgiven*, they met once a week for sushi, and Tulip told him that if he tried to turn her into a character she'd poison his fish. The third ghost is Tulip's mother, whom she remembers best feeding the arms and legs of long underwear into the clenched lips of the wringer washer, and then lugging those frozen limbs inside from the clothes line on December afternoons, imbued with the scent of heaven. Tulip's mother is the wild card in that threesome.

And her dead men will ride with her, Buell, talking talking talking to the horses, his low murmur making them prick their ears – he died easy, just keeled over with a heart attack. And her son, Sandy, killed here at the Rangeland Derby when his wagon broke an axle. In the pileup he somersaulted right over the horses' heads so they trampled him into the dirt track. Blood for the money. Every night these racers escape death by seconds cut finer than dust, and the crowd in the stand roars with the pleasure of possible disaster. Four teams of four horses hooked to a shrug-shouldered canvas-covered wagon, and at the sound of a claxon, required to do a figure eight around two barrels while four outriders mount their own rearing horses and follow the wagon around the dirt track.[3] Sort of like a driver guiding two thousand pounds of impatient race-horse stock with nothing more than dental floss, into a hell bent dash around the track they love to call "the half a mile of hell." Blood sports earn their reputations with mud and blood and dust and death. The chariot races in Rome were tame by comparison, they brag, and nobody in the business contradicts that claim.

Well, this parade route is tamer, a few blocks of driving through tiers of happy voyeurs waving and clapping. Tulip intends to do a good job as Marshall, to stick out her chest and look feisty. She suspects that they are honouring her this year because they have come up with a scheme to export chuckwagon races to Las Vegas, that even more spectacular carnival of death and desert and winning and losing and animal performance south of the border.

Ironies abound. Chuckwagon racing is an American game, promoted and domesticated in Calgary by a New Yorker (the much-cited Guy Weadick, who knew how to sell the idea of daredevils and rivalry) and now about to be exported to try and give the Canadian sport additional cash and cache. The first year, 1923, the Derby was won by a seventy-year-old driver who got the prize of a new Stetson hat.[4] And while the purse is fifty thousand dollars now, that's still not much to risk breaking your neck for.

But if the chucks catch on in Vegas, why wagon racing and its followers just might start to make some money. It's all about spectacle, that moment at the edge of a new hiatus when there's a brief attentive hush and everyone turns to look at what they think is the past, what they've decided to call history, without even knowing its inception or disguise.

No accounting for repetition, thinks Tulip Pane. No accounting for people's disgust and delight. Las Vegas here we come. First Cirque de Soleil and Céline Dion, and now chuckwagon racing. Free trade. Meanwhile, let's get this outfit rolling. It's starting to rain. The horses are restless and the parade is about to begin.

Questions to Ponder

1. What is the myth of the West to which van Herk refers?
2. What is significant about Tulip's ghosts?
3. What elements of this story are 'American'? What elements are Canadian?
4. What are the gender tensions in the story?
5. How does Tulip represent the mythic and the real West?

Must Reads

Belanger, Art J. *A Half Mile of Hell: The Story of Chuckwagon Racing*. Calgary: Frontier Publishing, 1970.

Breen, David H. *The Canadian West and the Ranching Frontier, 1874–1924*. Toronto: University of Toronto Press, 1983.

Elofson, Warren M. *Cowboys, Gentlemen, and Cattle Thieves: Ranching on the Western Frontier*. Montreal and Kingston: McGill-Queen's University Press, 2000.

King, Thomas. *Green Grass, Running Water*. Toronto: HarperCollins, 1993.

van Herk, Aritha. *Mavericks: An Incorrigible History of Alberta*. Toronto: Penguin, 2001.

Notes

1. Glen Mikkelsen, *Never Holler Whoa! The Cowboys of Chuckwagon Racing* (Toronto: Balmur Book Publishing, 2000); and *Checkered Courage* (Calgary: Johnson Gorman, 2002).
2. Leslie Fiedler, "Canada and the Invention of the Western," in *Crossing Frontiers*, edited by Dick Harrison (Edmonton: University of Alberta Press, 1979), p. 97.
3. See below, guide and diagram of Chuckwagon Rules and starting configuration, *2003 Spectators Guide and Yearbook*, The World Professional Chuckwagon Association (Calgary: Billy Melville Productions, 2003), p. 88.
4. Mikkelsen, p. 6.

appendix

The Significance of the Frontier in American History*[1]

Frederick J. Turner

In a recent bulletin of the Superintendent of the Census for 1890 appear these significant words: "Up to and including 1880 the country had a frontier of settlement, but at present the unsettled area has been so broken into by isolated bodies of settlement that there can hardly be said to be a frontier line. In the discussion of its extent, its westward movement, etc., it can not, therefore, any longer have a place in the census reports." This brief official statement marks the closing of a great historic movement. Up to our own day American history has been in a large degree the history of the colonization of the Great West. The existence of an area of free land, its continuous recession, and the advance of American settlement westward, explain American development.

Behind institutions, behind constitutional forms and modifications, lie the vital forces that call these organs into life and shape them to meet changing conditions. The peculiarity of American institutions is, the fact that they have been compelled to adapt themselves to the changes of an expanding people – to the changes involved in crossing a continent, in winning a wilderness, and in developing at each area of this progress out of the primitive economic and political conditions of the frontier into the complexity of city life. Said Calhoun in 1817, "We are great, and rapidly – I was about to say fearfully – growing!"[2] So saying, he touched the distinguishing feature of American

* Reprinted from the Report of the American Historical Association, 1893, pp. 199-277.

life. All peoples show development; the germ theory of politics has been sufficiently emphasized. In the case of most nations, however, the development has occurred in a limited area; and if the nation has expanded it has met other growing peoples whom it has conquered. But in the case of the United States we have a different phenomenon. Limiting our attention to the Atlantic coast, we have the familiar phenomenon of the evolution of institutions in a limited area, such as the rise of representative government; the differentiation of simple colonial governments into complex organs; the progress from primitive industrial society, without division of labor, up to manufacturing civilization. But we have in addition to this a recurrence of the process of evolution in each western area reached in the process of expansion. Thus American development has exhibited not merely advance along a single line, but a return to primitive conditions on a continually advancing frontier line, and a new development for that area. American social development has been continually beginning over again on the frontier. This perennial rebirth, this fluidity of American life, this expansion westward with its new opportunities, its continuous touch with the simplicity of primitive society, furnish the forces dominating American character. The true point of view in the history of this nation is not the Atlantic coast, it is the great West. Even the slavery struggle, which is made so exclusive an object of attention by writers like Prof. von Holst, occupies its important place in American history because of its relation to westward expansion.

In this advance, the frontier is the outer edge of the wave – the meeting point between savagery and civilization. Much has been written about the frontier from the point of view of border warfare and the chase, but as a field for the serious study of the economist and the historian it has been neglected.

The American frontier is sharply distinguished from the European frontier – a fortified boundary line running through dense populations. The most significant thing about the American frontier is, that it lies at the hither edge of free land. In the census reports it is treated as the margin of that settlement which has a density of two or more to the square mile. The term is an elastic one, and for our purposes does not need sharp definition. We shall consider the whole frontier belt, including the Indian country and the outer margin of the "settled area" of the census reports. This paper will make no attempt to treat the subject exhaustively; its aim is simply to call attention to the frontier as a fertile field for investigation, and to suggest some of the problems which arise in connection with it.

In the settlement of America we have to observe how European life entered the continent, and how America modified and developed that life and reacted on Europe. Our early history is the study of European germs developing in an American environment. Too exclusive attention has been paid by institutional students to the Germanic origins, too little to the American factors. The frontier is the line of most rapid and effective Americanization. The wilderness masters the colonist. It finds him a European in dress, industries, tools, modes of travel, and thought. It takes him from the railroad car and puts him in the birch canoe. It strips off the garments of civilization and arrays him in the hunting shirt and the moccasin. It puts him in the log cabin of the Cherokee and Iroquois and runs an Indian palisade around him. Before long he has gone to planting Indian corn and plowing with a sharp stick; he shouts the war cry and takes the scalp in orthodox Indian fashion. In short, at the frontier the environment is at first too strong for the man. He must accept the conditions which it furnishes, or perish, and so he fits himself into the Indian clearings and follows the Indian trails. Little by little he transforms the wilderness, but the outcome is not the old Europe, not simply the development of Germanic germs, any more than the first phenomenon was a case of reversion to the Germanic mark. The fact is, that here is a new product that is American. At first, the frontier was the Atlantic coast. It was the frontier of Europe in a very real sense. Moving westward, the frontier became more and more American. As successive terminal moraines result from successive glaciations, so each frontier leaves its traces behind it, and when it becomes a settled area the region still partakes of the frontier characteristics. Thus the advance of the frontier has meant a steady movement away from the influence of Europe, a steady growth of independence on American lines. And to study this advance, the men who grew up under these conditions, and the political, economic, and social results of it, is to study the really American part of our history.

Stages of Frontier Advance.

In the course of the seventeenth century the frontier was advanced up the Atlantic river courses, just beyond the "fall line," and the tidewater region became the settled area. In the first half of the eighteenth century another advance occurred. Traders followed the Delaware and Shawnese Indians to the Ohio as early as the end of the first quarter of the century.[3] Gov. Spotswood [*sic*], of Virginia, made an expedition in 1714 across the Blue Ridge. The end of the first quarter of the century saw the advance of the Scotch-Irish and the Palatine Germans up the Shenandoah Valley into the western part of Virginia, and along the Piedmont region of the Carolinas.[4] The Germans in New York pushed the frontier of settlement up the Mohawk to German Flats.[5] In Pennsylvania the town of Bedford indicates the line of settlement. Settlements had begun on New River, a branch of the Kanawha, and on the sources of the Yadkin and French Broad.[6] The King attempted to arrest the advance by his proclamation of 1763,[7] forbidding settlements beyond the sources of the rivers flowing into the Atlantic; but in vain. In the period of the Revolution the frontier crossed the Alleghanies into Kentucky and Tennessee, and the upper waters of the Ohio were settled.[8] When the first census was taken in 1790, the continuous settled area was bounded by a line which ran near the coast of Maine, and included New England except a portion of Vermont and New Hampshire, New York along the Hudson and up the Mohawk about Schenectady, eastern and southern Pennsylvania, Virginia well across the Shenandoah Valley, and the Carolinas and eastern Georgia.[9] Beyond this region of continuous settlement were the small settled areas of Kentucky and Tennessee, and the Ohio, with the mountains intervening between them and the Atlantic area, thus giving a new and important character to the frontier. The isolation of the region increased its peculiarly American tendencies, and the need of transportation facilities to connect it with the East called out important schemes of internal improvement, which will be noted farther on. The "West," as a self-conscious section, began to evolve.

From decade to decade distinct advances of the frontier occurred. By the census of 1820[10] the settled area included Ohio, southern Indiana and Illinois, southeastern Missouri, and about one-half of Louisiana. This settled area had surrounded Indian areas, and the management of these tribes became an object of political concern. The frontier region of the time lay along the Great Lakes, where Astor's American Fur Company operated in the Indian trade,[11] and beyond the Mississippi, where Indian traders extended their activity even to the Rocky Mountains; Florida also furnished frontier conditions. The Mississippi River region was the scene of typical frontier settlements.[12]

The rising steam navigation[13] on western waters, the opening of the Erie Canal, and the westward extension of cotton[14] culture added five frontier states to the Union in this period. Grund, writing in 1836, declares: "It appears then that the universal disposition of Americans to emigrate to the western wilderness, in order to enlarge their dominion over inanimate nature, is the actual result of an expansive power which is inherent in them, and which by continually agitating all classes of society is constantly throwing a large portion of the whole population on the extreme confines of the State, in order to gain space for its development. Hardly is a new State or Territory formed before the same principle manifests itself again and gives rise to a further emigration; and so is it destined to go on until a physical barrier must finally obstruct its progress."[15]

In the middle of this century the line indicated by the present eastern boundary of Indian Territory, Nebraska, and Kansas marked the frontier of the Indian country.[16] Minnesota and Wisconsin still exhibited frontier conditions,[17] but the distinctive frontier of the period is found in California, where the gold discoveries had sent a sudden tide of adventurous miners, and in Oregon, and the settlements in Utah.[18] As the frontier has leaped over the Alleghanies, so now it skipped the Great Plains and the Rocky Mountains; and in the same way that the advance of the frontiersmen beyond the Alleghanies had caused the rise of important questions of transportation and internal improvement, so now the settlers beyond the Rocky Mountains needed means of communication with the East, and in the furnishing of these arose the settlement of the Great Plains and the development of still another kind of frontier life. Railroads, fostered by land grants, sent an increasing tide of immigrants into the far West. The United States Army fought a series of Indian wars in Minnesota, Dakota, and the Indian Territory.

By 1880 the settled area had been pushed into northern Michigan, Wisconsin, and Minnesota, along Dakota rivers, and in the Black Hills region, and was ascending the rivers of Kansas and Nebraska. The development of mines in Colorado had drawn isolated frontier settlements into that region, and Montana and Idaho were receiving settlers. The frontier was found in these mining camps and the ranches of the Great Plains. The superintendent of the census for 1890 reports, as previously stated, that the settlements of the West lie so scattered over the region that there can no longer be said to be a frontier line.

In these successive frontiers we find natural boundary lines which have served to mark and to affect the characteristics of the frontiers, namely: The "fall line"; the Alleghany Mountains; the Mississippi; the Missouri, where its direction approximates north and south; the line of the arid lands, approximately the ninety-ninth meridian; and the Rocky Mountains. The fall line marked the frontier of the seventeenth century; the Alleghanies that of the eighteenth; the Mississippi that of the first quarter of the nineteenth; the Missouri that of the middle of this century (omitting the California movement); and the belt of the Rocky Mountains and the arid tract, the present frontier. Each was won by a series of Indian wars.

The Frontier Furnishes a Field for Comparative Study of Social Development.

At the Atlantic frontier one can study the germs of processes repeated at each successive frontier. "We have the complex European life sharply precipitated by the wilderness into the simplicity of primitive conditions. The first frontier had to meet its Indian question, its question of the disposition of the public domain, of the means of intercourse with older settlements, of the extension of political organization, of religious and educational activity. And the settlement of these and similar questions for one frontier served as a guide for the next. The American student needs not to go to the "prim little townships of Sleswick" for illustrations of the law of continuity and development. For example, he may study the origin of our land policies in the colonial land policy; he may see how the system grew by adapting the statutes to the customs of the successive frontiers.[19] He may see how the mining experience in the lead regions of Wisconsin, Illinois, and Iowa was applied to the mining laws of the Rockies,[20] and how our Indian policy has been a series of experimentations on successive frontiers. Each tier of new States has found in the older ones material for its constitutions.[21] Each frontier has made similar contributions to American character, as will be discussed farther on.

But with all these similarities there are essential differences, due to the place element and the time element. It is evident that the farming frontier of the Mississippi Valley presents different conditions from the mining frontier of the Rocky Mountains. The frontier reached by the Pacific Railroad, surveyed into rectangles, guarded by the United States Army, and recruited by the daily immigrant ship, moves forward at a swifter pace and in a different way than the frontier reached by the birch canoe or the pack horse. The geologist traces patiently the shores of ancient seas, maps their areas, and compares the older and the newer. It would be a work worth the historian's labors to mark these various frontiers and in detail compare one with another. Not only would there result a more adequate conception of American development and characteristics, but invaluable additions would be made to the history of society.

Loria[22] the Italian economist, has urged the study of colonial life as an aid in understanding the stages of European development, affirming that colonial settlement is for economic science what the mountain is for geology, bringing to light primitive stratifications. "America," he says, "has the key to a historical enigma which Europe has sought for centuries in vain and the land which has no history reveals luminously the course of universal history." There is much truth in this. The United States lies like a huge page in the history of society. Line by line as we read this continental page from west to east we find the record of social evolution. It begins with the Indian and the hunter; it goes on to tell of the disintegration of savagery by the entrance of the trader, the pathfinder of civilization; we read the annals of the pastoral stage in ranch life; the exploitation of the soil by the raising of unrotated crops of corn and wheat in sparsely settled farming communities; the intensive culture of the denser farm settlement; and finally the manufacturing organization with city and factory system.[23] This page is familiar to the student of census statistics, but how little of it has been used by our historians. Particularly in eastern States this page is a palimpsest. What is now a manufacturing State was in an earlier decade an area of intensive farming. Earlier yet it had been a wheat area and still earlier the "range" had attracted the cattle-herder Thus Wisconsin, now developing manufacture, is a State with varied agricultural interests. But earlier it was given over to almost exclusive grain-raising, like North Dakota at the present time.

Each of these areas has had an influence in our economic and political history; the evolution of each into a higher stage has worked political transformations. But what constitutional historian has made any adequate attempt to interpret political facts by the light of these social areas and changes?[24] The Atlantic frontier was compounded of fisherman, fur-trader, miner, cattle-raiser, and farmer. Excepting the fisherman, each type of industry was on the march toward the West, impelled by an irresistible attraction. Each passed in successive waves across the continent. Stand at Cumberland Gap and watch the procession of civilization, marching single file – the buffalo following the trail to the salt springs, the Indian, the fur-trader and hunter, the cattle-raiser, the pioneer farmer – and the frontier has passed by. Stand at South Pass in the Rockies a century later and see the same procession with wider intervals between. The unequal rate of advance compels us to distinguish the frontier into the trader's frontier, the rancher's frontier, or the miner's frontier, and the farmer's frontier. When the mines and the cow pens were still near the fall line the traders' pack trains were tinkling across the Alleghanies, and the French on the Great Lakes were fortifying their posts, alarmed by the British trader's birch canoe. When the trappers scaled the Rockies, the farmer was still near the mouth of the Missouri.

The Indian Trader's Frontier.

Why was it that the Indian trader passed so rapidly across the continent? What effects followed from the trader's frontier? The trade was coeval with American discovery. The Norsemen, Vespuccius, Verrazani, Hudson, John Smith, all trafficked for furs. The Plymouth pilgrims settled in Indian cornfields, and their first return cargo was of beaver and lumber. The records of the various New England colonies show how steadily exploration was carried into the wilderness by this trade. What is true for New England is, as would be expected, even plainer for the rest of the colonies. All along the coast from Maine to Georgia the Indian trade opened up the river courses. Steadily the trader passed westward, utilizing the older lines of French trade. The Ohio, the Great Lakes, the Mississippi, the Missouri, and the Platte, the lines of western advance, were ascended by traders. They found the passes in the Rocky Mountains and guided Lewis and Clarke,[25] Frémont, and Bidwell. The explanation of the rapidity of this advance is connected with the effects of the trader on the Indian. The trading post left the unarmed tribes at the mercy of those that had purchased fire-arms – a truth which the Iroquois Indians wrote in blood, and so the remote and unvisited tribes gave eager welcome to the trader. "The savages," wrote La Salle, "take better care of us French than of their own children; from us only can they get guns and goods." This accounts for the trader's power and the rapidity of his advance. Thus the disintegrating forces of civilization entered the wilderness. Every river valley and Indian trail became a fissure in Indian society, and so that society became honeycombed. Long before the pioneer farmer appeared on the scene, primitive Indian life had passed away. The farmers met Indians armed with guns. The trading frontier, while steadily undermining Indian power by making the tribes ultimately dependent on the whites, yet, through its sale of guns, gave to the Indian increased power of resistance to the farming frontier. French colonization was dominated by its trading frontier; English colonization by its farming frontier. There was an antagonism between the two frontiers as between the two nations. Said Duquesne to the Iroquois, "Are you ignorant of the difference between the king of England and the king of France? Go see the forts that our king has established and you will see that you can still hunt under their very walls. They have been placed for your advantage in places which you frequent. The English, on the contrary, are no sooner in possession of a place than the game is driven away. The forest falls before them as they advance, and the soil is laid bare so that you can scarce find the wherewithal to erect a shelter for the night."

And yet, in spite of this opposition of the interests of the trader and the farmer, the Indian trade pioneered the way for civilization. The buffalo trail became the Indian trail, and this became the trader's "trace;" the trails widened into roads, and the roads into turnpikes, and these in turn were transformed into railroads. The same origin can be shown for the railroads of the South, the far West, and the Dominion of Canada.[26] The trading posts reached by these trails were on the sites of Indian villages which had been placed in positions suggested by nature; and these trading posts, situated so as to command the water systems of the country, have grown into such cities as Albany, Pittsburg, Detroit, Chicago, St. Louis, Council Bluffs and Kansas City. Thus civilization in America has followed the arteries made by geology, pouring an ever richer tide through them, until at last the slender paths of aboriginal intercourse have been broadened and interwoven into the complex mazes of modern commercial lines; the wilderness has been interpenetrated by lines of civilization growing ever more numerous. It is like the steady growth of a complex nervous system for the originally, simple, inert continent. If one would understand why we are to-day one nation, rather than a collection of isolated states, he must study this economic and social consolidation of the country. In this progress from savage conditions lie topics for the evolutionist.

The effect of the Indian frontier as a consolidating agent in our history is important. From the close of the seventeenth century various intercolonial congresses have been called to treat with Indians and establish common measures of defense. Particularism was strongest in colonies with no Indian frontier. This frontier stretched along the western border like a cord of union.

The Indian was a common danger, demanding united action. Most celebrated of these conferences was the Albany congress of 1754, called to treat with the Six Nations, and to consider plans of union. Even a cursory reading of the plan proposed by the congress reveals the importance of the frontier. The powers of the general council and the officers were, chiefly, the determination of peace and war with the Indians, the regulation of Indian trade, the purchase of Indian lands, and the creation and government of new settlements as a security against the Indians. It is evident that the unifying tendencies of the Revolutionary period were facilitated by the previous cooperation in the regulation of the frontier. In this connection may be mentioned the importance of the frontier, from that day to this, as a military training school, keeping alive the power of resistance to aggression, and developing the stalwart and rugged qualities of the frontiersman.

The Rancher's Frontier.

It would not be possible in the limits of this paper to trace the other frontiers across the continent. Travelers of the eighteenth century found the "cowpens" among the canebrakes and peavine pastures of the South, and the "cow drivers" took their droves to Charleston, Philadelphia, and New York.[27] Travelers at the close of the War of 1812 met droves of more than a thousand cattle and swine from the interior of Ohio going to Pennsylvania to fatten for the Philadelphia market.[28] The ranges of the Great Plains, with ranch and cowboy and nomadic life, are things of yesterday and to-day. The experience of the Carolina cowpens guided the ranchers of Texas. One element favoring the rapid extension of the rancher's frontier is the fact that in a remote country lacking transportation facilities the product must be in small bulk, or must be able to transport itself, and the cattle raiser could easily drive his product to market. The effect of these great ranches on subsequent agrarian history of the localities in which they existed should be studied.

The Farmer's Frontier.

The maps of the census reports show an uneven advance of the farmer's frontier, with tongues of settlement pushed forward and with indentations of wilderness. In part this is due to Indian resistance, in part to the location of river valleys and passes, in part to the unequal force of the centers of frontier attraction. Among the important centers of attraction may be mentioned the following; fertile and favorably situated soils, salt springs, mines and army posts.

Army Posts.

The frontier army post, serving to protect the settlers from the Indians, has also acted as a wedge to open the Indian country, and has been a nucleus for settlement.[29] In this connection mention should also be made of the Government military and exploring expeditions in determining the lines of settlement. But all the more important expeditions were greatly indebted to the earliest pathmakers, the Indian guides, the traders and trappers, and the French voyageurs, who were inevitable parts of government expeditions from the days of Lewis and Clark.[30] Each expedition was an epitome of the previous factors in western advance.

Salt Springs.

In an interesting monograph, Victor Hehn[31] has traced the effect of salt upon the early European development, and has pointed out how it affected the lines of settlement and the form of administration. A similar study might be made for the salt springs of the United States. The early settlers were tied to the coast by the need for salt, without which they could not preserve their meats or live in comfort. Writing in 1752, Bishop Spangenburg says of a colony for which he was seeking lands in North Carolina, "They will require salt & other necessaries which they can neither manufacture nor raise. Either they must got to Charleston, which is 300 miles distant * * * or else they must go to Boling's Point in Vª on a branch of the James & is also 300 miles from here * * * Or else they must go down to Roanoke – I know not how many miles – where salt is brought up from the Cape Fear."[32] This may serve as a typical illustration. An annual pilgrimage to the coast for salt thus became essential. Taking flocks or furs and ginseng root, the early settlers sent their pack trains after seeding time each year to the coast.[33] This proved to be an important educational influence, since it was almost the only way in which the pioneer learned what was going on in the East. But when the discovery was made of the salt springs of the Kanawha, and the Holston, and Kentucky, and central New York, the West began to be freed from dependence on the coast. It was in part the effect of finding these salt springs that enabled settlement to cross the mountains.

From the time the mountains rose between the pioneer and the seaboard, a new order of Americanism arose. The West and the East began to get out of touch of each other. The settlements from the sea to the mountains kept connection with the rear and had a certain solidarity. But the over-mountain men grew more and more independent. The East took a narrow view of American advance, and nearly lost these men. Kentucky and Tennessee history bears abundant witness to the truth of this statement. The East began to try to hedge and limit westward expansion. Though Webster could declare that there were no Alleghanies in his politics, yet in politics in general they were a very solid factor.

Land.

The exploitation of the beasts took hunter and trader to the west, the exploitation of the grasses took the rancher west, and the exploitation of the virgin soil of the river valleys and prairies attracted the farmer. Good soils have been the most continuous attraction to the farmer's frontier. The land hunger of the Virginians drew them down the rivers into Carolina, in early colonial days; the search for soils took the Massachusetts men to Pennsylvania and to New York. As the eastern lands were taken up migration flowed across them to the west. Daniel Boone, the great backwoodsman, who combined the occupations of hunter, trader, cattle-raiser, farmer, and surveyor – learning, probably from the traders, of the fertility of the lands on the upper Yadkin, where the traders were wont to rest as they took their way to the Indians, left his Pennsylvania home with his father, and passed down the Great Valley road to that stream, Learning from a trader whose posts were on the Bed River in Kentucky of its game and rich pastures, he pioneered the way for the farmers to that region. Thence he passed to the frontier of Missouri, where his settlement was long a landmark on the frontier. Here again he helped to open the way for civilization, finding salt licks, and trails, and land. His son was among the earliest trappers in the passes of the Rocky Mountains, and his party are said to have been the first to camp on the present site of Denver. His grandson, Col. A. J. Boone, of Colorado, was a power among the Indians of the Rocky Mountains, and was appointed an agent by the Government. Kit Carson's mother was a Boone.[34] Thus this family epitomizes the backwoodsman's advance across the continent.

The farmer's advance came in a distinct series of waves. In Peck's New Guide to the West, published in Boston in 1837, occurs this suggestive passage:

> Generally, in all the western settlements, three classes, like the waves of the ocean, have rolled one after the other. First comes the pioneer, who depends for the subsistence of his family chiefly upon the natural growth of vegetation, called the "range," and the proceeds of hunting. His implements of agriculture are rude, chiefly of his own make, and his efforts directed mainly to a crop of corn and a "truck patch." The last is a rude garden for growing cabbage, beans, corn for roasting ears, cucumbers, and potatoes. A log cabin, and, occasionally, a stable and corn-crib, and a field of a dozen acres, the timber girdled or "deadened," and fenced, are enough for his occupancy. It is quite immaterial whether he ever becomes the owner of the soil. He is the occupant for the time being, pays no rent, and feels as independent as the "lord of the manor." With a horse, cow, and one or two breeders of swine, he strikes into the woods with his family, and becomes the founder of a new county, or perhaps state. He builds his cabin, gathers around him a few other families of similar tastes and habits, and occupies till the range is somewhat subdued, and hunting a little precarious, or, which is more frequently the case, till the neighbors crowd around, roads, bridges, and fields annoy him, and he lacks elbow room. The preemption law enables him to dispose of his cabin and cornfield to the next class of emigrants; and, to employ his own figures, he "breaks for the high timber," "clears out for the New Purchase," or migrates to Arkansas or Texas, to work the same process over.
>
> The next class of emigrants purchase the lands, add field to field, clear out the roads, throw rough bridges over the streams, put up hewn log houses with glass windows and brick or stone chimneys, occasionally plant orchards, build mills, schoolhouses, court-houses, etc., and exhibit the picture and forms of plain, frugal, civilized life.
>
> Another wave rolls on. The men of capital and enterprise come. The settler is ready to sell out and take the advantage of the rise in property, push farther into the interior and become, himself, a man of capital and enterprise in turn. The small village rises to a spacious town or city; substantial edifices of brick, extensive fields, orchards, gardens, colleges, and churches are seen. Broadcloths, silks, leghorns, crapes, and all the refinements, luxuries, elegancies, frivolities,

and fashions are in vogue. Thus wave after wave is rolling westward; the real Eldorado is still farther on.

A portion of the two first classes remain stationary amidst the general movement, improve their habits and condition, and rise in the scale of society.

The writer has traveled much amongst the first class, the real pioneers. He has lived many years in connection with the second grade; and now the third wave is sweeping over large districts of Indiana, Illinois, and Missouri. Migration has become almost a habit in the West. Hundreds of men can be found, not over 50 years of age, who have settled for the fourth, fifth, or sixth time on a new spot. To sell out and remove only a few hundred miles makes up a portion of the variety of backwoods life and manners.[35]

Omitting those of the pioneer farmers who move from the love of adventure, the advance of the more steady farmer is easy to understand. Obviously the immigrant was attracted by the cheap lands of the frontier, and even the native farmer felt their influence strongly. Year by year the farmers who lived on soil whose returns were diminished by unrotated crops were offered the virgin soil of the frontier at nominal prices. Their growing families demanded more lands, and these were dear. The competition of the unexhausted, cheap, and easily tilled prairie lands compelled the farmer either to go west and continue the exhaustion of the soil on a new frontier, or to adopt intensive culture. Thus the census of 1890 shows, in the Northwest, many counties in which there is an absolute or a relative decrease of population. These States have been sending farmers to advance the frontier on the plains, and have themselves begun to turn to intensive farming and to manufacture. A decade before this, Ohio had shown the same transition stage. Thus the demand for land and the love of wilderness freedom drew the frontier ever onward.

Having now roughly outlined the various kinds of frontiers, and their modes of advance, chiefly from the point of view of the frontier itself, we may next inquire what were the influences on the East and on the Old World. A rapid enumeration of some of the more noteworthy effects is all that I have time for.

Composite Nationality.

First, we note that the frontier promoted the formation of a composite nationality for the American people. The coast was preponderantly English, but the later tides of continental immigration flowed across to the free lands. This was the case from the early colonial days. The Scotch-Irish and the Palatine Germans, or "Pennsylvania Dutch," furnished the dominant element in the stock of the colonial frontier. With these peoples were also the freed indented servants, or redemptioners, who at the expiration of their time of service passed to the frontier. Governor Spottswood of Virginia writes in 1717, "The inhabitants of our frontiers are composed generally of such as have been transported hither as servants, and, being out of their time, settle themselves where land is to be taken up and that will produce the necessarys of life with little labour."[36] Very generally these redemptioners were of non-English stock. In the crucible of the frontier the immigrants were Americanized, liberated, and fused into a mixed race, English in neither nationality nor characteristics. The process has gone on from the early days to our own. Burke and other writers in the middle of the eighteenth century believed that Pennsylvania[37] was "threatened with the danger of being wholly foreign in language, manners, and perhaps even inclinations." The German and Scotch-Irish elements in the frontier of the South were only less great. In the middle of the present century the German element in Wisconsin was already so considerable that leading publicists looked to the creation of a German state out of the commonwealth by concentrating their colonization.[38] Such examples teach us to beware of misinterpreting the fact that there is a common English speech in America into a belief that the stock is also English.

Industrial Independence.

In another way the advance of the frontier decreased our dependence on England. The coast, particularly of the South, lacked diversified industries, and was dependent on England for the bulk of its supplies. In the South there was even a dependence on the Northern colonies for articles of food. Governor Glenn, of South Carolina, writes in the middle of the eighteenth century: "Our trade with New York and Philadelphia was of this sort, draining us of all the little money and bills we could gather from other places for their bread, flour, beer, hams, bacon, and other things of their produce, all which, except beer, our new townships begin to supply us with, which are settled with very industrious and thriving Germans. This no doubt diminishes the number of shipping and the appearance of our trade, but it is far from being a detriment to us."[39] Before long the frontier created a demand for merchants. As it retreated from the coast it became less and less possible for England to bring her supplies directly to the consumer's wharfs, and carry away staple crops, and staple crops began to give way to diversified agriculture for a time. The effect of this phase of the frontier action upon the northern section is perceived when we realize how the advance of the frontier aroused seaboard cities like Boston, New York, and Baltimore, to engage in rivalry for what Washington called "the extensive and valuable trade of a rising empire."

Effects on National Legislation.

The legislation which most developed the powers of the National Government, and played the largest part in its activity, was conditioned on the frontier. Writers have discussed the subjects of tariff, land, and internal improvement, as subsidiary to the slavery question. But when American history comes to be rightly viewed it will be seen that the slavery question is an incident. In the period from the end of the first half of the present century to the close of the Civil War slavery rose to primary, but far from exclusive, importance. But this does not justify Dr. von Holst (to take an example) in treating our constitutional history in its formative period down to 1828 in a single volume, giving six volumes chiefly to the history of slavery from 1828 to 1861, under the title "Constitutional History of the United States." The growth of nationalism and the evolution of American political institutions were dependent on the advance of the frontier. Even so recent a writer as Rhodes, in his "History of the United States since the compromise of 1850," has treated the legislation called out by the western advance as incidental to the slavery struggle.

This is a wrong perspective. The pioneer needed the goods of the coast, and so the grand series of internal improvement and railroad legislation began, with potent nationalizing effects. Over internal improvements occurred great debates, in which grave constitutional questions were discussed. Sectional groupings appear in the votes, profoundly significant for the historian. Loose construction increased as the nation marched westward.[40] But the West was not content with bringing the farm to the factory. Under the lead of Clay – "Harry of the West" – protective tariffs were passed, with the cry of bringing the factory to the farm. The disposition of the public lands was a third important subject of national legislation influenced by the frontier.

The Public Domain.

The public domain has been a force of profound importance in the nationalization and development of the Government. The effects of the struggle of the landed and the landless States, and of the ordinance of 1787, need no discussion,[41] Administratively the frontier called out some of the highest and most vitalizing activities of the General Government. The purchase of Louisiana was perhaps the constitutional turning point in the history of the Republic, inasmuch as it afforded both a new area for national legislation and the occasion of the downfall of the policy of strict construction. But the purchase of Louisiana was called out by frontier needs and demands. As frontier States accrued to the Union the national power grew. In a speech on the dedication of the Calhoun monument Mr. Lamar explained: "In 1789 the States were the creators of the Federal Government; in 1861 the Federal Government was the creator of a large majority of the States."

When we consider the public domain from the point of view of the sale and disposal of the public lands we are again brought face to face with the frontier. The policy of the United States in dealing with its lands is in sharp contrast with the European system of scientific administration. Efforts to make this domain a source of revenue, and to withhold it from emigrants in order that settlement might be compact, were in vain. The jealousy and the fears of the East were powerless in the face of the demands of the frontiersmen. John Quincy Adams was obliged to confess: "My own system of administration, which was to make the national domain the inexhaustible fund for progressive and unceasing internal improvement, has failed." The reason is obvious; a system of administration was not what the West demanded; it wanted land. Adams states the situation as follows: "The slaveholders of the South have bought the cooperation of the western country by the bribe of the western lands, abandoning to the new Western States their own proportion of the public property and aiding them in the design of grasping all the lands into their own hands. Thomas H. Benton was the author of this system, which he brought forward as a substitute for the American system of Mr. Clay, and to supplant him as the leading statesman of the West. Mr. Clay, by his tariff compromise with Mr. Calhoun, abandoned his own American system. At the same time he brought forward a plan for distributing among all the States of the Union the proceeds of the sales of the public lands. His bill for that purpose passed both Houses of Congress, but was vetoed *by* President Jackson, who, in his annual message of December, 1832, formally recommended that all public lands should be gratuitously given away to individual adventurers and to the States in which the lands are situated.[42]

"No subject," said Henry Clay, "which has presented itself to the present, or perhaps any preceding, Congress, is of greater magnitude than that of the public lands." When we consider the far-reaching effects of the Government's land policy upon political, economic, and social aspects of American life, we are disposed to agree with him. But this legislation was framed under frontier influences, and under the lead of Western statesmen like Benton and Jackson. Said Senator Scott of Indiana in 1841: "I consider the preemption law merely declaratory of the custom or common law of the settlers."

National Tendencies of the Frontier.

It is safe to say that the legislation with regard to land, tariff, and internal improvements – the American system of the nationalizing Whig party – was conditioned on frontier ideas and needs. But it was not merely in legislative action that the frontier worked against the sectionalism of the coast. The economic and social characteristics of the frontier worked against sectionalism. The men of the frontier had closer resemblances to the Middle region than to either of the other sections. Pennsylvania had been the seed-plot of frontier emigration, and, although she passed on her settlers along the Great Valley into the west of Virginia and the Carolinas, yet the industrial society of these Southern frontiersmen was always more like that of the Middle region than like that of the tide-water portion of the South, which later came to spread its industrial type throughout the South.

The Middle region, entered by New York harbor, was an open door to all Europe. The tide-water part of the South represented typical Englishmen, modified by a warm climate and servile labor, and living in baronial fashion on great plantations; New England stood for a special English movement – Puritanism. The Middle region was less English than the other sections. It had a wide mixture of nationalities, a varied society, the mixed town and county system of local government, a varied economic life, many religious sects. In short, it was a region mediating between New England and the South, and the East and the West. It represented that composite nationality which the contemporary United States exhibits, that juxtaposition of non-English groups, occupying a valley or a little settlement, and presenting reflections of the map of Europe in their variety. It was democratic and nonsectional, if not national; "easy, tolerant, and contented;" rooted strongly in material prosperity. It was typical of the modern United States. It was least sectional, not only because it lay between North and South, but also because with no barriers to shut out its frontiers from its settled region, and with a system of connecting waterways, the Middle region mediated between East and West as well as between North and South. Thus it became the typically American region. Even the New Englander, who was shut out from the frontier by the Middle region, tarrying in New York or Pennsylvania on his westward march, lost the acuteness of his sectionalism on the way.[43]

The spread of cotton culture into the interior of the South finally broke down the contrast between the "tide-water" region and the rest of the State, and based Southern interests on slavery. Before this process revealed its results the western portion of the South, which was akin to Pennsylvania in stock, society, and industry, showed tendencies to fall away from the faith of the fathers into internal improvement legislation and nationalism. In the Virginia convention of 1829–'30, called to revise the constitution, Mr. Leigh, of Chesterfield, one of the tide-water counties, declared:

> One of the main causes of discontent which led to this convention, that which had the strongest influence in overcoming our veneration for the work of our fathers, which taught us to contemn the sentiments of Henry and Mason and Pendleton, which weaned us from our reverence for the constituted authorities of the State, was an overweening passion for internal improvement. I say this with perfect knowledge, for it has been avowed to me by gentlemen from the West over and over again. And let me tell the gentleman from Albemarle (Mr. Gordon) that it has been another principal object of those who set this ball of revolution in motion, to overturn the doctrine of State rights, of which Virginia has been the very pillar, and to remove the barrier she has interposed to the interference of the Federal Government in that same work of internal improvement, by so reorganizing the legislature that Virginia, too, may be hitched to the Federal car.

It was this nationalizing tendency of the West that transformed the democracy of Jefferson into the national republicanism of Monroe and the democracy of Andrew Jackson. The West of the War of 1812, the West of Clay, and Benton, and Harrison, and Andrew Jackson, shut off by the Middle States and the mountains from the coast sections, had a solidarity of its own with national tendencies.[44] On the tide of the Father of Waters, North and South met and mingled into a nation. Interstate migration went steadily on – a process of cross-fertilization of ideas and institutions. The fierce struggle of the sections over slavery on the western frontier does not diminish the truth of this statement; it proves the truth of it. Slavery was a sectional trait that would not down, but in the West it could not remain sectional. It was the greatest of frontiersmen who declared: "I believe this Government can not endure permanently half slave and half free. It will become all of one thing or all of the other." Nothing works for nationalism like intercourse within the nation. Mobility of population is death to localism, and the western frontier worked irresistibly in unsettling population. The effects reached back from the frontier and affected profoundly the Atlantic coast and even the Old World.

Growth of Democracy.

But the most important effect of the frontier has been in the promotion of democracy here and in Europe. As has been indicated, the frontier is productive of individualism. Complex society is precipitated by the wilderness into a kind of primitive organization based on the family. The tendency is anti-social. It produces antipathy to control, and particularly to any direct control. The tax-gatherer is viewed as a representative of oppression. Prof. Osgood, in an able article,[45] has pointed out that the frontier conditions prevalent in the colonies are important factors in the explanation of the American Revolution, where individual liberty was sometimes confused with absence of all effective government. The same conditions aid in explaining the difficulty of instituting a strong government in the period of the confederacy. The frontier individualism has from the beginning promoted democracy.

The frontier States that came into the Union in the first quarter of a century of its existence came in with democratic suffrage provisions and had reactive effects of the highest importance upon the older States whose peoples were being attracted there. An extension of the franchise became essential.

It was *western* New York that forced an extension of suffrage in the constitutional convention of that State in 1821; and it was *western* Virginia that compelled the tide-water region to put a more liberal suffrage provision in the constitution framed in 1830, and to give to the frontier region a more nearly proportionate representation with the tide-water aristocracy. The rise of democracy as an effective force in the nation came in with western preponderance under Jackson and William Henry Harrison, and it meant the triumph of the frontier – with all of its good and with all of its evil elements.[46] An interesting illustration of the tone of frontier democracy in 1830 comes from the same debates in the Virginia convention already referred to. A representative from western Virginia declared:

> But, sir, it is not the increase of population in the West which this gentleman ought to fear. It is the energy which the mountain breeze and western habits impart to those emigrants. They are regenerated, politically I mean, sir. They soon become *working politicians*; and the difference, sir, between a *talking* and a *working* politician is immense. The Old Dominion has long been celebrated for producing great orators; the ablest metaphysicians in policy; men that can split hairs in all abstruse questions of political economy. But at home, or when they return from Congress, they have negroes to fan them asleep. But a Pennsylvania, a New York, an Ohio, or a western Virginia statesman, though far inferior in logic, metaphysics, and rhetoric to an old Virginia statesman, has this advantage, that when he returns home he takes off his coat and takes hold of the plow. This gives him bone and muscle, sir, and preserves his republican principles pure and uncontaminated.

So long as free land exists, the opportunity for a competency exists, and economic power secures political power. But the democracy born of free land, strong in selfishness and individualism, intolerant of administrative experience and education, and pressing individual liberty beyond its proper bounds, has its dangers as well as it benefits. Individualism in America has allowed a laxity in regard to governmental affairs which has rendered possible the spoils system and all the manifest evils that follow from the lack of a highly developed civic spirit. In this connection may be noted also the influence of frontier conditions in permitting lax business honor, inflated paper currency and wild-cat banking. The colonial and revolutionary frontier was the region whence emanated many of the worst forms of an evil currency.⁴⁷ The West in the War of 1812 repeated the phenomenon on the frontier of that day, while the speculation and wild-cat banking of the period of the crisis of 1837 occurred on the new frontier belt of the next tier of States. Thus each one of the periods of lax financial integrity coincides with periods when a new set of frontier communities had arisen, and coincides in area with these successive frontiers, for the most part. The recent Populist agitation is a case in point. Many a State that now declines any connection with the tenets of the Populists, itself adhered to such ideas in an earlier stage of the development of the State. A primitive society can hardly be expected to show the intelligent appreciation of the complexity of business interests in a developed society. The continual recurrence of these areas of paper-money agitation is another evidence that the frontier can be isolated and studied as a factor in American history of the highest importance.⁴⁸

Attempts to Check and Regulate the Frontier.

The East has always feared the result of an unregulated advance of the frontier, and has tried to check and guide it. The English authorities would have checked settlement at the headwaters of the Atlantic tributaries and allowed the "savages to enjoy their deserts in quiet lest the peltry trade should decrease." This called out Burke's splendid protest:

> If you stopped your grants, what would be the consequence? The people would occupy without grants. They have already so occupied in many places. You can not station garrisons in every part of these deserts. If you drive the people from one place, they will carry on their annual tillage and remove with their flocks and herds to another. Many of the people in the back settlements are already little attached to particular situations. Already they have topped the Appalachian mountains. From thence they behold before them an immense plain, one vast, rich, level meadow; a square of five hundred miles. Over this they would wander without a possibility of restraint; they would change their manners with their habits of life; would soon forget a government by which they were disowned; would become hordes of English Tartars; and, pouring down upon your unfortified frontiers a fierce and irresistible cavalry, become masters of your governors and your counselers, your collectors, and comptrollers, and of all the slaves that adhered to them. Such would, and in no long time must, be the effect of

attempting to forbid as a crime and to suppress as an evil the command and blessing of Providence, "Increase and multiply." Such would be the happy result of an endeavor to keep as a lair of wild beasts that earth which God, by an express charter, has given to the children of men.

But the English Government was not alone in its desire to limit the advance of the frontier and guide its destinies. Tidewater Virgina[49] and South Carolina[50] gerrymandered those colonies to insure the dominance of the coast in their legislatures. Washington desired to settle a State at a time in the Northwest; Jefferson would reserve from settlement the territory of his Louisiana purchase north of the thirty-second parallel, in order to offer it to the Indians in exchange for their settlements east of the Mississippi. "When we shall be full on this side," he writes, "we may lay off a range of States on the western bank from the head to the mouth, and so range after range, advancing compactly as we multiply." Madison went so far as to argue to the French minister that the Untied States had no interest in seeing population extend itself on the right bank of the Mississippi, but should rather fear it. When the Oregon question was under debate, in 1824, Smyth, of Virginia, would draw an unchangeable line for the limits of the United States at the outer limit of two tiers of States beyond the Mississippi, complaining that the seaboard States were being drained of the flower of their population by the bringing of too much land into market. Even Thomas Benton, the man of widest views of the destiny of the West, at this stage of his career declared that along the ridge of the Rocky mountains, "the western limits of the Republic should be drawn, and the statue of the fabled god Terminus should be raised upon its highest peak, never to be thrown down."[51] But the attempts to limit the boundaries, to restrict land sales and settlement, and to deprive the West of its share of political power were all in vain. Steadily the frontier of settlement advanced and carried with it individualism, democracy, and nationalism, and powerfully affected the East and the Old World.

Missionary Activity.

The most effective efforts of the East to regulate the frontier came through its educational and religious activity, exerted by interstate migration and by organized societies. Speaking in 1835, Dr. Lyman Beecher declared: "It is equally plain that the religious and political destiny of our nation is to be decided in the

West," and he pointed out that the population of the West "is assembled from all the States of the Union and from all the nations of Europe, and is rushing in like the waters of the flood, demanding for its moral preservation the immediate and universal action of those institutions which discipline the mind and arm the conscience and the heart. And so various are the opinions and habits, and so recent and imperfect is the acquaintance, and so sparse are the settlements of the West, that no homogeneous public sentiment can be formed to legislate immediately into being the requisite institutions. And yet they are all needed immediately in their utmost perfection and power. A nation is being 'born in a day.' * * * but what will become of the West if her prosperity rushes up to such a majesty of power, while those great institutions linger which are necessary to form the mind and the conscience and the heart of that vast world. It must not be permitted. * * * Let no man at the East quiet himself and dream of liberty, whatever may become of the West. * * * Her destiny is our destiny."[52]

With the appeal to the conscience of New England, he adds appeals to her fears lest other religious sects anticipate her own. The New England preacher and school-teacher left their mark on the West. The dread of Western emancipation from New England's political and economic control was paralleled by her fears lest the West cut loose from her religion. Commenting in 1850 on reports that settlement was rapidly extending northward in Wisconsin, the editor of the Home Missionary writes: "We scarcely know whether to rejoice or mourn over this extension of our settlements. While we sympathize in whatever tends to increase the physical resources and prosperity of our country, we can not forget that with all these dispersions into remote and still remoter corners of the land the supply of means of grace is becoming relatively less and less." Acting in accordance with such ideas, home missions were established and Western colleges were erected. As seaboard cities like Philadelphia, New York, and Baltimore strove for the mastery of Western trade, so the various denominations strove for possession of the West. Thus an intellectual stream from New England sources fertilized the West. Other sections sent their missionaries; but the real struggle was between sects. The contest for power and the expansive tendency furnished to the various sects by the existence of a moving frontier must have had important results on the character of religious organization in the United States. The multiplication of rival churches in the little frontier towns had deep and lasting social effects. The religious aspects of the frontier make a chapter in our history which needs more study.

Intellectual Traits.

From the conditions of frontier life came intellectual traits of profound importance. The works of travelers along each frontier from colonial days onward describe certain common traits, and these traits have, while softening down, still persisted as survivals in the place of their origin, even when a higher social organization succeeded. The result is that to the frontier the American intellect owes its striking characteristics. That coarseness and strength combined with acuteness and inquisitiveness; that practical, inventive turn of mind, quick to find expedients; that masterful grasp of material things, lacking the artistic but powerful to effect great ends; that restless, nervous energy;[53] that dominant individualism, working for good and for evil, and withal that buoyancy and exuberance which comes with freedom – these are traits of the frontier, or traits called out elsewhere because of the existence of the frontier. Since the days when the fleet of Columbus sailed in to the waters of the New World, America has been another name for opportunity, and the people of the United States have taken their tone from the incessant expansion which has not only been open but has even been forced upon them. He would be a rash prophet who should assert that the expansive character of American life has now entirely ceased. Movement has been its dominant fact, and , unless this training has no effect upon a people, the American energy will continually demand a wider field for its exercise. But never again will such gifts of free land offer themselves. For a moment, at the frontier, the bonds of custom are broken and unrestraint is triumphant. There is not *tabula rasa*. The stubborn American environment is there with its imperious summons to accept its conditions; the inherited ways of doing things are also there; and yet, in spite of the environment, and in spite of custom, each frontier did indeed furnish a new field of opportunity, a gate of escape from the bondage of the past; and freshness, and confidence, and scorn of older society, impatience of its restraints and its ideas, and indifference to its lessons, have accompanied the frontier. What the Mediterranean Sea was to the Greeks, breaking the bond of custom, offering new experiences, calling out new institutions and activities, that, and more, the ever retreating frontier has been to the United States directly, and to the nations of Europe remotely. And now, four centuries from the discovery of America, at the end of a hundred years of life under the Constitution, the frontier has gone, and with its going has closed the first period of American history.

Notes

1. Since the meeting of the American Historical Association, this paper has also been given as an address to the State Historical Society of Wisconsin, December 14, 1893. I have to thank the Secretary of the Society, Mr. Reuben G. Thwaites, for securing valuable material for my use in the preparation of the paper.
2. Abridgement of Debates of Congress, v, p. 706.
3. Bancroft (1860 ed.), iii, pp. 344, 345, citing Logan MSS.; [Mitchell] Contest in America, etc. (1752), p. 237.
4. Kercheval, *History of the Valley* ; Bernheim, *German Settlements in the Carolinas*; Winsor, *Narrative and Critical History of America*, v, p. 304; *Colonial Records of North Carolina*, iv, p. xx; Weston, *Documents Connected with the History of South Carolina*, p. 82; Ellis and Evans, *History of Lancaster County, Pa.*, chs. iii, xxvi.
5. Parkman, Pontiac, ii; Griffis, Sir William Johnson, p. 6; Simms's *Frontiersmen of New York*.
6. Monette, *Mississippi Valley*, i, p. 311.
7. Wis. Hist. Cols., xi, p. 50; Hinsdale, *Old Northwest*, p. 121; Burke, "Oration on Conciliation," Works (1872 ed.), i, p. 473.
8. Roosevelt, *Winning of the West*, and citations there given; Cutler's *Life of Cutler*.
9. Scribner's *Statistical Atlas*, xxxviii, pl. 13; MacMaster, *Hist. of People of U. S.*, i, pp. 4, 60, 61; Imlay and Filson, *Western Territory of America* (London, 1793); Rochefoucault-Liancourt, *Travels Through the United States of North America* (London, 1799); Michaux's "Journal," in *Proceedings American Philosophical Society*, xxvi, No. 129; Forman, *Narrative of a Journey Down the Ohio and Mississippi in 1780-'90* (Cincinnati, 1888); Bartram, *Travels Through North Carolina, etc.* (London, 1792); Pope, *Tour Through the Southern and Western Territories, etc.* (Richmond, 1792); Weld, *Travels Through the States of North America* (London, 1799); Baily, *Journal of a Tour in the Unsettled States of North America, 1796–'97* (London, 1856); *Pennsylvania Magazine of History*, July, 1886; Winsor, *Narrative and Critical History of America*, vii, pp. 491, 492, citations.
10. Scribner's *Statistical Atlas*, xxxix.
11. Turner, *Character and Influence of the Indian Trade in Wisconsin* (Johns Hopkins University Studies, Series ix), pp. 61ff.
12. Monette, *History of the Mississippi Valley*, ii; Flint, *Travels and Residence in Mississippi*; Flint, *Geography and History of the Western States*; Abridgment of Debates of Congress, vii, pp. 397, 398, 404; Holmes, *Account of the U. S.; Kingdom, America and the British Colonies* (London, 1820); Grund, *Americans*, ii, chs. i, iii, vi (although writing in 1836, he treats of conditions that grew out of western advance from the era of 1820 to that time); Peck, *Guide for Emigrants* (Boston, 1831); Darby, *Emigrants' Guide to Western and Southwestern States and Territories*; Dana, *Geographical Sketches in the Western Country*; Kinzie, Waubun; Keating, *Narrative of Long's Expedition*; Schoolcraft, *Discovery of the Sources of the Mississippi River, Travels in the Central Portions of the Mississippi Valley, and Lead Mines of the Missouri*; Andreas, *History of Illinois*, i, 86–99; Hurlbut, *Chicago Antiquities*; McKeuney, *Tour to the Lakes*; Thomas, *Travels through the Western Country, etc.* (Auburn, N. Y., 1819).
13. Darby, *Emigrants' Guide*, pp. 272ff.; Benton, Abridgment of Debates, vii, p. 397.
14. *DeBow's Review*, iv, p. 254; xvii, p. 428.

15 Grand, *Americans*, ii, p. 8.
16 Peck, *New Guide to the West* (Cincinnati, 1818), ch. iv; Parkman, *Oregon Trail*; Hall, *The West* (Cincinnati, 1848); Pierce, *Incidents of Western Travel*; Murray, *Travels in North America*; Lloyd, *Steamboat Directory* (Cincinnati, 1856); "Forty Days in a Western Hotel" (Chicago), in *Putnam's Magazine*, December, 1894; Mackay, *The Western World*, ii, ch. ii, iii; Meeker, *Life in the West*; Bogen, *German in America* (Boston, 1851); Olmstead, *Texas Journey*; Greeley, *Recollections of a Busy Life*; Schouler, *History of the United States*, v, 261–67; Peyton, *Over the Alleghanies and Across the Prairies* (London, 1870); Loughborough, *The Pacific Telegraph and Railway* (St. Louis, 1849); Whitney, *Project for a Railroad to the Pacific* (New York, 1849); Peyton, *Suggestions on Railroad Communication with the Pacific, and the Trade of China and the Indian Islands*; Benton, Highway to the Pacific (a speech delivered in the U. S. Senate, December 16, 1850).
17 A writer in *The Home Missionary* (1850), p. 239, reporting Wisconsin conditions, exclaims: "Think of this, people of the enlightened East. What an example, to come from the very frontiers of civilization! "But one of the missionaries writes: "In a few years Wisconsin will no longer be considered as the West, or as an outpost of civilization, any more than western New York, or the Western Reserve."
18 Bancroft (H. H.), *History of California, History of Oregon, and Popular Tribunals*; Shinn, *Mining Camps*.
19 See the suggestive paper by Prof. Jesse Macy, The *Institutional Beginnings of a Western State*,
20 Shinn, *Mining Camps*.
21 Compare Thorpe, in *Annals American Academy of Political and Social Science*, September, 1891; Bryce, *American Commonwealth* (1888), ii, p. 689.
22 Loria, *Analisi della Proprieta Capitalista*, ii, p. 15.
23 Compare *Observations on the North American Land Company*, London 1796, pp. xv, 144; Logan, *History of Upper South Carolina*, i, pp. 149–51, Turner, *Character and Influence of Indian Trade in Wisconsin*, p. 18; Peck, *New Guide for Emigrants* (Boston, 1837), ch. iv; Compendium Eleventh Census, i, p. xl.
24 See pages *post*, for illustrations of the political accompaniments of changed industrial conditions.
25 But Lewis and Clarke were the first to explore the route from the Missouri to the Columbia.
26 *Narrative and Critical History of America*, viii, p. 10; Sparks' *Washington Works*, ix, pp. 303, 327; Logan, *History of Upper South Carolina*, i; McDonald, *Life of Kenton*, p. 72; Cong. Record, xxiii, p. 57.
27 Lodge, *English Colonies*, p. 152 and citations; Logan, *Hist. of Upper South Carolina*, i, p. 151.
28 Flint, *Recollections*, p. 9.
29 See Monette, *Mississippi Valley*, i, p. 344.
30 Coues', *Lewis and Clark's Expedition*, i, pp. 2, 253–59; Benton, in Cong. Record, xxiii, p. 57.
31 Hehn, *Das Salz* (Berlin, 1873).
32 *Col. Records of N. C.*, v, p. 3.
33 Findley, *History of the Insurrection in the Four Western Counties of Pennsylvania in the Year 1794* (Philadelphia, 1796), p. 35.
34 Hale, *Daniel Boone* (pamphlet).
35 Compare Baily, *Tour in the Unsettled Parts of North America* (London, 1856), pp. 217–19, where a similar analysis is made for 1796. See also Collot, *Journey in North America* (Paris, 1826), p. 109; *Observations on the North American Land Company* (London, 1796), pp. xv, 144; Logan, *History of Upper South Carolina*.

36 "Spottswood Papers," in *Collections of Virginia Historical Society*, i, ii.
37 [Burke], *European Settlements, etc.* (1765 ed.), ii, p. 200.
38 Everest, in *Wisconsin Historical Collections*, xii, pp. 7ff.
39 Veston, *Documents connected with History of South Carolina*, p. 61.
40 See, for example, the speech of Clay, in the House of Representatives, January 30, 1824.
41 See the admirable monograph by Prof. H. B. Adams, *Maryland's Influence on the Land Cessions*; and also President Welling, in *Papers American Historical Association*, iii, p. 411.
42 *Adams' Memoirs*, ix, pp. 247, 248.
43 Author's article in *The Ægis* (Madison, Wis.), November 4, 1892.
44 Compare Roosevelt, *Thomas Benton*, ch. i.
45 *Political Science Quarterly*, ii, p. 457. Compare Sumner, *Alexander Hamilton*, chs. ii–vii.
46 Compare Wilson, *Division and Reunion*, pp. 15, 24.
47 On the relation of frontier conditions to Revolutionary taxation, see Sumner, *Alexander Hamilton*, ch. iii.
48 I have refrained from dwelling on the lawless characteristics of the frontier, because they are sufficiently well known. The gambler and desperado, the regulators of the Carolinas and the vigilantes of California, are types of that line of scum that the waves of advancing civilization bore before them, and of the growth of spontaneous organs of authority where legal authority was absent. Compare Barrowa, *United States of Yesterday and To-morrow*; Shinn, *Mining Camps*; and Bancroft, *Popular Tribunals*. The humor, bravery, and rude strength, as well as the vices of the frontier in its worst aspect, have left traces on American character, language, and literature, not soon to be effaced.
49 Debates in the Constitutional Convention, 1829–1830.
50 [McCrady] *Eminent and Representative Men of the Carolinas*, i, p. 43; Calhoun's Works, i, pp. 401–406.
51 Speech in the Senate, March 1, 1825; Register of Debates, i, 721.
52 *Plea for the West* (Cincinnati, 1835), pp. 11ff.
53 Colonial travelers agree in remarking on the phlegmatic characteristics of the colonists. It has frequently been asked how such a people could have developed that strained nervous energy now characteristic of them. Compare Sumner, *Alexander Hamilton*, p. 98; and Adams's *History of the United States*, i, p. 60; ix, pp. 240, 241. The transition appears to become marked at the close of the War of 1812, a period when interest centered upon the development of the West, and the West was noted for restless energy. Grund, *Americans*, ii, ch. i.

appendix

Frontierism, Metropolitanism, and Canadian History*

J. M. S. Careless

Like any other history, that of Canada has been written within the framework of intellectual concepts, some of which have been consciously applied by historians, while others have shaped their work more or less indirectly through the influence of the surrounding climate of opinion. It would obviously be impossible to draw out and catalogue all the concepts that have affected the writing of Canadian history, even in the most general way. Yet it does seem possible to discern certain underlying ideas or patterns of thought that have given character to various phases of Canadian historiography. And in more recent times, in particular, one can note the powerful influence of what might be called (for want of a more precise term) "frontierism" in the history of Canada.

The idea of the dynamic frontier as a great and distinctive force moulding North American development has left an enduring mark on the writing of history in Canada, just as it has in the United States. No doubt this frontier idea is no longer as fresh and vital in its application to this country as it was in the period before the Second World War: indeed, it is largely because its original influence has declined, and the concept has thus become a historical phenomenon in itself, that we are entitled to discuss and assess its influence. Nor was

---

* Canadian Historical Review 35, no. 1 (March 1954): 1-21. Reprinted by permission of University of Toronto Press Inc. (www.utpjournals.com).

the frontier thesis proper, as propounded by Frederick Jackson Turner and elaborated by his disciples, ever adopted as fully or dogmatically in Canada as it was in the United States – and there, of course, it has long been the subject of qualification and criticism. Nevertheless, the frontier interpretation broadly affected the thinking of a number of distinguished Canadian historians who in the main began their work about a quarter-century ago.[1] Today we can hardly examine the current state of Canadian historiography, and perhaps project its lines of growth, without giving heavy weight to the North American–environmentalist view of our history which stemmed originally from Turner's frontier thesis and which still leaves a rich heritage on both sides of the Canadian-American boundary.

There were other approaches to Canadian history before the rise of frontierism, and at present there are still others, which may involve the modification, complication, or even the virtual reversal of the frontier concept. Accordingly, in order to put frontierism in its proper context, it is first necessary to generalize – rather alarmingly, perhaps – on several "schools" of Canadian history. Each of these had some sort of interpretative approach, or at least some underlying assumptions, which gave a broadly similar character to the works its members produced.

These schools, however, are being set forth merely for convenience in tracing the general patterns of Canadian historiography and not as an all-inclusive filing system; for when individual historians are considered they do not always fit neatly into one particular classification. Some may change their school allegiance with the passage of time, while others, so to speak, may fall between schools. Furthermore, since the writing of history in French- and English-speaking Canada has largely been carried on as two separate enterprises, it would be of small consequence to try to link French-language schools with the English ones to be established below. And yet, despite these limitations, it can still be asserted that at various stages in Canadian historiography certain general approaches have been followed by important groups of historians, so that the designating of "schools" to illuminate that fact is by no means an unprofitable exercise.

I

The first school to be so designated might be termed the Britannic, or Blood is Thicker than Water School The writers of this group were often convinced imperialists of the later nineteenth or early twentieth centuries and were closely attached in sentiment and background to Great Britain. They tended, as William Kingsford, that dull dean of Canadian historians, said he did, to make their theme the emergence of a new Britannic community within the empire, a part of one imperial organism, whose people enjoyed the British institutions of their forefathers and were worthy members of that indefinable company, the "British race."[2] This Britannic School was inclined to ignore North American forces except when they were concentrated in the threatening power of the United States. The defeat of American pressure from without in 1776, 1812, and 1867 had "kept Canada British." So much for North America: a foe to be resisted.

Yet this group contributed something of lasting significance to the thought of Canadian history; the idea that Canada represented a declaration of independence from the United States, an attempt to build a second community in North America outside the American republic, and one marked off from it, indeed, by the longer persistence of the imperial tie. For some time this Canadian community would look to the bond with Britain to offset American dangers. But in the young twentieth century, when the days of actual threat had passed, that bond seemed to change increasingly in its implication – from protection to subordination. It was now that another school of Canadian historians began to arise, who viewed the imperial tie more critically in the light of the growing spirit of nationalism. And their main theme now became the march of Canada to political nationhood, through many a parliamentary manoeuvre and struggle of words as colonial limitations were progressively overcome.

This new School of Political Nationhood chiefly concentrated on the paper-strewn path to national status, directing Canadian history to Colonial Office dispatches, the records of imperial conferences, and tense questions of treaty-making powers. Two phases, however, may be discerned in the writings of this school, though both were concerned with the peaceful and piecemeal evolution of Canada to nationhood. The first of these mainly treated the achievement of responsible government and confederation, and on the whole was favourably disposed to things British, since leading historians like Chester Martin and R G. Trotter saw these national advances as being considerably aided by British advocacy and still as taking shape within the general framework of British institutions.[3] As this indicates, there was really no sharp break here between the Britannic and Nationhood schools, and contemporary opinion in Canada largely tended to think in terms both of national development and of maintaining some degree of connection with Britain. Yet gradually a watershed was being crossed, as more and more stress was laid on the winning of national rights. Thus came the second phase, which dealt primarily with the achievement of autonomy in external affairs, and the motto of most of its authors might well have been, A Canadian Citizen I will Die.

Sometimes, it is true, these historians might welcome the emergence of the new British Commonwealth as the concomitant of Canada's advance to nationhood.[4] But generally they were less friendly to British influences, and the nationalist note was clear, as in the writings of J. W. Dafoe or O. D. Skelton. British influences, in short, were largely equated with imperial leading strings, and the more nationalistic writers were ever on guard against imperialist designs to enmesh pure young Canada in a web of power politics – though one might wonder why gentlemen so keenly perceptive of the harsh realities of power in the European world could not recognize, in fixing their watchful eye on the British menace, that, after 1918, at least, the fearsome British lion had become rather a straw-stuffed beast. Still, this preoccupation with straw men or straw lions may perhaps be explained by the fact that much of their writing was done amidst the somewhat unreal atmosphere of Mackenzie King's bold crusade of the 1920's for Canada's right to have no foreign policy. And these authors were often strongly Liberal in sympathies. At times they seemed to write as if Canadian history was in essence a steady Liberal broadening-down of freedom to the ultimate end of national status – after which absolutely memorable History would come to a dead stop.[5]

Nevertheless the Political Nationhood group, first phase or second, did solid service in uncovering the process whereby Canada obtained the various attributes of self-government. Moreover, in stressing the theme of nationhood they were themselves expressing the basic truth that a society distinct from that of Britain had taken shape in Canada and was demanding recognition and the full right to manage its own affairs. As these historians, however, generally talked in political and constitutional terms, they did not effectively analyze the social, economic, and intellectual forces within North America which were creating a Canadian community increasingly conscious that it was far from being an overseas projection of Britain.

To fill this gap, a new school of historians began to take shape in the later 1920's, although it is important to note that its members were often closely related to the nationalist authors of the day. Indeed, this was nationalism in another sphere, seeking to demonstrate that Canadian desires for nationhood were rooted in the native North American environment: that Canadian institutions and viewpoints were not simply British, but were in their own way as American as those of the United States. The environment had done it. This, then, was the Environmentalist School, or North Americans All.

It was this group that built particularly on the concept of the frontier in North American history derived from Turner and his followers in the United States. The frontier, where man came most immediately into contact with the North American physical environment, was the great seed-bed for the growth of a truly North American society. From the start, as the United States and Canada had spread across the continent, environmental influences that first began on the frontier had worked to shape a native American character different from that of the Old World, left far behind. Here was the key principle to be applied by Canadian environmentalist historians: that thanks to the continuous process of adaptation to the environment, an American content had steadily grown in Canada within external forms of government, society, or culture inherited from Britain or France.[6]

It followed that Canadian history could be most fruitfully compared to that of the United States in its essentially North American nature and course of development. In pursuing this promising theme, however, these writers took over the general approach and mood of Turner and company – the frontier and its agrarian population as emblematic of native democratic, progressive, perhaps even of "Good" forces in the history of the continent – rather than the precise frontier thesis, which received little direct application in Canada. Yet because that original thesis was so powerful in its impact and so pervasive in its influence, it requires examination here; although, admittedly, the subject is hardly a new one.[7]

II

Turner had held in his frontier thesis that "the greatest formative influence" in American history had been the long existence of "the open frontier, the hither edge of free land," continually moving westwards.[8] The conditions of frontier society had determined the character of western institutions, and these in turn had reacted on the East. Out of the frontier, in fact, had come American individualism, democracy, inventiveness, coarseness, and idealism. Turner wrote that the seeds of American democracy were not carried to the New World in the *Mayflower* but sprang up out of the native forest. The effect of the frontier was to make Americans out of Europeans. In brief, the West was the true America, that ever taught the populous but effete East the American way of life.

This was environmental determinism at its most forthright. The wilderness and the men it produced had made America. Defenders of Turner might claim that he had not proposed a frontier hypothesis as the only key to American history, but it was widely seized upon as the true explanation, especially as its nationalist and romantic implications gripped the American imagination.[9] Its effects may still be found today, on different cultural levels in the United States. Indeed, it may not be irrelevant to note that Hollywood, that lowest common denominator of the American mind where myths are mass-produced, still pours forth a flood of highly technicoloured Westerns each purporting to touch the very soul of America, as some pioneer rugged individualist with iron hands and blazing guns "carves out an empire" for the nation at various points west, while Indians in their thousands from Central Casting Office go down before the onward march of democracy.

Of course Hollywood is a far cry from the academic world of history, and here there have been repeated and detailed criticisms of the frontier thesis as applied in the United States. Nevertheless the stimulus it gave to environmentalist – at times even isolationist – study of American history remained a powerful one. Moreover, a broad survey of the opinions of American historians made a little over a decade ago revealed that the majority would still accept the frontier thesis, with qualifications, although the trend seemed to be turning against it.[10] In this trend were men like Carleton Hayes, who asked, concerning the American frontier, "frontier of what?" and answered that America was essentially the western edge of European civilization. Accordingly, its story could be read as part of the expansion of Europe; and its culture and institutions should be studied not solely in national isolation as native products, but rather as elements transferred from Europe, adjusting – no doubt – to a somewhat different environment.[11]

Dixon Ryan Fox also pursued this theme of transfer, finding that the ideas and institutions transmitted from Europe bulked far larger in American development than any modifications of them or new contributions made on this side of the Atlantic. He observed, in fact, that ideas and institutions had steadily been carried west to the frontier, and considered that the East had far more shaped the West in America than *vice versa* – that the real story of the United States was the progressive turning of pioneer Wests into developed Easts.[12] Further in this vein, Arthur M. Schlesinger Jr. sought to demonstrate that the upsurge of Jacksonian Democracy, long regarded as the very incarnation and triumph of the free farming frontier, was instead far more strongly based amid the urban masses of the East.[13]

The frontiersmen among American historians have, however, struck back. One of them, W. P. Webb, has recently launched a most dazzling counter-attack on all fronts by proclaiming that the whole expansion of Europe since 1500 was one "Age of the Great Frontier."[14] He contends that most of modern Western European civilization as we know it, with its characteristic capitalism, democracy, and individualism, is the product of world frontiers that opened up to Europe when its peoples began to go adventuring across the oceans. He speaks of a four-hundred-year frontier boom, now ended, when Europe grew rich and developed the twin luxuries of freedom and the all-important individual, a boom that resulted from the "windfalls" of vast natural resources that were found in the empty Americas, Australasia, and South Africa. Europe became a dominating metropolis – a word we shall return to later – organizing, controlling, and exploiting these tremendous overseas frontiers, but in consequence having its development moulded by them.

How does all this relate to Canadian history? To some extent there have been similar stages in the use of the frontier interpretation, though these, indeed, might overlap. In the first stage, there were stimulating applications of frontierist themes and concepts to the Canadian half of the North American environment, seen most clearly perhaps in W. N. Sage's paper of 1928, "Some Aspects of the Frontier in Canadian History." This treated Canadian expansion across the continent as an integral part of a total North American frontier movement that ignored the international boundary.[15] Then there were the valuable investigations of F. H. Underhill into the nature of Canadian political parties, and especially the Clear Grit Liberal movement directed by George Brown and the Toronto *Globe*. With regard to Canadian parties, Professor Underhill traced their development according to conflicts between western agrarian areas and eastern business interests, in sound Turnerian fashion (1935).[16] With regard to the Clear Grits, he saw them as "an expression of the 'frontier' in Canadian politics" (1927).[17] E. H. Oliver applied frontierism to Canadian religious development, and in his *Winning the Frontier* (1930) depicted the Canadian churches as being moulded by a frontier environment.[18] Somewhat later A. S. Morton emphasized the dominant power of the environment in the extension of settlement into the Prairie West (1938).[19] And A. L. Burt effectively used a frontier interpretation to show how the people of New France were shaped by North American forces to become truly an indigenous people, not just a seeming copy of Old World "feudal" France (1940).[20]

In the second stage, there came criticisms and modifications of the frontier interpretation, although the environmentalist emphasis was still much in evidence.[21] A. R. M. Lower noted in a paper of 1930, "The Origins of Democracy in Canada," that "There can be little question but that American democracy had a forest birth." Yet he went on to assert that frontier equality might not result in political democracy unless "theoretical positions as to its nature" had already been projected into the frontier environment. In Canada's case, the egalitarian conditions of pioneer life had interacted with traditions brought from across the Atlantic; and Canadian democracy had developed more slowly than American because of Canada's briefer, more limited frontier experience, its stronger attachments to the Old World, and the long-enduring, overriding power of the imperial authority in government.[22] Nevertheless, despite this recognition of non-environmental, transferred influences, Professor Lower, in his *Colony to Nation* (1946) continued to stress the power of the New World "to change old institutions and give them new form and spirit"[23] North American democracy, he reiterated, was "forest-born." In short, though this was modification, environmentalism sprung from the frontier concept still remained strong.

In the third stage, as in the United States, new emphasis was given to the role of eastern rather than western forces in Canada, to urban interests and to the dominating power of the organizing, controlling metropolis. Thus Professor Underhill, for example, noted in 1946 that the original frontier agrarianism of the Clear Grits had subsequently been qualified by urban and business leadership introduced to the party by George Brown and other Toronto worthies.[24] And Professor Lower in his same *Colony to Nation* paid marked attention to the economic power wielded by metropolitan centres like Montreal and London, which, he made clear, did much to affect the course of events in raw Canadian settlements.[25] On another tack, Professor Fred Landon, in describing the frontier era in western Ontario, gave chief place to the transmitted influence of

American democratic ideas and practices rather than to actual frontier conditions in forming the outlook of the pioneer community.²⁶ But this only pushed the influence of the environment one stage back, to patterns of life worked out in the former frontier states below the Great Lakes. In any case it was evident that, despite qualifications and shifts of emphasis, environmentalism was still flourishing in Canadian history.

Still, it should be plain from this discussion that Canadian environmentalists did not generally follow any rigid frontier dogma and did show regard for other than native or western forces in analysing Canadian developments. After all, in a country which had obviously maintained many transatlantic ties and long continued as a colony there could not be as strong an assertion as in the United States of a separate North American growth in isolation from the world. And yet there was an inclination for environmentalists to see as much as possible of the history of Canada terms of common North American experience in driving back the wilds – to suggest that the really important features in Canada development had in truth been "forest-born"; in other words, that the various Wests had been the principal source of transforms energy and of national progress, in which they had pulled along and supported the conservative, exploitative East.

There was, moreover, a certain tendency to fix values. That pioneer society, the West, and simple farmers became virtuous and forward-looking to the beholder, while town society, the East, an. un-simple business men became selfish and reactionary. There might be an element of truth here, but moral overtones somewhat coloured the picture, so that western farmers who wanted free trade established in their interests were Good, while eastern business men who wanted a protective tariff enacted in theirs were Evil. Similarly, the West appeared as the true home of Canadianism, while the East, which worked out a distinctive Canadian economic nationalism in railway and tariff policy, was hardly Canada at all. No doubt powerful eastern business interests fattened themselves considerably through these arrangements. But could environmentalists properly become moral about business elements adjusting themselves to problems of the environment in their own way?

In sum, Canadian environmentalists frequently displayed the compelling mood of the frontier school, with its moral implications of a struggle between sound native democratic forces and elements that clung to privilege, exploitation, and empty Old-World forms. In so doing they often oversimplified a conflict between West and East, or better, between pioneer agrarian interests and exploitative urban centres. As a result, major Canadian movements for political change might be viewed too narrowly in the light of frontierism. For example, Upper Canadian radicalism of the 1830's, Clear Grit Liberalism of the mid-century, and Progressivism of the 1920's might all be explained in terms of the upsurge of the then newest West, as western forces of pioneer individualism launched crusades against privilege and urban business domination.[27] Yet it could also be shown that Mackenzie radicalism was probably more influenced by the working model of American political democracy and the ideas of British radicalism; that Clear Grittism was closely organized about the rising urban centre of Toronto; and that Western Progressivism was not based on self-sufficient pioneer farmers but on organized grain specialists engaged in a highly complex kind of agricultural business, whose goals involved not the triumph of individualism but the replacement of a set of unfavourable government controls centred in the tariff with another represented by Wheat Boards and government provision of major services.

Furthermore, it might well be a result of frontierism, sprung as it was from the mid-western heart of the continent, that a viewpoint characteristic of mid-western isolationism often appeared among environmentalist writers in Canada. Their view of the environment, like Turner's, was primarily continental. Thus it tended to neglect the influence of the seas beyond, the "maritime environment" that had always tied the continent to Europe. Canada might be treated as a northern extension of certain continental physiographic provinces, without due consideration of geographic and historic forces that had from the beginning of white penetration made this country an east-to-west projection from Europe. And logically it would follow that geography – in the continental sense only – had shaped Canada as a number of disparate American regions, held out of the American republic by mainly emotional forces and by the chance of history: in short, a loose grouping of less well-favoured, somewhat backward, American states. A rather paradoxical basis, this, for the nationalism environmentalists usually professed.

However, it is worth repeating that leading contemporary historians who have been referred to here in connection with the vigorous environmentalist phase of Canadian history have themselves, in more recent writings, not only shown awareness of the shortcomings of interpretations stemming from frontierism but have also done much to reconsider and to correct them. Nor, certainly, have their ideas ceased to develop beyond this one approach. None the less it may be hazarded that the effects of frontierist teachings remain strong today in suggesting for Canadian history, and doubtless for its readers, certain stereotypes about the dynamic West and the torpid East, and about the nature of Canada as a more restricted, backward version of the American model to the south. And frontierism may still leave a tendency to overvalue the influence of native North American forces and the material environment, and a tendency to undervalue forces transferred from Europe and the non-material environment: that of ideas, traditions and institutions. Yet these latter factors were particularly important in a portion of North America that did not undergo a revolutionary upheaval, emotional as well as political, to break ties with Europe, and which continued to place a special premium on the word "British" as applied to institutions and ideas. In fact, it is these very things which chiefly mark off the development of Canada from that of the United States. They give validity to the study of a separate Canadian history, one which is not just a counterpart of United States history in having a similar North American content.

Accordingly, while in no way underrating the very great contributions which frontierism and environmentalism have made to the understanding of Canada as a part of North America, it does seem necessary to look for a wider framework for Canadian history. But this, indeed, was already taking shape while the frontier interpretation was being usefully applied, and to a certain extent grew out of it, as an examination will show.

III

This next framework was in some ways a qualified version of environmentalism and in others the frontier concept reversed. It has appeared in most explicit form in the writings of D. G. Creighton, particularly in his *Commercial Empire of the St. Lawrence* (1938) and *Dominion of the North* (1944), but its foundations were laid in earlier works by H. A. Innis which broke rich new ground in Canadian economic history, notably *A History of the Canadian Pacific Railway* (1923) and *The Fur Trade in Canada* (1930). These studies of major Canadian economic enterprises, which were essentially great systems of continent-wide communications, pointed the way to a new general interpretation of Canadian history that would be forcefully developed by Professor Creighton.

His approach, in fact, has been said to establish a "Laurentian School" of Canadian historiography, since it largely rests on the idea that the long St. Lawrence water route and its connections across the continent became the basis of an extensive communications system around which Canada itself took shape. The commercial empire of the St. Lawrence, the broad domain of Montreal, first flung a Canadian fur trade across the continent, then competed vigorously with New York and the American seaboard through canal and railway enterprises for control of the trade of the mid-western heartlands of America, and finally built a new economic dominion across the northwestern plains to the Pacific that was, in fact, the Dominion of Canada. It followed that the existence of a separate Canada was not just a fortuitous result of the American Revolution, of French determination to survive, nor of Loyalist emotional resolves to "stay British" – despite the hard facts of the environment – nor again of the mere continuance of the imperial tie. It was also rooted in powerful factors of geography and commerce that underlay the whole Canadian development.

This, in a sense, was environmentalism, since the St. Lawrence was as real a feature of the North American environment as the North American forest, and a good deal more permanent. Environmentalists had stressed before that the main natural lines of North American geography ran north and south, linking the regions of Canada more effectively with their United States counterparts below the border than with their Canadian neighbours to east and west. But the St. Lawrence, the Great Lakes, the Saskatchewan, and the Fraser traced lines across the continent that were quite as natural; and, as the writings of Professors Innis and Creighton indicated, they made possible the east-to-west linking of Canadian regions from the earliest days of the fur trade, as communications spread by the lakes and river valleys from sea to sea. Perhaps we could even call this the Waterways School, especially since it made clear that the environment did not stop short at the Atlantic edge of North America. For the St. Lawrence system that funnelled traffic from the continental interior out to the sea was closely connected with British finance and markets across the waters in an east-west trading network that thus reached halfway around the world.[28]

Yet the Laurentian interpretation did not mean just a new emphasis on material environmentalism, since it also revealed that this huge communications and transport system could transfer immigrants, ideas, and impulses in one direct channel from Britain deep into the heart of the continent. As a result, the Ontario frontier of the earlier nineteenth century might actually be in closer contact with the sea and the mind of Europe than were the mid-western regions of the United States, more isolated behind the Appalachian barrier in a Mississippi Valley world of their own.

The Laurentian School, however, tended to go even further, and to reverse the earlier environmentalist position in this respect: it looked not from the forest-born frontiers for its perspective of Canadian history but from developing eastern centres of commerce and industry. Indeed, it primarily studied the effects of the East on the West, and largely regarded business men and conservative urban political elements as agents of national expansion who might well be more far-sighted in their outlook than were their agrarian opponents. Here then was a metropolitan rather than a frontier viewpoint. Moreover, this Laurentian view could be effectively linked with the monumental studies of H. A. Innis on the organization of the staple products trade of broad North American areas through costly and complex transport systems controlled in large urban centres.[29] The result was virtually to establish "metropolitanism" in Canadian historiography, the study of the role of metropolitan forces in this country, a vitalizing approach that may yet undergo considerable development.

Metropolitanism is at root a socio-economic concept that has already seen some application in Canadian history. As mentioned earlier, Professor Lower has made use of it in *Colony to Nation*, and elsewhere as well,[30] but it has been most closely applied in D. C. Masters' work, *The Rise of Toronto, 1850–1890* (1947).[31] In this he traced the rise of the city to a position of metropolitan dominance over Ontario, while at the same time it entered into vigorous competition with Montreal business interests for control of a broader Canadian hinterland. Toronto's climb to metropolitan stature is an instructive particular theme in Canadian history, but the rise of the metropolis in general is one of the most striking features of modern Western society. Briefly this implies the emergence of a city of outstanding size to dominate not only its surrounding countryside but other cities and their countrysides, the whole area being organized by the metropolis, through control of communications, trade, and finance, into one economic and social unit that is focussed on the metropolitan "centre of dominance" and through it trades with the world.[32] Political activity, too, may often become centred on the metropolis.

London and New York are of course the classic examples of modern metropolitanism. But the metropolitan relationship is a chain, almost a feudal chain of vassalage, wherein one city may stand tributary to a bigger centre and yet be the metropolis of a sizable region of its own. Thus, for example, Winnipeg is Montreal's subsidiary but is the metropolis of a large area of the prairie West. The Toronto metropolis is a subsidiary of both New York and Montreal, while Canada's main metropolitan centre, Montreal, has traditionally been bound to London. These facts are not new in themselves; but when it is remembered that the metropolitan pattern includes not only economic ties but social and cultural associations also, then many effective lines of inquiry may present themselves. For example, one might suggest that the survival of British customs sometimes noted in the English-speaking ruling class of Montreal, or Toronto's split personality, whereby it strives both to be a minor New York and to maintain its "British" character, may be comprehended through the weighing of various metropolitan connections and influences in these cities' history.

At present, however, the chief point to observe is that the rise of metropolitanism is the other side of the coin to frontier expansion. One may speak of the constant expansion of the frontier, or of the constant extension of the metropolitan power that is pushing out the frontier. What Webb called the "Age of the Great Frontier," might just as well be called the "Age of the Great Metropolis," when western Europe in general, by spreading out its system of communications and commerce, organized the world about itself. The age of this great European metropolis has passed away. Its predominant focus, London, has yielded in primacy of economic power to New York – though now there is no one main world metropolitan region, since, despite the rise of North America, Europe still maintains a vast overseas economic network, while a far-flung separate trading system is emerging in the Communist-dominated world.

Returning to the frontier itself, one might say that it is developed by a metropolitan centre of dominance which supplies its capital, organizes its communications and transport, and markets its products. The frontier's culture, too, originally stems from a metropolitan community; at root, learning and ideas radiate from there – and thus is Turner answered. True, there may be frontier religious movements, but these begin with preachers going out to the frontier and end in the focusing of the sect on the city.[33] The economic and cultural metropolitan processes go hand in hand, as newspapers, books, and men of education spread from the centre. Frontiers may often supply grievances for political movements. Urban centres as often supply the intellectual leadership; so that frontier demands take form at the hands of urban journalists and professional men.

It may be seen when this analysis is carried through that the frontier, far from being essentially independent and self-reliant, is in the largest sense a dependent. It constantly requires metropolitan aid and control, though by the same token it may come to resent and resist it. Frontier protest movements are a natural accompaniment of the extension of metropolitan power into new areas. The dynamic, organizing, hard-pressing forces of metropolitanism bring reaction on themselves. This may occur either at moments when the frontier as such is rapidly expanding, and full of problems of adjustment, or when it is actually declining; that is, becoming organized into a more mature and integrated region with a new metropolitan centre of its own, which hopes to wrest control of the local economy away from the older centre, and therefore gives voice and leadership to a regional protest movement.

How does this pattern fit Canadian history? No good historian would try to make it fit too exactly: if we reject a frontier determinism we should hardly replace it with a metropolitan determinism. Still, there may be an approach here as instructive for Canadian historiography as the frontier interpretation was in its day. For example, one might examine the unrest in Upper Canada in the 1830's, when this frontier area was rapidly expanding with the tide of British immigration, as a result of the vigorous extension of powerful business interests into a broad new domain, and of the spread of educated men and stimulating ideas from older communities, displayed notably in the rising power of the press and the journalist on the Upper Canada scene. On the other hand, the Clear Grit movement of the 1850's would appear as the organizing of the maturing western community around Toronto, the rising young metropolis, in a common campaign against the domination of the region by Montreal, the older centre. In this campaign Toronto supplied both intellectual leadership, in the form of the *Globe*, and strong party direction, in the form of George Brown and other wealthy and prominent business or professional men: the urban element was critically important. And as for Western Progressivism in the 1920's, was it not bound up with the rise of Winnipeg as a prairie metropolitan centre, was not a good deal of intellectual leadership centred in that city, and is there not evidence that here was a maturing western community now ready to contest outside metropolitan domination on a large scale?[34]

Metropolitanism can be seen operating even more clearly in Canadian history where there are no frontiers of actual settlement to block the view, so to speak, and by their undoubted colour and liveliness rather steal the centre of the stage. In the Canadian fur trade, from earliest French times on, the role of the dominant organizing metropolis is plain: Montreal and Quebec the metropolitan centres for the posts of the whole fur-trading West, Paris and later London the metropolis for these Canadian towns. On the Canadian lumbering and mining frontiers, in our present northern expansion, the directing, extending, organizing, and exploiting functions of metropolitan interests are evident once more. In fact metropolitanism has shown itself even more clearly in Canadian development than in American, precisely because we have had far less fertile acreage for agricultural settlement than has the United States. Hence the agrarian frontier of the sort that Turner described has played proportionately less part in our history. This, then, is a distinctive attribute of Canada's own version of the North American story.

Furthermore, in Canada, with its small population heavily concentrated in certain areas, metropolitan influences have had a particularly free sweep. The United States, of course, has much bigger metropolitan cities like Chicago, Philadelphia, and New York. But it also has many more large centres, each organizing its own region, though all ultimately subordinate to New York. Canada, however, has only three first-ranking metropolitan centres today: Montreal, the greatest, Vancouver, which by organizing effective communications has extended its hinterland eastward into the prairies, and Toronto, which controls wealthy southern Ontario and is steadily advancing its empire in the mining North. In Canada, therefore, metropolitan power is in comparison to the United States more directly centralized and more immediately apparent.

Historically speaking, the functioning of metropolitanism may do more to explain the course of Canadian history than concepts of frontierism borrowed from the United States and set forth before the significance of the modern metropolis was clear. For example, the greater conservatism of Canada as compared to the United States may be read as a mark of the much stronger influence exercised in this country by conservative-minded eastern urban centres

– which were certainly far removed from any impulses of forest democracy. Moreover, the stronger influence of British ideas and institutions – and even of colonialism – must have been fostered in Canada by its long and close focusing on the British metropolis itself. Finally, the fact that Canada has pioneered not so much in democracy as in the large-scale combination of public and private interests to overcome the problems raised by a difficult environment, again suggests the greater power throughout Canadian history of the forces seeking to organize communication systems and extend commerce. One might well say that the building of the C.P.R. so far ahead of settlement, and Macdonald's policies of economic nationalism in general, were plain manifestations of the power of metropolitan influences in Canadian politics. And many other instances might also be brought to mind.[35]

It could be objected with regard to some of the foregoing examples that applying a metropolitan interpretation only restates old problems in somewhat different terms. It may be so: but what is particularly needed is a restatement, a new perspective that may disclose new vistas and produce new patterns for Canadian history. At any rate, frontierism, along with earlier schools and approaches, has had its use and its day. Environmentalism needs recasting, and is being recast. The metropolitan approach largely recognizes what is already going on in Canadian historiography and provides a new framework – one which pays heed both to the distinctive features of the history of this country and to a notable modern phenomenon, the rise of metropolitanism all around the world.

Notes

1. It is worthy of note that the *Canadian Historical Review* for September, 1932 (XII, no. 3, 343), in recording the death of F. J. Turner in March of that year, observed: "His emphasis on the importance of the frontier was the greatest single influence in the re-interpretation of the history of the United States during the past generation. The application of his views to Canadian history has scarcely begun but it is safe to say that they will have a profound effect – perhaps not less in emphasizing the differences than the similarities in the development of the two countries."
2. William Kingsford, *The History of Canada* (10 vols., Toronto, 1887–98). For his declaration of purpose, see particularly the prefaces to volumes VII, VIII, and X. Other historians who might be named to the Britannic school are Sir George Parkin, J. C. Dent, A. G. Bradley, Archibald MacMechan, and James Hannay, Of the works of the last-named, see especially

How Canada Was Held for the Empire: The Story of the War of 1812 (Toronto, 1905), a later edition of his *War of 1812* (1901), whose very title is significant.

3   See especially Chester Martin, *Empire and Commonwealth* (Oxford, 1929) and R. G. Trotter, *Canadian Federation* (Toronto, 1924). Others who might be considered members of this school are Adam Shortt, in his writings outside the specialized field of economic history, William Smith, G. E. Wilson, D. C. Harvey, Chester New, and perhaps G. M. Wrong. It will be seen, of course, that one school may overlap another in point of time, and draw its members from more than one generation. It bears repeating, however, that no attempt will or can be made to classify all major historians in one school or another. Some by virtue of fairly specialized subject-matter may defy a broad classification, despite the importance of their work. Scholars primarily concerned with the French regime, the federal system, or regional developments, for example, may not fit easily into a general school, though some aspects of their writings may suggest a possible affiliation. Then again, some authors may display elements of more than one school. In this regard, the imposing figure of G. M. Wrong seems to stand between the Britannic and Nationhood schools, and indeed suggests the transition from one to the other. Professor Wrong assuredly wrote with a consciousness of developing Canadian nationalism. But perhaps the "Britannic" element in his thought was well expressed in these words from an article of 1920 discussing the sometimes difficult advances made by Dominion nationalism during the First World War: "Yet in spite of this the British peoples were one. Probably we tend in smooth and easy days to underestimate the effects of the deep roots of unbroken tradition which nourish the life of a nation. The liberties of Canada have come, not without struggle, slowly from precedent to precedent based on parallel changes within Britain herself. It is the same in Australia. What these young states thus prize most in their own life is what Britain herself prizes most and it has involved no rupture of the long past or with the parent state. There is among all of them a continued unity in tradition and in political development." *Canadian Historical Review*, I, no. 1, "Canada and the Imperial War Cabinet," 23.

4   For example, W. P. M. Kennedy. See particularly his many reviews of the 1920's, and annual review articles of the earlier 1930's, in the *Canadian Historical Review* on aspects of imperial constitutional law and Canada's relations therewith.

5   See particularly J. W. Dafoe, *Laurier, a Study in Canadian Politics* (Toronto, 1922), and *Canada, an American Nation* (New York, 1935); and O. D. Skelton, *The Life and Letters of Sir Wilfrid Laurier* (2 vols., Toronto, 1921). See also, of course, the work of J. S. Ewart, who although a lawyer – as Dafoe was an editor, and Skelton became a civil servant – no less followed a nationalist historical approach in dealing with questions of autonomy. Writers of the young *Canadian Forum* "school," rather left of Liberalism, also expressed a deep suspicion of British imperial entanglements. (See the unpublished M.A. thesis by Margaret Prang at the University of Toronto, 1953, "Some Aspects of Political Radicalism in Canada between the Two World Wars.") Others less nationalist in tone but still notably concerned with Canada's developing autonomy were A. G. Dewey *(The Dominions and Diplomacy,* 2 vols., London, 1929) and R. M. Dawson (ed. and introd. to *Development of Dominion Status, 1900–36,* Toronto, 1937). G. P. Glazebrook and F. H. Soward might also be mentioned as later "affiliates" of this school, but only in the sense that they did valuable work in its field of primary

interest, the development of Canadian external relations, rather than that they carried on its earlier mood of eager nationalism.

6 The work of this school will be discussed in detail in subsequent pages, but for now let it be said that, at one time or another, its membership might be held to include W. B. Munro, F. H. Underhill, W. N. Sage, A. R. M. Lower, F. Landon, A. S. Morton, and A. L. Burt. Qualifications will of course be necessary, but at any rate the above authors made good use of frontier-environmentalist concepts in various writings, whatever else they may also have done. Furthermore, J. B. Brebner worked in the environmentalist vein to some extent, and might be regarded as an "affiliate" of this school during much of the 1930's, while W. L. Morton might be deemed a somewhat later affiliate. It should be plain that no tight determinism is intended in thus naming these authors, nor, on the whole, did they display any. Yet the influence of environmentalism upon them may well be remarked, and hence it seems instructive to try to class them in this fashion for the purposes of this paper, even though many of them might subsequently move on to different perspectives when the peak of the Environmentalist School had passed.

7 See M. Zaslow, "The Frontier Hypothesis in Recent Historiography," *Canadian Historical Review*, XXIX, no. 2, 1948, for a fairly recent examination.

8 Turner's thesis was first embodied in his paper, "The Significance of the Frontier in American History," read before the American Historical Association in 1893, and ultimately reprinted in his *Frontier in American History* (New York, 1920). I am indebted here to the succinct description of Turnerism in G. F. G. Stanley's paper, "Western Canada and the Frontier Thesis," *Canadian Historical Association Report*, 1940, 105. See also Zaslow, "The Frontier Hypothesis,"' 154–55.

9 See F. L. Paxson, "A Generation of the Frontier Hypothesis, 1893–1932," *Pacific Historical Review*, II, no. 1, 1933, and also H. N. Smith, *Virgin Land: The American West as Symbol and Myth* (Cambridge, 1950), especially the concluding chapter on Turner.

10 G. W. Pierson, "American Historians and the Frontier Hypothesis in 1941," *Wisconsin Magazine of History*, XXVI, nos. 1 and 2, 1942.

11 C. J. H. Hayes, "The American Frontier – Frontier of What?" *American Historical Review*, LI, no. 2, 1946.

12 D. R. Fox, *Ideas in Motion* (New York, 1935). See also his introduction to *Sources of Culture in the Middle West* (D. R. Fox, ed., New York, 1934).

13 A. M. Schlesinger, Jr., *The Age of Jackson* (Boston, 1945).

14 W. P. Webb, *The Great Frontier* (Boston, 1953).

15 *Canadian Historical Association Report*, 1928. See also M. L. Hansen and J. B. Brebner, *The Mingling of the Canadian and American Peoples* (Toronto, 1940), for a general integration of Canadian settlement into the whole theme of North American frontier expansion. Professor Brebner also followed this approach in his essay, "The Survival of Canada," in *Essays in Canadian History Presented to G. M. Wrong* (R. Flenley, ed., Toronto, 1939). In this he ascribed Canadian survival to the cross-pulls of American sectionalism and to the British connection rather than "predominantly to Canadian resistance," so that the emergence of a Canadian nation was largely an externally produced modification of the general North American process of settlement: for, "... to the student of population the settled regions of Canada, with the great exception of Quebec, appear on the whole to be outward projections

of the settled regions of the United States ... rather than interlocked units of a separate people which has systematically expanded its occupation from Atlantic to Pacific" (272–73).

16 F. H. Underhill, "The Development of National Political Parties in Canada," *Canadian Historical Review*, XVI, no. 4, 1935. See also W. B. Munro, *American Influences on Canadian Government* (Toronto, 1929), for the influence of frontier environment on party organization and politics.

17 F. H. Underhill, "Some Aspects of Upper Canadian Radical Opinion in the Decade before Confederation," *Canadian Historical Association Report*, 1927, 47. See also G. W. Brown, "The Grit Party and the Great Reform Convention of 1859," *Canadian Historical Review*, XVI, no. 3, 1935.

18 E. H. Oliver, *The Winning of the Frontier* (Toronto, 1930).

19 A. S. Morton, *History of Prairie Settlement* (Canadian Frontiers of Settlement, VII, part 1, Toronto, 1938). See also, but to lesser extent because of its largely pre-settlement theme, A. S. Morton, *A History of the Canadian West to 1870–1* (Toronto, 1939). The attention paid to environmental forces at this period is well suggested by the whole Canadian Frontiers of Settlement series of the later thirties, a nine-volume project under the Canadian Pioneer Problems Committee, begun in 1934.

20 A. L. Burt, "The Frontier in the History of New France," *Canadian Historical Association Report*, 1940. See also his *Short History of Canada for Americans* (Minneapolis, 1942), 23–31. In a more recent work, however, his presidential address before the Canadian Historical Association, "Broad Horizons" (*Report*, 1950), Professor Burt sought a broadening of approach, beyond the continent of North America, to take in Canada's background in imperial history. And he noted that wider views in history had largely been replaced in Canada after the First World War by a heavy concentration on developments in the narrowly Canadian scene, thanks to "the rising tide of Canadian nationalism" – a statement which might well sum up the whole environmentalist phase. See also his study, *The United States, Great Britain, and British North America from the Revolution to the Establishment of Peace after the War of 1812* (Toronto, 1940), which rejects a frontier expansionist view of the causes of the War of 1812, stressing rather the maritime clashes between Britain and the United States.

21 Examples of criticism of the application of the frontier thesis to Canada are J. L. McDougall, "The Frontier School and Canadian History," *Canadian Historical Association Report*, 1929, and G. F. G. Stanley, "Western Canada and the Frontier Thesis."

22 *Canadian Historical Association Report*, 1930, 66–70. "It must therefore be a modified or adapted version of the [Turner] thesis which can be fitted to Canada" (66). See also Professor Lower's paper, "Some Neglected Aspects of Canadian History," *Canadian Historical Association Report*, 1929, 67–68. These articles indicate that from the start, so to speak, the author was concerned about the weight to be given to tradition and political structure as well as to environment in explaining the course of Canadian history.

23 *Colony to Nation* (Toronto, 1946), 48–49. See also J. B. Brebner, "Canadian and North American History," *Canadian Historical Association Report*, 1931, in which the author noted the "identities of contour between Canadian history and North American" produced by the continental environment (42), but also remarked on points of difference, for example, in the administration of justice, where "The frontier theory of North American history, that

enthusiastic elaboration of Prof. F. J. Turner's reasonable suggestions, obviously will not serve" (45).

24   F. H. Underhill, "Some Reflections on the Liberal Tradition in Canada," *Canadian Historical Association Report*, 1946.

25   *Colony to Nation*, 198–200. See also Professor Lower's *North American Assault on the Canadian Forest* (Toronto, 1938), in which organizing, dominating, metropolitan economic forces are shown in action in the forest environment. Another significant volume bearing on the relation of frontier areas to urban business interests is his earlier *Settlement and the Forest Frontier in Eastern Canada* (Canadian Frontiers of Settlement, IX, part 1, Toronto, 1936).

26   Fred Landon, *Western Ontario and the American Frontier* (Toronto, 1941).

27   Note, for example, W. L. Morton, "Direct Legislation and the Origins of the Progressive Movement," *Canadian Historical Review*, XXV, no. 3, 1944: "It [Pro-gressivism] was the latest upsurge of agrarian and frontier democracy" (279).

28   The growing emphasis on "maritime factors" in Canadian and indeed North American history was a major development of the 1940's that extended and greatly recast environmentalist thinking, or – as it might also be put – marked the transition to a newer, wider interpretation of Canadian history. Perhaps the growing recognition of "extra-continental" forces could be linked to the impact of the Second World War, which sharply checked isolationist tendencies in Canadian thought, as the outside world was borne in upon it: a different result from that of the First World War, already noted, which enhanced a rather inward-looking nationalism. The significance of broad strategic factors, many of imperial or at least extra-continental origin, was newly observed in Canadian history, largely owing to the rise of a "military" school, if the name be permitted, in which the rather neglected military and naval side of Canadian development were dealt with by such historians as C. P. Stacey, G. S. Graham, and G. N. Tucker. On the primarily economic side, H. A. Innis' *The Cod Fisheries* (Toronto, 1940) was of critical importance in showing the Atlantic not as a dividing waste of waters but as a linking network of waterways that served an international and intercontinental economy. As Dr. J. T. Shotwell said in its preface, "it extends the frontiers of North America over a vast area that we have never thought of before as constituting a part – and a fundamental part – of the continent." In more general terms than just the economic, G. W. Brown had answered the question of whether the Americas had a common history by asserting that they had, as integral parts of an Atlantic world ("Have the Americas a Common History? A Canadian View," *Canadian Historical Review*, XXIII, no. 2, 1942). And J. B. Brebner, in closing and climaxing the great Carnegie series of studies in Canadian-American relations with his *North Atlantic Triangle* (Toronto, 1945), had found, strikingly enough, that his original plan to "set forth the interplay between Canada and the United States" had had to be extended to take in transatlantic influences stemming from Britain – and thus his significant title. His book was of double importance. Not only did it markedly reveal the transfer of forces and culture across the Atlantic lake and around the great triangle of Britain, the United States, and Canada; it also indicated that a massive set of studies on Canadian-American relations, whose very inception in the early thirties expressed the then-current concern with North American environmentalism, had ended in the forties in a new awareness of forces that reached far beyond the continental limits. Certainly a new approach to Canadian and North American historiography was taking shape.

29 See, as well as works of Professor Innis already cited, *Problems of Staple Production in Canada* (Toronto, 1933); *Settlement and the Mining Frontier* (Canadian Frontiers of Settlement, IX, part 2, Toronto, 1936); "Transportation as a Factor in Canadian Economic History/' *Proceedings of the, Canadian Political Science Association*, 1931; and "Significant Factors in Canadian Economic Development," *Canadian Historical Review*, XVIII, no. 4, 1937.

30 See note 25 above. Also, for a stimulating outline of the roles of Canadian metropolitan centres, Montreal, Toronto and Vancouver, and their competition for "hinterlands," see Professor Lower's essay, "Geographical Determinants in Canadian History," in *Essays Presented to G. M. Wrong*, 245–51. Indeed, he discerns in the whole pattern of Canadian economic development, "the characteristic expression of the staple trade, the metropolitan-hinterland relationship" ("Two Ways of Life: The Primary Antithesis of Canadian History," *Canadian Historical Association Report*, 1943, 13).

31 Professor Masters here applies the concept of economic metropolitan dominance put forward by N. S. B. Gras in his *Introduction to Economic History* (New York, 1922) though he extends it as well to social and cultural fields. According to Gras, a city rises to metropolitan dominance over a hinterland region through four stages: first, it creates a well-organized marketing system for the whole area; second, manufacturing develops in the metropolis or the hinterland; third, there is an active programme of transportation development; and fourth, a mature financial system is constructed to provide for the trade both with the hinterland and with the outside world (See preface to *The Rise of Toronto*, Toronto, 1947).

32 See C. A. Dawson and W. E. Gettys, *An Introduction to Sociology* (New York, 1948), 154–71.

33 S. D. Clark, *Church and Sect in Canada* (Toronto, 1949), especially 90–173.

34 W. L. Morton, in his admirable recent study, *The Progressive Party in Canada* (Toronto, 1950), has written of the whole Progressive movement in strongly western environmental terms. Yet while interpreting Progressivism in the light of a frontier agrarian background, he has also showed awareness of the impact of metropolitan forces throughout. See also the foreword to this volume by S. D. Clark, noting that this western sectional protest ended by "becoming accommodated to the power structure of the metropolitan-federal system" (ix).

35 It has been said by J. B. Brebner that "the most substantial Canadian nationalism in time of peace has been economic nationalism" ("Canadianism," *Canadian Historical Association Report*, 1940, 8), and others, such as W. S. MacNutt, have echoed that view (see his letter to the editors of the *Canadian Historical Review*, XXXIV, no. 1, 1953, 108). Since economic nationalism is pre-eminently the result of metropolitan forces, it might appear that the way to the "national" heart of Canadian development, if that is a desirable goal, lies not through the frontiers of field and forest, where the environmentalists sought it, but rather through the metropolitan approach.

Bibliographic Essay

In 1987, the summer before I began graduate school, I picked up a book by one of my future advisors. Howard Lamar and Leonard Thompson's work, *The Frontier in History: North America and South Africa Compared*, draws a comparison between the American West (meaning the United States) and South Africa.[1] The concept intrigued me, particularly because I saw many parallels between the settling of the western United States and what little I knew of the colonial administration of India. A book that compared such seemingly disparate entities as the North American West and South Africa appealed to me.

Initially, the book disappointed me. The authors did not provide a comparative narrative. Instead, they organized the book around common themes and alternated chapters between the two areas chosen. And because it is not a comparative narrative, much of the comparative analysis falls to the reader to tease out. I did not realize at the time that graduate programs did not train people around questions but rather around countries or regions within countries. This narrow geographical training in turned hampered people from exploring beyond their regions or geographic areas. Lamar and Thompson attempted to solve this problem by co-authoring a book so that each could represent the side they knew best.

Despite my initial disappointment, I have referred back to the book over the years. The individual essays themselves provide much context for the two areas. And the comparison, while not explicit, works in the sense that both authors saw and say new things about their areas as they see similarities and differences between the two areas. Lamar and Thompson see similarities between the indigenous populations, between the colonial administrations, and between the settlers that would be lost without the comparison. Therefore, this work underscores one of the main reasons for doing comparative work: it helps you see what might be hidden in a non-comparative context.

In 1994, James O. Gump wrote *The Dust Rose like Smoke: The Subjugation of the Zulu and the Sioux*.[2] Like Lamar and Thompson, he compares the United States' West to South Africa. But unlike them, he creates a comparative narrative and narrows the regions to the homelands as defined by the indigenous peoples involved: the Sioux and the Zulu. This methodology, though, invited criticism that such narrowly defined regions are not representative of the larger countries or national trends. But as we will see below, historians of the borderlands will tell you national trends may not matter as much as regional ones.

There are two very basic methodologies for setting up a comparison. One is to choose cases that appear to be similar and examine the differences. The other is to choose cases that appear to be different and examine the similarities. In both cases, the comparison should yield a new understanding of each of the original cases. The problem is: who defines what is different and what is similar? In the case of Lamar and Thompson, it would seem that everyone would agree that North America and South Africa are very different cases: geographically, culturally, politically, historically. But what happens when you choose cases that some people perceive as similar where you perceive them as different, or vice versa?

For those of us who study either the Canada-U.S. West or the Mexico-U.S. comparisons, this problem crops up continuously. In the case of Canada and the United States, many people think of the nations as basically the same: democracies, Anglo-European heritage, capitalist, etc. But for historians and others, they seem radically different. The Mexico-U.S. comparison has the opposite problem: they seem radically different and people are loath to admit to similarities. Some historians have taken these preconceptions on head-first. Roger Nichols and his work *Indians in the United States and Canada*, and Jill St. Germain and her book *Indians Treaty-Making Policy in the United States and Canada* both examine Canadian and United States policy and actions toward the Indians.[3] Both point out the similarities between the two countries when it comes to settlement policy and policy toward Indians. And through that assumption of similarity, both see important differences and, most important, new similarities that have been missed in the past. Nichols seeks to provide a broad overview of Canadian and U.S. interactions with Indians since colonial days. He writes on cogent comparative narrative that leads the reader back and forth across the border. St. Germain focuses her study more narrowly both through her subject and her chronology. She focuses on a ten-year period

(1867–77) and teases out how Canadian and U.S. policy become more similar when starting from different points and arguing for different outcomes. Again, a comparative narrative leads the reader through the complexities of the two countries' interrelationship with native peoples.

Both Nichols and St. Germain treat the border as a hard boundary between Canada and the United States because the actors they are interested in, governments, treat the border in that manner. In reality, historians know that people, goods, ideas, rivers and weather all flow over borders as if they do not exist. Therefore, when one studies the border between Canada and the U. S. or Mexico and the U. S. comparative history begins to become transnational or borderlands history as well.

Several books illustrate this phenomenon. My own work, *Noble, Wretched and Redeemable*, while comparing Protestant missionaries in Canada and the United States and their attitudes toward Indians, uncovered a transnational image of the Indian.[4] In other words, by comparing how Protestant missionaries in the two countries portrayed Indians in their writings, I found that they depicted Indians in similar ways and actually read and copied each other's works. Ideas and images flowed over borders. As far as Protestant missionaries were concerned, the "heathen" frontier did not possess a nation-state border, just a moral one. Thus, comparison can highlight a transnational trend.

But when does something transnational become a borderland issue? Or when is something a comparative history versus a borderlands history versus a transnational history? A comparative history can be a borderlands study and/or a transnational history. Through comparison of two adjacent countries, a borderlands can be explored or a transnational trend or theme discovered. But a borderlands history does not have to be comparative nor does a transnational history.

One of the earliest comparative/borderlands histories is Paul Sharp's *Whoop-Up Country*[5]. In some ways, it has become a contested text. To some scholars, it is one of the first borderlands books. To others, it is an early example of comparative work. In my mind, it is both. While looking at the whiskey trade between Canada and the United States, he explores how the two countries tried to regulate it and exploit it while establishing that there was a place called "Whoop-Up Country" that straddled the border. Studying the whiskey trade only in Canada or only in the United States would not have yielded such an interesting answer or conclusion.

What it comes down to is definitions. In the past few years, several historians have produced excellent comparative works that are grounded in the study of the borderlands. The trick is that they have looked outside of the nation-state paradigm to do it. Hana Samek's work, *The Blackfoot Confederacy*, represents a first attempt at reconstructing the border through other player's eyes and definitions.[6] In her study of the Blackfoot Confederacy, she lets the Blackfoot provide the definition of what is the border, not Canada or the United States. For the Confederacy, the border existed merely as speed bump, not an impediment, until they developed conflicts with the powers that respected and enforced the border: Canada and the United States. By letting historical actors define the term and usage of "border," she was able to study a culture and society that revolved around a border without being limited or dominated by it.

Other authors employed this methodology as well. Beth LaDow makes a similar argument about the Sioux and their treatment of the border.[7] By letting individual actors define the border, not governments or historians, these scholars help illuminate and embrace the complexity of borderland communities. Borderlands both help and confuse comparisons. The similarities may make it seem as if the border does not matter until one demonstrates that to the people involved the border meant something. It is much like comparing cousins: same gene pool, different results. And Sheila McManus has shown us that national expectations as to how a region should act may not play out in that region.[8] By tracing the transition from Blackfoot country to borderlands, McManus discovered that definitions of space, race and gender followed borderland areas, not national boundaries.

As you will see in the list below, comparisons come in all shapes and sizes. Some are regional, some are national, some are cultural, some are political. All open our eyes to new ideas we had not seen or thought of before. Though we may not always agree with their conclusions, these authors at least challenge us to view the world through multiple lenses rather than just the one we usually carry around.

Comparative Frontiers: World

Allen, H. C. *Bush and Backwoods: A Comparison of the Frontier in Australia and the United States*. Westport, CT: Greenwood Press, 1975.

Dunlap, Thomas. *Nature and the English Diaspora*. Cambridge: Cambridge University Press, 1999.

Frederickson, George. *White Supremacy: A Comparative Study in American and South African History*. Oxford: Oxford University Press, 1981.

Gump, James O. *The Dust Rose Like Smoke: The Subjugation of the Zulu and the Sioux*. Lincoln: University of Nebraska Press, 1994.

Hartz. Louis. *The Founding of New Societies: Studies in the history of the United States, Latin America, South Africa, Canada, and Australia*. New York: Harcourt, Brace and World, 1964.

Lamar, Howard and Leonard Thompson. *The Frontier in History: North America and South Compared*. New Haven: Yale University Press, 1981.

Paullada, Stephen. *Rawhide and Song: A Comparative Study of the Cattle Cultures of the Argentina Pampas and North American Great Plains*. New York: Vantage Press, 1963.

Slatta, Richard. *Comparing Cowboys and Frontiers*. Norman: University of Oklahoma Press, 1997.

Comparative Frontiers: Canada and the United States

Bennett, John and Seena Kohl. *Settling the Canadian-American West, 1890–1915*. Lincoln: University of Nebraska Press, 1995.

Findlay, John M. and Ken S. Coates, *Parallel Destinies: Canadian-American Relations West of the Rockies*. Seattle/Montreal: University of Washington Press/McGill-Queen's University Press, 2002.

Evans, Sterling, ed. *The Borderlands of the American and Canadian Wests: Essays on Regional History of the Forty-ninth Parallel*. Lincoln: University of Nebraska Press, 2006.

Higham, C. L. *Noble, Wretched and Redeemable: Protestant Missionaries to the India in Canada and the United States, 1820–1900*. (Albuquerque/Calgary: University of New Mexico Press/University of Calgary Press, 2000

LaDow, Beth. *The Medicine Line: Life and Death on a North American Borderlands*. New York: Routledge, 2002.

McManus, Sheila. *The Line Which Separates: Race, Gender, and the Making of the Alberta-Montana Borderlands*. Lincoln: University of Nebraska Press, 2005.

Nichols, Roger. *Indians in the United States and Canada: A Comparative History*. Lincoln: University of Nebraska Press, 1998.

Samek, Hana. *The Blackfoot Confederacy, 1880-1920: A Comparative Study of Canadian and United States Indian Policy*. Albuquerque, NM: University of New Mexico Press, 1987.

Sharp, Paul. *Whoop-Up Country: The Canadian-American West, 1865–1885*. Helena, MT: Historical Society of Montana, 1960.

St. Germain, Jill. *Indian Treaty-Making Policy in the United States and Canada, 1867–1877*. Lincoln: University of Nebraska Press, 2001.

Notes

1 Howard Lamar and Leonard Thompson, *The Frontier in History: North America and Southern Africa Compared* (New Haven, CT: Yale University Press, 198?).

2 James Gump, *The Dust Rose Like Smoke: The Subjugation of the Zulu and the Sioux*. (Lincoln: University of Nebraska Press, 1994.)

3 Roger Nichols, *Indians in the United States and Canada: A Comparative History* (Lincoln: University of Nebraska Press, 1998.); Jill St. Germain, *Indian Treaty-Making in the Untied States and Canada, 1867–1877* (Lincoln: University of Nebraska Press, 2001).

4 C. L. Higham, *Noble, Wretched and Redeemable: Protestant Missionaries to the Indians in Canada and the United States, 1820–1900*. (Albuquerque/Calgary: University of New Mexico Press/University of Calgary Press, 2000).

5 Paul Sharp, *Whoop-Up Country: The Canadian-American West, 1865–1885* (Helena, MT: Historical Society of Montana, 1960).

6 Hana Samek, *The Blackfoot Confederacy, 1880–1920: A Comparative Study of Canadian and U. S. Indian policy* (Albuquerque, NM: University of New Mexico Press, 1987).

7 Beth LaDow, *The Medicine Line: Life and Death on a North American Borderlands* (New York: Routledge, 2000).

8 Sheila McManus, *The Line that Separates: Race, Gender, and the Making of the Alberta-Montana Borderlands* (Lincoln, NE: University of Nebraska Press, 2005).

Index

Aboriginals/aboriginal women (nations/people), 86
  government policies, 92–95
  and La Verendrye, 134–35
Adams, John Quincy, 181–82
Administration, system of, 181
Albany congress of 1754, 174
Alberta (southern), 32, 33, 34, 35, 51, 54–55n9, 97
  Calgary Stampede, 36
  homestead regulations, 107
  oil boom, 75
  and Russell, 37
Alleghanies (Alleghany Mountains), 169, 170
Allen, John L., 1, 6
American and Canadian Wests, historiographies/histories of, 15, 109
American character, 16–17
American development, 166
American heroes/mythic Western figures, 149
American historians and frontier thesis, 198–99
American Homestead Act, 105
American institutions, peculiarity of, 165–66
Anderson, Benedict, 74
Anti-American sentiments, 100–103
Arizona, 117

Army posts, 175
Asbury, Kelly, 139
Aspdin, Mary, 92–93, 94
Aspdin, Thomas, 92, 93
Assiniboine Massacre, Cypress Hills, 8
Assiniboines, 134
Atherton, Lewis, 33
Atlantic (frontier, the), 170, 171, 213n28
Atwood, Margaret, 10
Audubon, John James, 88, 89

Babel, Tower of, 25–26
Barrows, John R., 33, 56n11
Beadle, Erastus, 147, 149
Beecher, Lyman, 187–88
Benton, Thomas, 181, 187
Berger, Carl, 72
Berton, Pierre, 3
Beveridge, R.W., Rev., 106–7, 108
"Big Four," 35, 36, 39
Binnie-Clark, Georgina, 104–5, 106
Blackfoot, 87–88, 218
Blackfoot Confederacy, 218
"Blood-and-thunder romances"/dime westerns, 147
Blood Indians. *See* Kainai
Blood Meridian, 5
Boone, Daniel, 144, 147, 176
Border, 218
Borderland issue/history, 217

223

Borderlands, 218
Borein, Edward, 36
The Boy's Own Annual, 59n29
Bradley, A.G., 99
Brebner, J.B., 76
Britain (Britannia)/British (tradition, cultural heritage, influences), 32, 67–68, 96–97, 195–96. *See also* England/English
Britannic School, Canadian history, 194–95
Bronco, 41–43
Brown, George, 199, 207
Bryant, William Cullen, 47
Buffalo Bill (Hon. William F.) Cody, 146, 147
Buntline, Ned, 147, 149
Burns, Patrick, 39
Burt, A.L, 200, 212n20
Bush, George W., 76, 149

Calgary Stampede, 35–39
  and Indians, 45
  parade, 51, 153–52
Canada, eastern forces in, 200
Canada in the Twentieth Century, 99
Canada–U.S. West comparisons, 216–17
Canadian and American Wests, historiographies/histories of, 15, 109
Canadian Dominion Lands Act, 105–7
Canadian history, "maritime factors," 213n28
Canadian history, schools of, 194, 210n3
  Britannic, 194–95
  Environmentalist, 197–203
  Laurentian, 204–5
  Metropolitanism, 205–9
  School of Political Nationhood, 195–96
Canadian National Railway, 50–51
Canadian Pacific Railway, 19, 71, 203

Captivity narratives, 99–103
Cardinal, Harold, 117
Careless, J.M.S., 17–18, 19–20
  metropolitan-hinterland paradigm, 20, 69, 70–71
Carson, Kit, 144
Cartier, Jacques, 22
Cather, Willa, 31
Catlin, George, 2, 3, 5, 6–7, 8, 11
  Indian Gallery, 45–46, 49
Cattle industry/trade, 33, 57n14, 140
Cavanaugh, Catherine, 95–96
Centralized control, Canada. *See* Metropolitanism/metropolitan centers (of dominance)
Character (consciousness)
  American, 16–17
  national, 143
  and environment/geography, 72, 73
Chuckwagon (races, racing), 153, 154–55, 157–58, 161–62
Civilization, North American (as) an extension of European civilization, 18
Clark, William/Lewis and Clark expedition, 1, 2, 3–4, 131
Clay, Henry, 181, 182
Clear Grit Liberal movement/Clear Grits, 199, 202, 207
Coburn, Wallace, 41
Coburn, Walt, 33, 56n12
Cody, Hon. William F. *See* Buffalo Bill Cody
Colonial life and European development, 171
Colony to Nation, 200
Combet, Denis, 134
Communications and transport systems, 203, 204–5
Comparative history (narrative, histories, work)/comparisons, 215–18. *See*

also Native peoples' experience, comparative history
Composite nationality, 178–79, 182–83
Continentalist myth, 127
Cook, Lorna, 139
Cooper (Russell), Nancy, 37
Cooper, James Fenimore, 4, 149
Cooperation, 129
Country Born/"half-breed"/Métis, 122–23, 135
Cowboy(s)/cowhands, 34, 35, 140–41
   Barrows, 56n11
   ideal/mythic figure, 41–45
   and moving pictures, 147–48
   Remington, 40, 41–44
   respectable, 55n10
   Russell, 38
Cowboy Sport—Roping a Wolf, 34–35, 57–58n17
Crane, Stephen, 145
Crawford, Max, 116
Cree, 90
Creighton, Donald G., 17, 203–4
Cross-border work/scholarship. *See* Native peoples' experience, comparative history
Culbertson, Alexander, 86–89, 91
Custer Died for Your Sins, 117
Cypress Hills Assiniboine Massacre, 8

Dafoe, J.W., 196
Damon, Matt, 139
Davis, Richard Harding, 146
Dawes Severalty Act, 94
Delaney, Theresa, 103
Deloria, Vine, Jr., 117
Democracy, growth of, and frontier, 184–86
Development
   American, 166
   European, and colonial life, 171
   social, frontier, comparative study of, 170–72
Dime westerns/"blood-and-thunder romances," 147
Dippie, Brian W., 6–7
Dominant images of the West, 144
Dominion (of Canada), 67, 72, 204. *See also* Canadian Dominion Lands Act
Dust Rose like Smoke, The: The Subjugation of the Zulu and the Sioux, 216

East
   efforts to regulate the frontier, 187–88
   and West, 199, 201–2, 205
Eastern forces in Canada, 200
Eastwood, Clint, 147, 160
Educated Imagination, The, 25–26
Educational and religious activity, 187–88
Elofson, Warren, 33
Emerson, Ralph Waldo/Emersonian, 129, 130
End of the Trail, The, 46
England/English (Englishmen), 182
   authorities/government, attempts to check and regulate the frontier, 186–87
   dependence on, 179–80
   in the West, the, 55n9. *See also* Britain (Britannia)/British
The Englishman's Boy, 8–10, 11
Environmentalism/environmentalists, 200, 201–3, 204–5, 213n28
Environmentalist School, Canadian history, 197–203
Europe/European, 167, 202
   and America, 131
   development and colonial life, 171
   and frontiers, 199
   gender norms, imposition of, 92

ideas and institutions transmitted from, 198–99, 203
and North American civilization, 18

Farmers/farming frontier, 172–73, 174–75, 176–77, 178
Federal Acknowledgement Program, 123
Feminine Canadian West, 96–99
Ference, Ermeline, 51
Fiedler, Leslie, 77, 147–48, 159
Filson, John, 144, 147, 149
First Nations/Native civilization, 20–21. See also Indians
Fitzgerald, F. Scott, 5–6
Flaherty, Robert, 73
Ford, John, 145
Fort Benton, 87, 89
Fox, Dixon Ryan, 198–99
Francis, Daniel, 63, 65
Francis, Douglas, 32
Franklin, Benjamin, 133
Fraser, James Earle, 46
Free land, 185, 141, 143, 146
French, 132, 133, 134, 135
Fripp, Charles, 49–50
Frontier, northern, 135
Frontier, significance of in American history, 141–42, 165–67
  army posts, 175
  attempts to check and regulate, 186–87
  comparative study of social development, 170–72
  composite nationality, 178–79
  effects on national legislation, 180
  farmer's frontier, 174–75
  growth of democracy, 184–86
  Indian trader's frontier, 172–74
  industrial independence, 179–80
  intellectual traits, 189
  land, 176–78
  missionary activity, 187–88
  national tendencies, 182–84
  public domain, 181–82
  rancher's frontier, 174
  salt springs, 175–76
  stages of advance, 167–70. See also Turner, Frederick Jackson
Frontier and metropolitanism, 206–7
Frontier in History, The: North America and South Africa Compared, 215
Frontier interpretation, criticisms and modifications of, 200
Frontier myth, Stegner, 129, 130–31
Frontier studies, 119
Frontier thesis
  American, 68, 71
  Canadian, 68–71. See also Turner, Frederick Jackson
Frye, Northrop, 22, 25–26
The Fur Trade in Canada, 18, 69, 71–72, 203
Fur trade, Canada, 203, 204
Fusco, John, 139

Garceau, Dee, 107–8
Gender and land policy, 103–9
Gender norms, European, imposition of, 92
Gendered dimensions, two Wests, 95–98
Gendered Western identity, 95
Geography, physical, 119–20
Germanic (origins, germs, mark)/German(s), 167, 179
Gjerde, Jon, 24
Goetzmann, William H., 5
Goodnight, Charles, 158
Government and Native peoples, 120, 121
Government policies, Aboriginal women, 92–95
Gowanlock, Theresa, 103
"The Greatest Show on Earth," 153–62

Great Plains, 169
Great West, the, 16, 17
Gressley, Gene, 33
Grey, Zane, 51
Grove, Frederick Philip, 31
Gump, James O., 216

"Half-breed"/Country Born/Métis, 122–23, 135
Haliburton, Robert Grant, 72
Ham, George, 91
Harper, J. Russell, 2
Hartz, Louis, 142
Hayes, Carleton, 198
Hehn, Victor, 175
Heroes, American/mythic Western figures, 149
Higham, Carol, 95
Hingston, William Hales, 72–73
Hinterland. *See* Metropolitan-hinterland paradigm/perspective/myth
Historians
   and myths, 145
   American, and frontier thesis, 198–99
Historical materials/literature, Native peoples, 118–19
Historiographies/histories, Canadian and American Wests, 15, 109
History, Canadian, schools of. *See* Canadian history, schools of
History of the Canadian Pacific Railway, 19, 203 *A*
Hofstadter, Richard, 142
Hollywood, 198
Homestead (land, regulations), 104–9
Hudson's Bay Company, 2, 6, 66, 120
Huffman, L.A., 40

Identities: national, regional, and international, 74, 76, 82nn47, 50

Illustrations and promotional literature/booklet, 31–32, 50–51
Imagined Communities, 74
Imperialist(s)/imperial (designs), 195, 196
Indian agents, 91–92, 93
Indian Gallery, Catlin, 45–46
Indians, 216, 217
   Albany congress of 1754, 174
   and Canada, 66
   and frontier, 168, 169
   and Mounted Police, 53n6
   Native/First Nations civilization, 20–21
   Plains, 37
   in stampedes, touring shows, etc., 45, 61n52
   as touchstones to a common myth, 45–51. *See also* Native peoples' experiences, comparative history
Indians in the United States and Canada, 216, 217
Indian trader's frontier, 172–74
Indian Treaty-Making Policy in the United States and Canada, 216–17
Individualism, 184, 185–86
Industrial independence, 179–80
Innes, John, 49
Innis, Harold Adams, 15, 203, 204, 205
   "northern vision," 71–72
   perspective of the West/Laurentian thesis, 17–20, 21, 22–23
   and Native civilization, 20–21
   staples thesis, 70–71
   versus Turner, 15, 18–19, 20–23
Institutions, American, peculiarity of, 165–66
Intellectual traits and frontier, 189
Intermarriages, descendants of, 122–23
Iroquois, 172, 173
Irvine, Fanny, 91
Irvine, L.S., 91

Index   227

Jameson, Sheilagh, 33
Jefferson, Thomas, 1–2, 3, 6, 8, 11, 187

Kainai (Blood), 86, 87, 90, 91
Kane, Paul, 2, 3, 5, 6–7, 8, 11, 46
Kanouse, Henry Alfred (Fred), 90, 91
Kaye, Frances, 20
Kelly, Fanny, 99–102, 103
Kelly, Leroy V., 51
King, Mackenzie, 196
Kingsford, William, 195
Kurz, Rudolph Friederich, 88–89

LaDow, Beth, 86, 218
Lakota, 92–93, 99, 101–3
Lamar, Howard, 215, 216
Lame Bull Treaty, 87–88
Land allotments, 94–95
Land in Her Own Name: Women as Homesteaders in North Dakota, 108
Landon, Fred, 200–201
Land policy and gender, 103–9
Land(s) and frontier, 176–78, 181–82
Lane, George, 34–35, 38
Laurentian School, Canadian history, 204–5
Laurentian thesis/perspective. *See* Innis, Harold Adams
La Verendrye, Pierre Gaultier de Varennes et Sieur de, 131, 134–35
Legal position of Indians, 121–22
Legislation, national, effects of frontier on, 189
Lewis, Meriwether/Lewis and Clark expedition, 1, 2, 3–4, 131
Lewis, R.W.B., 145
Liberal movement/Liberalism, Clear Grit, 199, 202, 207
Libraries, research, 117
Lightfoot, Gordon, 3
Limerick, Patricia Nelson, 142, 143

Lindgren, H. Elaine, 108
Literature, American and Canadian, 31
  "blood-and-thunder" romances, 147
Literature (booklet), promotional, and illustrations, 31–32, 50–51
Literature/historical materials, Native peoples, 118–19
London, 206
Longabaugh, Henry (the Sundance Kid), 160
Louisiana purchase, 181
Lower, A.R.M., 69, 200, 205

Macdonald, John A., Sir, 48, 66, 96–97, 98
Mackenzie, Alexander, 1, 3, 6, 8, 11
MacLaren, I.S., 7
MacMillan, Jessie de Prado, 104
Manly space, West as, 95–96
Many Guns, Cecily, 94
March toward the West, 171–72
"Maritime factors," Canadian and North American history, 213n28
Marshall, John, Chief Justice, 121
Martin, Chester, 195
Marx, Leo, 145
Masculine U.S. West, 96, 97–99
Masters, D.C., 205
Matteson, Tompkins, 47
McCarthy, Cormac, 5
McClintock, Anne, 97, 103–4
McManus, Sheila, 218
McMurtry, Larry, 9
Merk, Frederick, 149
Métis/Country Born/"half-breed," 122–23, 135
Metropolitan-hinterland paradigm/perspective/myth, 20, 22, 23, 69
Metropolitanism/metropolitan centers (of dominance), 17–20, 70–71, 205–209
Mexico, 140, 150

Mexico–U.S. comparisons, 216–17
Middle region, 182–83
Mild West and Wild West, 33–34, 65–68, 74, 76
Minds of the West: Ethnocultural Evolution in the Rural Middle West, 1870–1917, 24
Minority groups, 23
Missionaries, Protestant, 217
Missionary activity, 187–88
Monolithic view (of the West), 23, 24, 25
"Montana face," 147–48
Montreal, 205, 206, 208
Morgan, Lewis Henry, 86
Morton, A.S., 200
Morton, William L., 73, 115–17
   northern frontier, 135
   trans-Atlantic myth, 127
Mountains, 169, 170, 176
Mounted Police (Mounties), North West, 2–3, 7–8, 11, 36, 66, 121, 141, 155–56
   and Indians, 53n6
   Remington, 41
   Russell, 38–39, 40–41
"Move On, Maroon Brother, Move on!", 48
Moving pictures and cowboys (cowhands), 147–48
Murray, W.H.H., 98
Mythic Western figures/American heroes, 149

Narrative of My Captivity Among the Sioux Indians, 99–102, 103
Nation building and gender, 95
National character (consciousness), 143
   and environment/geography, 72, 73
Nationalism, 196–197
Nationality, composite, 178–79, 182–83

National legislation, effects of frontier on, 180
National tendencies, frontier, 182–84
Nationhood, Political, School of, Canadian history, 195–96
Native culture, differing orientation to, 135
Native/First Nations civilization, 20–21. *See also* Indians
Native peoples' experience, comparative history, 115, 124
   academic and intellectual obstacles, 118
   Canadian academics/historians, 115–16
   descendants of intermarriages, 122–23
   differing historiographies, 118–19
   government, 120, 121
   legal position of Indians, 121–22
   literature/historical materials available, 118–19
   myths, 116
   national chronologies, 120–21
   physical geography, 119–20
   population densities, 120
   practical issues, 117–18
   tribal recognition, 123–24
   warfare, 121
Natoyist-Siksina (Holy Snake/Natawista), 86–92
Nevitt, Richard B., 90–91
New England/New Englander, 182, 183, 188
New York, 206, 208
Nichols, Roger, 216, 217
"No Place for a Woman: Engendering Western Canadian Settlement," 95–96
Noble, Wretched and Redeemable, 217
Noel, Jan, 85

North American (environment, society, common experience), 197, 201
North American history, "maritime factors," 213n28
North and West in Canadian mythology, 71–74, 76–77
North West Mounted Police. *See* Mounted Police (Mounties), North West
Northern culture/civilization, 127
Northern frontier, 135
"Northern vision", 71–74
Northwest, 127, 128, 135
North-West Resistance/Riel Rebellion, 103

Ohio, 167–68
Oil, 75
Oliver, E.H., 199–200
Oliver, Frank, 106, 107
"One West, Two Myths: Comparing Canadian and American Perspectives," 95
Opper, Frederick, 48
Ostenso, Martha, 31

Parade Marshall, Calgary Stampede, 153, 154–55, 158, 159
Peck's New Guide to the West, 177–78
Peigan, 94
Pennsylvania, 182, 183
Perry, Adele, 98
Physical geography, 119–20
Pioneer(s), 120, 121, 177, 178
Pitts, Jonathan, 5, 6, 10
Plains Indians, 37
Pocklington, William, 91–92
Policy studies, Native peoples, 118–19
Political Nationhood, School of, Canadian history, 195–96
Politicians and frontier democracy, 185
Population densities, 120
Prairie Provinces, 107

Prairie West, 67
Prince of Wales, 39
Progressivism, Western, 202, 207–208
Promotional literature/booklet and illustrations, 31–32, 50–51
Protestant missionaries, 217
Protest movements, regional, 75–76
Public domain, 181–82
Pullen-Burry, Bessie, 97–98
Purchase of Louisiana, 181

Quebec Act of 1774, 132–33
"Queen of the Sioux," 101–2

Race/racialist (thread, rhetoric), 72, 73, 104
Radicalism, Upper Canadian, 202
Railways, 19, 50–51, 71, 203
Ranching/ranch culture/ranchers, 32, 33, 51, 52n2, 54nn8–9
rancher's frontier, 174
Rangeland Derby, 155
Reagan, Ronald, 63, 65, 149
Red River (Winnipeg), 96
Regional protest movements, 75–76
Religious and educational activity, 188–87
Remington, Frederic, 2–3, 5, 6–7, 8, 11, 39–40, 149
and cowboys, 40, 41–44
and Sivell, 44
Research libraries, 117
Riel, Louis, 7, 8, 66, 135
Riel Rebellion/North-West Resistance, 103
Rise of Toronto, 205
Robert (Hewitt), Ida, 108
Rocky Mountains, 169, 170
Roosevelt, Theodore (Teddy), 149
and cowboys, 40, 41, 42, 43, 45
Rouse, A.L., 116
Russell (Cooper), Nancy, 37
Russell, Charles M., 33, 36–37

Barrows on, 56n11
and Calgary Stampede, 36–39
Cowboy Sport—Roping a Wolf, 34–35, 57–58n17
and Indians, 48–49
and Sivell, 44
and violence, 56–57n13

"Safety valve," West as, 144–45
Sage, W.N., 199
Salt springs, 175–76
Samek, Hana, 218
Samuels, Harold, 3
Samuels, Peggy, 3
San Juan Island dispute, 101
Saskatchewan, 4
Schlesinger, Arthur M., Jr., 199
Schools of Canadian history. *See* Canadian history, schools of
Scotch-Irish, 179
Sectionalism/sectional (trait, etc.), 182, 183, 184
Service, Robert, 63–65, 77
Settlement(s), 165, 168
Shameful side of westward movement, 142
Sharp, Paul, 217
"The Shooting of Dan McGrew," 63–65
Simpson, George, Sir, 2, 6
Sioux, 101–2, 216, 218
Sitting Bull, 7, 8, 66
Sivell, Rhoda, 44–45
Skelton, O.D., 196
Slavery, 183, 184
Slotkin, Richard, 149
Smalley (Bangs), Etta, 108
Smith, Goldwin, 22
Smith, Henry Nash, 1, 24–25, 131, 143–46
Snell, James, 103
Social development, comparative study of, frontier, 170–72

South, the, 182, 183, 184
South Africa, 215, 216
Spirit: Stallion of the Cimarron, 139–40, 150
St. Germain, Jill, 216–17
St. Lawrence, 204
Stages of frontier advance, 167–70
Stanley, John Mix, 47, 88
Staples thesis, 70–71
Stegner, Wallace, *Wolf Willow*, 4–5, 6, 7, 8–9, 10–11
prairies and plains, levelling of difference, 128–34
Stevens, Isaac, 87
Sundance Kid (Henry Longabaugh), 160
Sykes, Violet Pearl, 93–94

Tanner, Tony, 145
Thomas, Lewis G., 32, 38, 51
Thompson, John Herd, 95, 96
Thompson, Leonard, 215, 216
Tide-water (region), 182, 183, 185
Toronto, 205, 206, 207, 208
Tower of Babel, 25–26
Trachtenberg, Alan, 145
Trader(s), Indian, 172–174
Trails and trade, 173
Trans-Atlantic myth, 127
Transnational issue/history, 217
Transport and communications systems, 203, 204–5
Tribal recognition, 123–24
Trotter, R.G., 195
Turner, Frederick Jackson, 5, 144, 209n1
architect of Western American myth, 141–43
continentalist myth, 127
frontier thesis (hypothesis), 15–17, 23, 24, 25, 68
frontier thesis and American historians, 198–99

frontier thesis and Canadian history, 194, 197–200
versus Innis, 15, 18–19, 20–23. *See also* Frontier, significance of in American history
Two Months in the Camp of Big Bear, 103

Uncle Sam, 96, 98
Underhill, F.H., 199
United States and metropolitan power, 208
Upper Canada, unrest in, 207
Upper Canadian radicalism, 202

Vanderhaeghe, Guy, 8–10, 11
Van Kirk, Sylvia, 87
Violence, 149
and Charles M. Russell, 56–57n13
Virginia, 168
convention of 1829–1830, 183, 185
Virgin land, 97, 143–44
Virgin Land: The American West as Symbol and Myth, 24–25, 144
Vorpahl, Ben Merchant, 3
Voyages from Montreal, on the River St. Lawrence, through the Continent of North America to the Frozen and Pacific Oceans in the Years 1789 and 1793, 1–2

Wagon racing. *See* Chuckwagon
Ward, John William, 145
Warfare, 121
Washington, George, 132–33
Weadick, Guy, 35–37, 58n21
Webb, W.P., 71, 199, 206
West
Canada–U.S., comparisons, 216–17
dominant images of, 144
and East, 199, 201–2, 205
Great, the, 16, 17
as manly space, 95–96

march toward the, 171–72
nationalizing tendency of, 184
and North in Canadian mythology, 71–74, 76–77
Peck's New Guide to, 177–78
religious and educational activity, 187–88
as "safety valve," 144–45
visions (myths) of/imagined, 74–77. *See also* Wild West and Mild West
Western figures, mythic/American heroes, 149
Western Progressivism, 202, 207–8
Westerns, dime/"blood-and-thunder romances," 147
The West from a Car Window, 146
Wests
Canadian and American, histories of, 109
feminine Canadian and masculine U.S., 96–99
two, gendered dimensions, 95–98
Westward movement, shameful side of, 142
"What It Must Come To," 46, 47
Wheat and Woman, 104–5
Whiskey trade, 217
White, Richard, 17, 23
White women, 92, 93–94, 100
the ideal, 103
and land policy, 103–9
Whoop-Up Country, 217
Wild West and Mild West, 33–34, 65–68, 74, 76
Wild West show, 146, 147
Wister, Owen, 42, 43, 60n44, 146, 149
Wolf Willow, 4–5, 7, 8–9, 10–11
prairies and plains, levelling of difference, 128–34
Worster, Donald, 143, 149

Zulu, 216

www.ingramcontent.com/pod-product-compliance
Lightning Source LLC
Chambersburg PA
CBHW052059300426
44117CB00013B/2195